Discovery Travel Adventures™

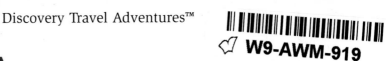

ALASKAN
WILDERNESS

Tricia Brown
Editor

John Gattuso
Series Editor

Discovery Communications, Inc.

INSIGHT GUIDES

Discovery Communications, Inc.
John S. Hendricks, Founder, Chairman, and
   Chief Executive Officer
Judith A. McHale, President and Chief Operating
   Officer
Michela English, President, Discovery Enterprises
   Worldwide
Raymond Cooper, Senior Vice President, Discovery
   Enterprises Worldwide

Discovery Publishing
Natalie Chapman, *Publishing Director*
Rita Thievon Mullin, *Editorial Director*
Mary Kalamaras, *Senior Editor*
Maria Mihalik Higgins, *Editor*
Kimberly Small, *Senior Marketing Manager*
Chris Alvarez, *Business Development*

Discovery Channel Retail
Tracy Fortini, *Product Development*
Steve Manning, *Naturalist*

Insight Guides
Jeremy Westwood, *Managing Director*
Brian Bell, *Editorial Director*
John Gattuso, *Series Editor*
Siu-Li Low, *General Manager, Books*

Distribution
United States
Langenscheidt Publishers, Inc.
46-35 54th Road
Maspeth, NY 11378
Fax: 718-784-0640

Worldwide
APA Publications GmbH & Co.
Verlag KG Singapore Branch, Singapore
38 Joo Koon Road, Singapore 628990
Tel: 65-865-1600. Fax: 65-861-6438

Discovery Communications produces high-quality
nonfiction television programming, interactive
media, books, films, and consumer products.
Discovery Networks, a division of Discovery
Communications, Inc., operates and manages the
Discovery Channel, TLC, Animal Planet, and
Travel Channel. Visit Discovery Channel Online
at http://www.discovery.com.

Although every effort is made to provide accurate information in this publication, we would
appreciate readers calling our attention to any
errors or outdated information by writing us at:
Insight Guides, PO Box 7910, London SE1 1WE,
England; fax: 44-171-403-0290; email:
insight@apaguide.demon.co.uk

Printed by Insight Print Services (Pte) Ltd, 38
Joo Koon Road, Singapore 628990.

Alaskan wilderness / Tricia Brown, editor.
       p.   cm. -- (Discovery travel adventures)
    Includes bibliographical references and index.
    ISBN 1-56331-837-7 (pb. : alk. paper)
    1. Alaska Guidebooks. 2. Alaska Pictorial works.
  3. Wilderness areas -- Alaska Guidebooks. 4. Wilderness
  areas -- Alaska Pictorial works. I. Brown, Tricia. II. Series.
F902.3.A657 1999
917.9804'51 -- dc21   99-27645
                                                   CIP

T his guidebook combines the interests and enthusiasm of two of the world's best-known information providers: **Insight Guides**, whose titles have set the standard for visual travel guides since 1970, and **Discovery Communications**, the world's premier source of nonfiction television programming. The editors of Insight Guides provide both practical advice and general understanding about a destination's history, culture, institutions, and people. Discovery Communications and its website, www.Discovery.com, help millions of viewers explore their world from the comfort of their home and encourage them to explore it firsthand.

About This Book

Alaskan Wilderness reflects the work of dedicated editors and writers who have firsthand knowledge of adventuring in and dreaming about Alaska's wild places. **John Gattuso**, of Stone Creek Publications in New Jersey, worked with Insight Guides and Discovery Communications to conceive and direct the series. Gattuso chose **Tricia Brown**, an Anchorage author and editor with many books to her credit, to manage the project. "For creative people all over this state, Alaska is both subject and inspiration," says Brown, who drove up the Alaska Highway from the Chicago area in 1978. "I never imagined a place could be so captivating." Brown is the author of a critically acclaimed book, *Children of the Midnight Sun*, which profiles Eskimo and Indian cultures through interviews with children.

Much of Alaska's population is made up of settlers, like Brown, who came north with a plan to stay a year or two. The same is true of many of the contributors to *Alaskan Wilderness*. A one- or two-year adventure is what writer **Andromeda Romano-Lax** was thinking when she arrived in 1994, but somehow she never left. Romano-Lax usually brings along her two preschoolers when she's researching an assignment: "My hobbies include hiking (with kids on my back), sea kayaking (with kids under deck), and writing (with kids on my lap, until I kick them out of my office)." She lends her vast experience in hiking and kayaking to her chapter on the Kenai Peninsula.

Dan Joling is a Midwesterner who in 1978 left Wisconsin behind to begin a new life. He accepted a job at a Fairbanks newspaper when the state was 19 and he was just a few years older. "I stayed because I liked the people, opportunities, the state's youthfulness," Joling says, "plus the miles and miles of country without 'No Trespassing' signs." Joling happily hopped a floatplane to Misty Fiords National Monument to research his chapter on Alaska's southernmost park.

Consider the irony of a former California girl writing about adventuring in the snow. But when it comes to snow, Anchorage resident **Nan Elliot** knows her stuff. After all, she once traveled the 1,100-mile route of the Iditarod Trail to Nome by dog team. That extraordinary feat, coupled with her love of skiing, made her a clear choice to write about ways to explore the state in winter. Montana was home for **Kaylene Johnson** before she settled in Eagle River with her pilot-husband. Not surprisingly, she's seen a lot of the state from the air, so she was assigned to write about flightseeing expeditions as well as Kodiak Island.

If you're like most travelers, you look to the locals for the best advice on how to pack and what you can expect to see. For that reason, we sought out several contributors who could write about their own little piece of Alaska. Among them is **Nick Jans**, who has lived in the Noatak and Kobuk Valleys for nearly 20 years. As a contributing editor to *Alaska* magazine, he has gained a national following with monthly columns about living in modern bush Alaska. **Kris Capps**, an experienced kayaker and river guide, was selected to author chapters on float trips and Prince William Sound. **Kathleen McCoy**, an editor for the *Anchorage Daily News*, makes her home near the border of Chugach State Park, which she covered for this book. As author of a guidebook on Alaska's parks, Anchorage writer **Bill Sherwonit** has probably traveled through more of the state's national parks than most veteran rangers. He penned chapters on three far-flung locations: Admiralty Island National Monument, Katmai National Park, and the Pribilof Islands.

Ken Marsh grew up just north of Anchorage and now writes about his Alaskan journeys for a variety of magazines. With all that experience in backcountry hiking and camping, Marsh was eminently qualified to write a chapter about "Roughing It" in the wilderness. **John Murray**, author of more than a dozen nature books and a former professor of English at the University of Alaska, covered several of his favorite wilderness destinations, including Lake Clark and Denali National Parks.

Magazine assignments and book contracts have taken **Kim Heacox** all over Alaska — and all over the world. As glamorous as that sounds, he's a homebody at heart. "I always enjoy coming home to tidewater glaciers, sea kayaks, and my acoustic guitar," he says, all of which are waiting for him in Gustavus, a tiny town at the edge of Glacier Bay National Park. Heacox authored the chapter on Wrangell-St. Elias National Park, just around the corner from Glacier Bay. **Tom Walker** is another world traveler who jokes that he's been "self-unemployed" since 1972, but in reality he's a successful writer and photographer with 13 books and numerous magazine articles to his credit. For this book, he's written about one of his favorite places, the Brooks Range, and describes the caribou migrations that have long captivated his imagination.

Thanks to the many park rangers who reviewed the text and to the members of Stone Creek's editorial team: Michael Castagna, Nicole Buchenholz, Bruce Hopkins, Judith Dunham, and Edward A. Jardim.

Parasailing (above) off the mountains above Juneau offers incomparable views of Gastineau Channel in Southeast Alaska.

Ice climbers (opposite) find plenty of opportunity in Alaska, which is covered by nearly 30,000 square miles of glaciers.

Dog mushing (below) is the state's official sport. You can book a mushing adventure through kennels outside Anchorage or Fairbanks.

Backcountry camping (following pages) on Thunder Mountain in the Tongass National Forest brings with it the spectacle of one of Alaska's most accessible glaciers, the Mendenhall.

Table of Contents

MAPS

Alaska does not belong to Alaskans alone, although it is easy for us to think so. Rather it is America's last wild place, the treasure of a nation, and the retreat of a society that's weary of hurtling through life by the appointment book. Imagine it: a single state equivalent in size to one-fifth of the combined Lower 48 states, and most of it uninhabited by humans. To own one's thoughts and to slow time in such a wide, expansive landscape is the stuff of imagination, as compelling as a child's desire to run and tumble across a field of newly mown grass. The Alaskan wilderness inspires running wild – and poetry, art, curiosity, and dreams of beginning again, as many of its people know firsthand. The Far North, wrote poet Robert Service, forever ensnares the heart: "The freshness, the freedom, the far-ness; My God, how I'm stuck on it all!" ◆ America's 49th state is so broad, so unpeopled, and so roadless that small airplanes are more

Alone at the top of the world, Alaska remains a powerful magnet for seekers of purity, beauty, and solitude.

common than cabs in other states. There are more private pilots than truck drivers and cabbies combined. Men outnumber women (and women have coined the phrase, "The odds are good, but the goods are odd"). Consider, too, that the population numbers just over 600,000, and almost half of them live in one city: Anchorage. Nearly the entire state – all 365 million acres – is raw, wondrous wilderness. ◆ Alaska really *is* the Last Frontier, just as the license plates say, full of places where you can stand on your toes and howl at the northern lights, and nobody will be around to look at you funny. But you are not alone. A wolf pack observes a group of canoeists from atop a ridge. Bald eagles feast on salmon as photographers

Walrus (left) return during their spring migration to haul-outs on Round Island in the southern Bering Sea.

Previous pages: Fly-fishing on Rabbit Creek north of Anchorage; extreme skiing in the Chugach Mountains near Valdez; Mount McKinley, awash in morning light.

engaged in balancing the dual missions of protecting the wilderness while allowing people to use it.

Like other animals, humans will always require wild spaces, but perhaps for more complex reasons. Spiritual nourishment is just one. In the wild, we grasp the mysterious interdependence of place, people, and wildlife, and we comprehend the stark reality of the food chain by entering it. Wilderness reminds us how much we need each other, too, an attitude that's pervasive in a state with so few people and so much country. It's why lost mountaineers usually aren't lost for long, why hikers share whatever they have, and why remote cabins are left stocked and unlocked. In the wild, we learn about our own thin-skinned, mortal bodies, our need for healthy food and clean water, planning and preparedness. And finally, in the wild, we reawaken long-forgotten instincts and rediscover a world that's delicate yet durable.

Alaska's great, wild spaces must always be protected, Margaret E. Murie once wrote. "This is the great gift Alaska can give to a harassed world."

maneuver for a better shot. Flightseers gaze down upon a colony of slumbering walrus, their overlapping bodies woven into a carpet of fat. Dall sheep skitter across a steep mountainside as small stones rain down on backpackers. Bears and caribou and moose go about their business as if you don't exist, because the reality is, you don't matter to them. All they need is the space they've always had and the freedom to use it. Guaranteeing that space and freedom – for animals and for humans –

is a matter of politics.

Look at a map of Alaska with all of the federal, state, and Native Alaskan lands inked in different colors, and you may need a magnifying glass to see what is *not* in color. Less than one percent of the state lies in private hands. In 1980, President Jimmy Carter signed the Alaska National Interest Lands Conservation Act that added millions of acres and wild rivers to areas already under federal jurisdiction. In the decades since the law was approved, state and federal agencies have

Adventuring In Alaska

Throw away your day planner and enter a wilderness where backcountry skills are more valuable than greenbacks. Whether you're hiking the Brooks Range, running the Yukon River, or setting up camp under the midnight sun, your "real" life will be the last thing on your mind.

Natural Wonders

A new arrival to Alaska steps out of an airplane, a cruise ship, or a mud- and bug-encrusted car. Immediately the neck cranes back, the eyes sweep upward. There, in the upside-down bowl of the sky, a horizon-to-horizon drama demands attention: The huge northern sky is choreographing the clouds and wind, light and shadow.　◆　This magnificent Alaska skyscape makes an opening statement about the vastness of the rest of the state. It's a humbling experience. You can't help but feel insignificant in the face of so much wild space.　◆　Alaska is made for wonder. There is room here for massive mountain ranges that include 17 of the highest peaks in the United States, 47 steaming volcanoes, and 100,000 glaciers. There are more than three million lakes, 1,800 named islands plus thousands more unnamed, and rolling river drainages that include 1,400 miles of the mighty Yukon River.　◆　Amazingly, the entire place

In a state larger than most European countries, the possibilities are as boundless as the imagination.

was once under water. The state's varied geologic texture is evidence of a violent episode about 140 million years ago when the Earth's crust buckled, fractured, and tossed up whole mountain ranges from the sea.　◆　Volcanic eruptions occurred periodically for millions of years and were followed by periods of sagging and eroding and then building again. But about 60 million years ago, the whole of what we now call Alaska was finally above sea level, and another period of volcanic activity followed. An almost subtropical climate allowed trees to flourish on today's Arctic Slope.　◆　Final shapers of Alaska's scenery were the glaciers that covered fully half of the state a million years ago. Glaciers put

Gray wolves watch without being seen, making even a glimpse of the skittish animals a rarity.

Preceding pages: Breaking trail in the backcountry isn't for the ill-prepared.

Night Light

Baseball games at midnight. Camping on Flattop Mountain to honor the summer solstice. Backyard gardening into the wee hours. City workers leaving jobs in the afternoon to fish prime salmon streams all night, then driving back to work in the morning. These are symptoms, one and all, of a curious relationship Alaskans have with light in summer.

The midnight sun (above) seems to bounce along the horizon in this timed-exposure image.

Spruce trees (opposite, top) are dominant in the boreal forests of Alaska's interior.

The common loon (opposite, bottom) is known for its eerie call.

Barren ground caribou (below), found in 13 distinct herds that migrate regionally, are commonly sighted in Denali National Park.

Alaska's far-north place on the globe ensures that as the Earth's axis tilts closer to the sun in June, July, and August, the state basks in hours and hours of rich summer light. So significant is the annual ebb and flow of light to Alaskans that newspapers and radio commentators report how many minutes of light the state gains (or loses) each day.

Anchorage sees a late-night sunset throughout the summer. At and above the Arctic Circle, night disappears. In Barrow, almost 300 miles north of the Circle, the sun rises on May 10 and does not set again until August 1.

their signature on the place as they carved and filed immense swathes of land into smooth valleys and deep fjords, burying forever in permafrost such bizarre prehistoric creatures as the hairy mammoth, saber-toothed tiger, and woolly rhinoceros.

Glaciers are still at work. Southeast Alaska has 16 active tidewater glaciers, and the Juneau Icefield in the Coast Mountains, just 25 miles north of the capital city, is the world's largest glacial accumulation outside of Greenland and Antarctica.

The catalogue of Alaska superlatives is impressive indeed:

● Mount McKinley, rising 20,300 feet above sea level out of the 500-mile-long, intensely glaciated Alaska Range, is the highest mountain in North America.

● The Wrangells, a compact cluster of volcanic mountains in east-central Alaska, is considered by many to be the most beautiful in the nation.

● Alaska's tidal shoreline (31,383 miles) is greater than the shoreline of the Lower 48 states, and Alaska's land mass (570,374 square miles) is larger than the next three largest states combined.

● Tongass, the largest national forest in the United States, encompasses nearly 17 million acres and covers more than 73 percent of Southeast Alaska.

● Malaspina Glacier is North America's largest piedmont glacier, a type in which two or more glaciers flow from confined valleys to form a large fan.

● Cook Inlet's tidal flux of nearly 40 feet is one of the greatest in the world, second only to the Bay of Fundy.

Bountiful Wildlife

No discussion of Alaskan wonders should overlook the teeming wildlife. Among the best known are the brown, or grizzly, bears that roam most of the state; the black bears that inhabit forested areas; the nomadic caribou; Alaska's own native Dall sheep; the Sitka black-tailed deer in the coastal rain forests of the Southeast and Prince William Sound; and the deer family's largest member, the moose. In smaller numbers are wolves, bison, musk oxen, wolverines, coyotes, foxes, lynx, polar bears, and whales.

And that's all without mentioning the bird population. More than 420 species have been recorded in Alaska; birders enjoy unparalleled opportunities to see North American and Asian species. The numbers are staggering: 24 million migrating waterfowl gather annually on the Yukon-Kuskokwim Delta in western Alaska. So are the varieties: swans, brants, cackling Canada geese, emperor geese, lesser golden plovers, snipes, jaegers, godwits, sandpipers, and sandhill cranes. To the Copper River Delta east and south, add tiny dunlins, western sandpipers, trumpeter swans, and dusky Canada geese. The high country in Denali National Park is home to raptors and ptarmigans. The Brooks Range sustains owl species and peregrine falcons. The largest concentration of bald eagles in North America inhabits the Chilkat River Valley northwest of Haines. The Pribilof Islands, 200 miles off the west coast of Alaska, and Prince William Sound in south-central Alaska, provide prime habitat for seabirds, including red- and black-

legged kittiwakes, horned and tufted puffins, northern fulmars, common and thick-billed murres, pigeon guillemots, and others.

Beyond the annual bird migrations, three-quarters of a million marine mammals spend spring and summer in the waters off Alaska. Again the numbers are imposing: 4,400 bowhead whales, 15,000 beluga whales, and a quarter of a million walrus.

Alaska defines natural wonder. It seduces with glorious landscapes and wild spirit, and it offers what few places can – a palpable realization that there's something in this world greater than ourselves.

Roughing It

Home this evening is a mountain tent huddled upon alpine tundra bordering a high-country lake. The view is incredible. Up above, heading the valley beyond the lake's far side, a hanging glacier clings to the face of a rising peak. Below, the valley falls away gently into head-high alders, then wind-stunted spruce, and finally, far, far below, into a great boreal forest through which a silver river flows. The air here is thinner and clean. Lighter. And the openness – the 360-degree "big sky" view – reveals a wilder, older world. For now, your isolation is complete. ◆ It's tough to imagine, in this contemporary, electronic age, stepping into a new country, one with expansive areas that remain unsettled and raw, unchanged for millennia. Yet here in Alaska, where wilderness in its truest form lives on, you may find such country. And until you've seen it, felt it, heard it, smelled it – lived it – you can't possibly grasp its true magnitude. ◆ In that sense, Alaska is a land waiting to be explored.

Hiking and camping in Alaska's backcountry require thorough planning and preparation, and a commitment to low-impact travel.

And if you're willing to get out, to get a little wet, a little cold, a little sweaty, a little swept off your feet by the natural power of it all, then you've found a country that will grow in your heart and become part of you – a powerful, longing part. ◆ It's not difficult to "get remote" in Alaska. The state is famous for its paucity of roads, with scarcely more than 9,000 miles of highways and city streets, many of them unpaved. These sparse threads don't begin to cover Alaska's 570,374 square miles. This great wilderness is isolated from the outside world by its own sprawling bulk. ◆ The point is this: When you're ready to leave

Campers atop Ruth Glacier enjoy spectacular mountain vistas. Camping in the clouds, at the top of the world, usually requires the services of an experienced guide or outfitter.

civilization and step into wild Alaska, you may find yourself completely alone in a big, primitive land. Chances are that's just the way you like it. And that's fine, as long as you're prepared to survive in a place without convenience stores, hospitals, and central heat.

Be Prepared

It's easy to get into trouble out here. Say you've chartered a bush-plane drop-off on a remote river. You'll spend a week drifting downstream in a raft watching the country slip by, getting out now and then to camp for the night, doing a little fishing, or hiking for a spell into the hills. Your pilot will meet you 100 miles downriver at a designated

pickup point. But the plane has just roared off and the seclusion is beginning to fall around you like snow. Silence. Nothing to hear but the purling river and your own breathing. You're gathering your gear, getting prepared, when you realize that you've forgotten something: toilet paper! Or, perhaps, insect repellent. Or, on a more tragic level, the raft pump. What will you do?

The moral of the story is to be prepared. And that means planning. Every detail of your trip must be considered prior to your departure. Are you ready for all weather possibilities? If you're camping in the Brooks Range in June, for instance, you may experience warm,

sunny days, or you may wake up in a snowstorm. As for rain, raw wind, and blood-sucking mosquitoes and flies… well, count on them all. If you're back-packing, how much food and gear can you reasonably carry? Enough to reach your destination? Are you in decent physical shape? Will you need a lightweight, wind-resistant tent? Will it keep you dry on a rainy day? Because Alaska is so many places, and since each place changes by season, preparation depends on where and when you're going, and what you plan to do.

Prince of Wales Island in southeast Alaska can be a gentle place in April. Expect some rain (perhaps a lot of it) and a few days of shirt-sleeve sunshine. Black bears are out on the tidal flats poking their noses into beach grass, and rufous hummingbirds are buzzing among salmonberry blossoms. Meanwhile, in the hills of the Alaska Range, the lakes and streams are frozen and the nights are frigid. Rain gear and rubber boots appropriate for one place are necessarily replaced by parkas and snowshoes in the other.

So some knowledge of the region you wish to visit, especially its climate and geography, is mandatory. The best advice is to research your destination in advance. Read. A bookstore and library are good places to start. Phone or stop by the offices of the Alaska State Parks, Bureau of Land Management, U.S. Forest Service, or National Park Service. Talk to rangers, guides, air taxi operators; these people know their country and can lend advice on terrain, average temperatures, rainfall, snow pack, and the like.

You'll need maps. Check out the U.S. Geological Survey for detailed topographical maps of the region you'll be exploring. Examine the contours, lakes, and streams. Know beforehand what's out there, and plan accordingly.

How will you reach your

destination? In a roadless wilderness, you often have to fly. Where will you land? Is there a lake long enough to accommodate a floatplane? Perhaps a gravel bar, open tundra, or even a rough airstrip is present. Call air

A lone hiker (opposite) takes a break at a waterfall in Tongass National Forest. But solo travel in Alaska's backcountry can be risky.

River crossing (above) is one more case where there's safety in numbers.

Staying dry (top) is essential for a comfortable hike and healthy feet.

Choosing an Outfitter

If you're new to camping, or even new to camping in Alaska, you would be wise to take your first trek in the company of a reputable outfitter. But how to choose? Your money, and maybe even your life, are on the line. It's critical that you find the right people for the job.

Start your search by asking the following questions:

● How long has the outfitter been in business? Longevity is often an indicator of reliability.

● Are the guides experienced? River rafting, sea kayaking, mountain climbing, and other wilderness activities involve some risk. You'll want to go only with seasoned guides who know how to avoid trouble – or get out of it.

● Are the guides certified in advanced first aid? Do they carry emergency medical supplies, and do they know how to use them?

● What gear does the outfitter provide? You don't want to find out at the last minute that you have to pay extra for an essential piece of equipment.

● How much will the trip cost? Are the outfitter's fees in line with his or her competitors? If not, find out why.

● Can the outfitter supply references? A reputable outfitter will gladly provide names and telephone numbers of previous clients.

taxi operators and ask. If you're hiking off the highway system, will you follow an established, maintained trail? Or will you "bust brush"?

All of which leads to another question: Just how *will* you get around once you reach your destination? If you plan to raft a wild river, your research should focus on dangerous rapids and falls. How many river miles can you expect to cover each day? Figure this into the length of your float when planning a pickup at the far end. Similarly, whether you're kayaking the coast, traversing a mountain range on foot, or cross-country skiing through the wilderness in March, your research should determine the length of the trip and what gear you bring.

In the end, Alaska's wilderness is bigger and far more powerful than the most skilled trekker. Unforeseen problems, the kind that even detailed planning can't prevent, will surely arise. To be safe, do some soul-searching before entering the field – and be honest with yourself: Are your survival skills, physical condition, and equipment up to the task? Don't cave in to pride or peer pressure. Bravado can get you into serious trouble.

The Right Stuff

Proper physical conditioning may mean a dedicated running or hiking program three to four days a week for at least three months prior to your trek. If you arrive in the backcountry overweight and out of shape, you will be miserable at best. At worst, over-stressed bones and muscles will leave you prone to injuries. All trekkers – and particularly those over age 30 – should visit the doctor beforehand for physical checkups.

Don't cut corners when it comes to outdoor clothing and equipment. You'll need good gear to survive. If you can't afford the right stuff, borrow from a friend or rent from an outfitter or outdoor retailer. And if those tactics fail, cancel your trip. Camping in the wilderness with inadequate gear is a recipe for disaster.

Backpacks must be sturdy, light, and comfortable. Speak with outfitters, guides, and outdoor retailers for brand and model suggestions. Try on new packs and get help fitting straps, belts, and hinges. Add some weight and see how the pack

Mountain bikers (opposite) are welcome on the first 15 miles of the sole road into Denali National Park.

Mosquito myths (below) are almost as big as the bugs themselves, which hold the tongue-in-cheek title of "Alaska State Bird."

Beating the Bugs

In most areas of Alaska from May through September, you will find them: buzzing, pestering, blood-sucking insects. And in legendary numbers. Most notorious are the mosquitoes, blackflies, no-see-ums, and horseflies. Without protection against them, a dream trip through scenic wilderness can become a nightmare.

Your first line of defense is insect repellent. Nearly all chemical repellents contain Deet, although some are more concentrated than others. For complete coverage, however, you should consider a mesh "bug jacket" and head net. Blackflies and tiny, biting no-see-ums tend to crawl into hidden spots along hairlines and under watchbands, shirt-sleeves, and pants legs. When these insects are prevalent, experienced campers sometimes tape cuffs and carefully apply repellent around these areas and behind ears, collars, and other places that gnats can reach.

Also make certain that your tent fly and vents are fitted with extra-small, insect-proof mesh. Examine mesh prior to camping for tears or holes that might allow bugs to enter and make for irritatingly sleepless nights.

Bear Sense

"Bearanoia" is a term commonly applied to those with an unreasonable fear of bears. Others, usually inexperienced in the ways of the Alaskan wilderness, sometimes lack a healthy respect for these powerful, if generally shy, animals. Treading a middle ground, seasoned bear-country trekkers use common sense and a basic understanding of bear behavior to avoid close encounters.

All three North American bear species are found in Alaska: black bear, brown (grizzly) bear, and polar bear. All can be dangerous, particularly when surprised at close quarters or while protecting food caches or cubs. The best insurance against bear attacks is to avoid close contact. Here are some tips:

● Avoid surprising bears. Talk loudly or carry "bear bells," and hike in groups of three or more whenever possible. Announcing your presence allows bears to avoid *you*.

● Don't camp on or near bear paths. Trails along salmon streams, for example, should be avoided. Find out how to identify other common locations.

● Don't keep food in or near tents. Store food in sealed containers well away from camp. If possible, hoist containers high up in a tree.

● Avoid bear kills. Bears can remain in the area of a kill for days and can be highly protective of it.

● Give bears their space. If you happen upon a bear, turn and give it a wide berth. *Walk* away; never run. Running can trigger a predatory reflex in an otherwise peaceful animal.

Bears (above) are more interested in fish than sleeping fishermen, but a sloppy campsite is asking for trouble.

Topographical maps (opposite, top) and a compass or global positioning system (GPS) are essential aids.

Comfort camping (opposite, bottom), even in winter, is no problem with forethought and smart packing.

rides. Comfort is paramount. Camp stoves, headlamps, and tents must be sturdy and as lightweight as possible.

What about water? It's everywhere in Alaska, but it's not always safe to drink. Waterborne bacteria and protozoa, most notably *Giardia lamblia*, are present throughout the state. Various compact water-purifying systems are available; most have a filter and manual pump to make drinking water safe.

Clothing should be light, warm, and functional even when wet. Rain jackets, pants, and shells will be needed in wet weather: Gore-Tex and similar fabrics are popular and reliable. Inner clothing should consist of several layers. Avoid cotton, which tends to retain moisture and loses its insulation value when wet. Polyester and polypropylene fabrics (including PolarFleece, Polartec, Capilene) are tough

to beat. They are light, and they retain warmth even when wet. Most veteran trekkers wear this stuff from head to toe.

The footwear you choose depends largely on the terrain, season, and type of traveling you intend to do. Comfort, traction, and ankle support are always top considerations. In rocky, mountainous country, leather hiking boots with Vibram soles may be the best choice.

On a float trip, knee-high rubber boots or hip boots may be more appropriate. On a snowshoe trek in March, foam-insulated boots (often called "packs") may be needed to keep your feet warm. Choose packs with removable liners that can be taken out and quickly dried.

Sleeping bags must be compact, light, and warm. Down fillings that were popular 20 years ago have been largely replaced by synthetic fillings that, like today's outdoor clothing fabrics, dry quickly and remain warm even when wet. Also important to warmth and comfort is a decent sleeping pad. Corrugated foams and inflatables of various lengths and thicknesses are available.

A compass – or, even better, a hand-held global positioning system (GPS) – is an important tool for cross-country travelers. Today's GPS units are light,

extremely accurate, and affordable. A compass is still an effective direction-finder, but a GPS allows campers to program landmarks and receive readings on elevations and distances.

So, you've got good gear and top-notch physical conditioning on your side for safe and enjoyable camping. But no matter how prepared you may be, emergencies can – and will – occur. Always carry a lightweight, well-stocked first-aid kit. Also, hand-held two-way radios (or, in some circumstances, cell phones) save lives. Lightweight radios take up little space and cost as little as $300. Campers who have become injured or ill in the field will vouch for the value of these inexpensive devices.

Alaska, you will find, is a pristine place, and you surely will want to keep it that way. Practice low-impact camping, and, when in doubt, follow the old rule: If you pack it in, pack it out. Make certain that campfires are fully extinguished, and when "nature calls," bury the evidence. This place is unique; to stand here is to be, as Charles Kuralt wrote, "alone in the universe." Leave nothing behind to betray your presence, and Alaska will remain a great, wild land for a long time to come.

Weaving among the rugged mountains of the Alaska Range, the Nenana River outside Denali National Park is a mighty chute of water that runs through a wilderness paradise. Rain swells its banks. The summer sun melts glaciers, and the glacial silt turns the dark, green water a chocolate brown. Early in the season – May or early June – whitewater kayakers dodge icebergs the size of car hoods. As summer progresses, the water warms up to a balmy 45°F, and canoeists head for the river's gentler stretches. Hillside carpets of blue lupine eventually yield to the magenta-colored fireweed that provides a sharp contrast to the yellow-leaved birch trees of autumn. Moose munching onshore silently watch boats float by. On nearby slopes, grizzly bears might be gobbling down berries. ◆ This is accessible wilderness, easy to get to and easy to enjoy. A string of river companies just outside the national park offers two-hour or longer raft rides down the

For the thrill of kayaking through frothy rapids or a leisurely float on a placid river, Alaska has lots of the essential ingredients.

Nenana. As one outfitter points out, you can choose mild or wild on this river. If you go for wild, be prepared to tear your eyes away from the scenery and grant full attention to the churning, angry waves at rapids like Terror Corner. Bracing into the waves, most boaters emerge upright as sputtering victors. But sometimes the river wins, and paddlers are dumped into the icy water, only to be tugged this way and that by the currents before finally, feebly, gratefully making their way to shore. ◆ Alaska rivers like the Nenana are intensely cold and powerful. Many are in remote, roadless locations, and a number require paddlers to have whitewater

Raft adventures on the Nenana River are available near the entrance to Denali National Park, where the choices range from flat-water floats to white-knuckle rides.

Sea kayakers (above) explore the protected waters of the Inside Passage.

Beginners to kayaking (below) can learn in the calm waters of Ketchikan's Creek Street.

Waterproof cameras (opposite, top) are available in "disposable" form.

Two-man kayaks (opposite, bottom) offer more power and much better maneuverability.

experience or at least enlist the services of a professional guide. For these reasons – and especially if this is your first Alaska float trip – it's good to know in advance where you want to go and what kind of float you want to take. Do you crave a heart-thumping whitewater trip down Class IV rapids, or do you envision yourself paddling serenely through a cove occupied by curious sea otters? Consulting guidebooks covering the state's wildlands, parks, and waterways is a good way to begin your research. Consider the trips on pages 40 and 41; they offer a range of experiences and scenic possibilities. And contact the nearest Alaska Public Lands Information Office, which can provide valuable, up-to-date information on Alaska's rivers.

Multiple Choices

Even if you're an experienced whitewater aficionado, it's important never to paddle alone. Paddling clubs in Fairbanks and Anchorage will gladly connect you with local boaters who know a river and its moods at different levels. The

paddling community in Alaska is small, particularly in the interior, so you'll likely get an invitation to join local paddlers as they head downstream. All you need to do is rent a kayak and arrange to join the group.

Like a carnival ride, wild water can be exhilarating, but some travelers may prefer to seek a more sedate or controlled water excursion. There are more miles of rivers than roads in Alaska, and many of them are calm ribbons offering relatively quiet journeys through the wilderness. A few, like the Chena River, even wind through urban Alaska; several local businesses rent canoes for this popular paddle through downtown Fairbanks.

Alaska also is a land of lakes, any number of which can easily provide seclusion and maybe even a tug or two on a fishing line. You can make arrangements with a bush pilot to fly you and your gear, including an inflatable kayak or raft, to a lake, or you can secure a rental at a remote lodge. On the Kenai Peninsula and also north of Anchorage, some lakes interconnect to form a canoe trail system, inviting extended explorations.

Sea kayaks are the best mode of travel on many of these lakes, on easy-flowing rivers, and in areas like Prince William Sound, Misty Fiords National Monument, and the Inside Passage.

High and Dry

When a disposable waterproof camera washed onshore in front of Shortie Schmidt's home on the Nenana River, he developed the film and took the photos to the annual summer river festival. He found the camera owner at once. Hooray for waterproof cameras!

But what happens when the camera isn't disposable or waterproof? Your best bet is to go to a local army surplus store and spend a few bucks on an ammo can. Then buy a small insulated pad and make a little box, held together with duct tape, to fit the can. Besides keeping your equipment dry, the container floats.

Plastic Pelican boxes, also handy for camera storage, come with or without padding. These waterproof boxes protect a camera and other gear if dropped on rocks or handled roughly. More expensive waterproof cases also are available commercially.

Thanks to modern technology, you can keep the rest of your gear dry, too. Kayakers use waterproof storage sacks known as "dry bags." A large bag is roomy enough for a sleeping bag, pad, and tent. Smaller bags are available for extra clothes, food, and personal items. But don't take the term "dry bag" literally. Always add extra protection by first wrapping everything in plastic.

Sleek yet stable and easy to maneuver, they become silent transport. They also have lots of storage room for camera gear, lunch, and more. Tour boats will often drop off passengers for an afternoon of paddling and then pick them up at the end of the day.

As you plan your Alaska float, consider hiring a guide to take you down a river or through coastal waters. With a guide's experience and organization, you can put aside some of your concerns about preparing for the trip. Outfitters provide all necessary boating and safety equipment, give you an

introductory lesson, and, for multiple-day trips, can supply food and camping gear. Packages may include flying to a remote put-in site followed by a week or more of paddling and camping, hiking, and photography

along a designated Wild and Scenic River. Other outfitters can take you paddling and camping through the Inside Passage or Prince William Sound, or they can drop you and your party, along with kayaks, camping gear, and supplies, at a base camp. Some trips combine paddling with whale watching, bear viewing, and other wildlife explorations.

Sometimes it's best to let someone else take the helm. Day boats and cruise ships ply the Inside Passage, and all that's left for you to do is to stare at the scenery and use up your film. A few river options let you sit back and just watch the scenery go by, too. In Fairbanks, operators of the riverboat *Discovery* offer narrated historical and cultural tours of the Chena and Tanana Rivers. The *Yukon Queen II* regularly cruises the Yukon River between Eagle and Dawson City in the Yukon Territory, Canada.

Time Out

Many paddlers who opt for long trips find themselves tucking away their watches as they adjust their schedule to the ebbs and flows of the water. Even whitewater junkies don't miss the excitement of wild water on these trips. They discover that some of the best adventures are on water with hardly a ripple. While paddling on the Noatak River in the southern Brooks Range, for example, canoeists may see hundreds of caribou stream over a hillside as if some invisible hand were pouring them out of a giant pitcher. They may hear the distinct *click-click-click* of the animals' ankles as they move en masse, pausing now and then to munch on lichen. Or perhaps they'll see a herd of musk oxen huddling on a coastal plain, or the silhouette of a grizzly bear standing upright against the snow-covered slopes of 8,855-foot Mount Michelson.

These waterways offer a pathway into another world. The water is alive, and it's never the same twice. One river excursion may be memorable for the clouds of pesky mosquitoes. Another trip on the very same river may be remarkable for balmy weather and abundant wildlife.

But these are merely incidentals. The real focus on these trips is the water and where it leads – a journey that is always good for the soul.

Canoeists (top) find a remote campsite on Byers Lake in Denali State Park.

Waterfalls (left) and other seldom-seen beauties lure kayakers along the jagged coastline of Southeast Alaska.

Boaters (opposite) get a close-up view of South Sawyer Glacier in Tracy Arm.

THE FLOAT	Difficulty	Paddler's Promise

Prince William Sound
Sea kayakers may choose from two points of entry that are road-accessible: Valdez (eastern Sound) or Whittier (western Sound).

The region is an ideal choice for novices on a one-day excursion. Veteran kayakers will enjoy the challenge of an extended trip combined with backcountry camping.

Unique to this trip is the opportunity to paddle among crackling icebergs. Be prepared for some of the best wildlife-viewing afloat. Watch for bald eagles, puffins, sea otters, and orca whales. Keep an eye on the mountainsides for mountain goats and Dall sheep.

Kenai Fjords National Park
Sea kayakers can put in at Seward and paddle through one of the most wildlife-rich regions of Alaska.

This trip is rated easy to moderate. Depending on your available time, you can plan for a single day on the water or book an extended kayaking/camping excursion.

Get ready for spectacular views of fjords and sea arches. Listen for calving icebergs. Watch for seals and sea lions dozing on ice floes and for colonies of seabirds. Birders will find this an excellent opportunity to add to their life list.

Misty Fiords National Monument
Sea kayak through protected waterways out of Ketchikan along the Inside Passage.

Make it as easy or difficult as you like, depending on whether you go out for a day, a week, or longer. Novices should seek out a guide for multiday trips.

Load your waterproof camera for fantastic shots of the Inside Passage, where mist hangs moodily over glacier-formed fjords and volcanic formations. Sit back for a leisurely and scenic paddle through one of the state's largest wilderness areas. Depending on the season, you may spot a whale or two.

Copper River
Drive to Chitina in south-central Alaska for the put-in, and raft or kayak this exciting glacier-fed river. Pass between snowcapped mountains, view Childs Glacier, and drop into a broad river valley.

The river is rated Class II with Class III sections (moderate with some difficult stretches). The ratings often are upgraded one more level to account for the danger of extremely cold water.

This is Alaska's fourth-largest river, flowing from the mountainous interior to coastal rain forest. In some places, it is broad and lazy; in others, wild and challenging. Guaranteed, you'll enjoy the jaw-dropping cross section of scenery, including 16,000-foot snow-covered peaks.

Gulkana River
Drive to Mile 175 or 179.5 of the Richardson Highway and put in at Paxon Lake. Easy access makes this one of the most popular whitewater trips in Alaska.

This is a multiday trip rated Class II (moderate) with one Class III (difficult) canyon. For a one-day family trip, put in at the Sourdough campground and gently float the 13 miles to Poplar Grove.

Flowing from headwaters at the foot of the Alaska Range, this national wild and scenic river offers several levels of difficulty. Expect great fishing, especially for king salmon, from mid-June to mid-July. Know how to maneuver a canoe and you'll have a rewarding trip.

Lake Creek
Hire a bush pilot in Anchorage or Talkeetna and fly to Chelatna Lake. Arrange for a pickup at the confluence of the Yentna River after two or more days of exciting whitewater.

This two-day trip is rated Class II to Class III (moderate to difficult), depending on the section. Two sets of challenging rapids are set about midway through the journey.

Lake Creek is a clearwater stream with plenty of good campsites along the way. There are miles of exciting rapids and outstanding views of Mount McKinley and other mountain giants of the Alaska Range. Fishing is excellent from mid-June through early August.

THE FLOAT	Difficulty	Paddler's Promise
Nenana River A beautiful glacial stream that flows through boreal forest in the heart of Alaska. There are several options for put-ins from Parks Highway just outside of Denali National Park. 	Go easy or make it tough, depending on which stretch you choose. There are three, each 8 to 10 miles long, that are ranked Class II to IV (moderate to very difficult)	Expect big, powerful water, exploding waves, and giant holes — some friendly, some not-so-friendly. Take time on the mellow sections to admire some of Alaska's most spectacular scenery. Novices should hire a guide or go with a rafting-trip operator.
Charley River If you're looking for a lively whitewater experience, this is the float for you. Arrange a bush flight out of Fairbanks, Tok, or Eagle to the Upper Charley airstrip and a pickup at Circle City on the Yukon River.	This is for experienced paddlers who are looking for a 7- to 10-day trip. The water is rated Class III (difficult), perhaps Class IV (very difficult) at high water. The best water is in late May and early June.	You'll want to make this an annual trip. The Charley is a pristine wilderness river that flows through the Yukon-Charley Rivers National Preserve. You'll travel from open tundra upland into forested valleys. Mosquitoes are a sure thing. And watch for the occasional moose.
Hulahula River This is whitewater at its finest through the starkly beautiful Brooks Range north of the Arctic Circle. Arrange a flight from Fairbanks and a pickup on the coast.	Much of the river is Class III (difficult), with Class IV (very difficult) sections, depending on rain and snowmelt. The 70-mile float, combined with hiking, is a memorable two-week trip.	A raft or inflatable kayak is best for maneuvering through boulder fields. You'll be too busy to admire the spectacular scenery while you're on the river, so leave extra time to absorb the beauty of this treeless landscape.
Willow Creek Veteran kayakers will find challenging whitewater on this lively waterway in the Talkeetna Mountains. Turn east onto Hatcher Pass Road at Milepost 71 of the Parks Highway, then left on an unpaved road just past Milepost 41.	This day trip calls for every bit of your attention. There are three sections, ranging in difficulty from Class III (difficult) to Class IV (very difficult) and even Class V (extremely difficult).	This is a small, technical, clearwater stream with plenty of thrilling whitewater for seasoned paddlers. You'll share the stream with some of Alaska's biggest fish from late June through mid-July.
Newhalen River Experienced paddlers will find some of the state's best whitewater on this Alaska Peninsula powerhouse. Catch a commercial flight to the village of Iliamna, then an air taxi to the put-in at Upper Landing. 	This run is a good day trip but not for beginners, as it includes Class IV (very difficult) rapids with a Class V (experts) drop. You can portage around the drop on a mile-long trail.	The Newhalen is a huge, muscular river with big rapids. The water is warm, clear as a gem, and filled with salmon. This is the best big-water surfing in Alaska.
Talkeetna River Rafters and kayakers will find good fun and challenging whitewater on this stream in the Talkeetna Mountains. The put-ins are reached by bush plane out of Talkeetna or Anchorage. Rafters should land at the Yellowjacket airstrip; kayakers should land at Stephan Lake.	The Talkeetna is a swift, glacier-fed stream. Nearly a quarter of the 60-mile run is continuous whitewater. It's rated Class IV (very difficult) to Class V (extremely difficult).	This is a premier wilderness trip with brown bears, salmon, and whitewater all in one float. Be prepared to share the river with motorboats and anglers during peak king salmon season, mid-June to mid-July. Take your time and make it a three-day trip.

Alaska from Above

Flying through the Knik Valley in south-central Alaska, a Cessna 185 descends into the Gorge, a canyon with a glacier on one side and a sheer rock face on the other. The landscape dwarfs the buzzing aircraft, giving passengers the sense that they're riding inside the hull of a fragile flying insect. They drink in the astonishing view. Pastel-blue cracks on the face of the glacier are deep enough to swallow a 17-story building. No one speaks. Words can't capture the raw beauty outside or the feelings of wonder within. ◆ Even long-time Alaskans are awestruck by the view from the air. Who wouldn't be? Wild places stretch from horizon to horizon, untouched by human hands. From the lush rain forest of the southeastern panhandle to the delta wetlands of the western coast and the tapestry of the far northern tundra, **Flightseers can travel** much of Alaska is accessible only by air. And it **with two guarantees:** may never look more spectacular than **The view will be incomparable,** it does from above. ◆ Travel by airplane **and there's not a bad** is almost always a breathtaking journey, but it's also **seat in the house.** a crucial mode of transportation. Beyond the major cities and towns, many communities can't be reached by road. Most bush villages appear on the map like disconnected specks without the usual web of asphalt connecting them to the outside world. Just about everything that goes in or comes out – people, mail, groceries, medicine – travels by air. ◆ Given the importance of air travel, Alaska has been dubbed the "flyingest" state in the Union. One out of 58 Alaskans is a registered pilot, and one out of 59 owns an airplane. Lake Hood in Anchorage is the largest and busiest seaplane base in the world, averaging 234 landings and takeoffs a day; 800 per day

Bush pilots offer a wide range of services, from flying campers and climbers to remote sites to specializing in half-day flightseeing trips over Mount McKinley.

in the most rugged settings. Depending on season and terrain, they may be equipped with pontoons, skis, or tundra tires. Pontoons on an aircraft make convenient landing strips of coves, lakes, and streams; skis are used on ice and snow; and tundra tires, like big rubber donuts, cushion landings on gravel bars or soft, spongy tundra. Helicopters also are an option for backcountry travel, especially for close-up views of the terrain and extremely tight landings.

Bush pilots are an equally rugged and colorful bunch. Their courageous, comic, and sometimes tragic stories have been told and retold until they've become the stuff of legend. Take Paul Claus, one of Alaska's most celebrated bush pilots. He's been known to land on a glacier so steep that he had to anchor the plane with an ice screw to keep it from sliding off the edge. To take off, he leaned out the window, cut the tether with a knife, and throttled off the slope.

Passenger's Checklist

Before you decide to fly into the wilderness, there are a few things you should keep in mind. First, air taxis aren't cheap. Cost varies widely depending on the destination, amount of gear, and the number of passengers, and is usually based on flight hours. Even a relatively short hop into the bush can cost as much as a flight from the Lower 48 states to Alaska.

are not uncommon in summer. Merrill Field, also in Anchorage, is home to hundreds of small aircraft and considered one of the nation's busiest regional airports.

Arranging a flight is a fairly straightforward matter. Air taxi and bush operators are listed in the Yellow Pages of any Alaskan telephone directory. Some companies offer a regular schedule of flights and destinations. Others operate on a charter basis and will take you just about anywhere you want

to go. Still others specialize in flightseeing tours of the region's most scenic places. Want to spend a day or two fishing in complete solitude at a remote mountain lake, or perhaps a few hours trekking across an otherwise inaccessible glacier? If so, these are the people you need to see.

Bush planes range in size from a two-person Piper Super Cub to a 20-passenger DeHavilland Twin Otter. They are remarkably versatile aircraft designed to operate

Second, patience is a virtue. Bad weather and mechanical problems often delay flights for hours or days, so bring extra provisions, a deck of cards, and a sense of humor. Impatience, which some pilots call "get-home-itis," is a leading factor in small-aircraft accidents.

Finally, put safety first. Don't hesitate to ask your pilot if he or she has insurance and a commercial license, which requires a higher standard of training and aircraft maintenance than a private license. And be sure the plane has life vests, an emergency locator transmitter (ELT), and other essential safety equipment. Never challenge a pilot's decision to cancel a flight; the sun may be

Floatplanes like this Bellanca Scout (opposite) can land on distant lakes such as this one in Chugach National Forest.

Super Cubs (left) are the smallest of the fleet, so seating is cramped.

Watery runways such as this one (below) near Fairbanks freeze each winter. Some owners swap floats for wheels.

shining where you are, but the weather at your destination could be dramatically different – and unsafe. Nor should you pressure a pilot to carry more people or gear than the aircraft can handle. Weight and balance are critical for safe flying.

Flying in Alaska is routine but almost never boring. An airplane may be the only practical means of getting from one place to another, but it also provides an encounter with the Alaskan wilderness unlike any other. Perhaps the only way truly to grasp a land of such vast dimensions is to view it from above.

So you want to come in winter to see the "real" Alaska. Where do you go, what do you do, and how do you prepare? First, in this land of extremes, you need to remember that two of these extremes are cold and dark. How cold is it? Veteran gold miners in the North Country say that at 65°F below zero, spit freezes in midair and cracks before it hits the ground. Though the inconveniences and hazards of winter travel in Alaska are many, so too are the pleasures. Winter in the north, while demanding a healthy respect, returns beauty and excitement unmatched elsewhere in the world. ◆ Because Alaska is huge, winter plays out very differently from south to north. Whereas Anchorage gets only a flurry of minus temperatures and a few serious cold snaps, the mercury in the interior and along the northern coast routinely plunges below zero. Crystals of ice float in the air and sparkle like little dancing rainbows. Snow squeaks underfoot, chill

"Seward's Icebox" becomes a polar playground as Alaska embraces the upside of snow, ice, and extraordinary cold.

seems to seep into every crevice of clothing, and the sun is merely a decorative orb in the sky. ◆ Winter gets increasingly dark and cold the farther north you go. Contrary to popular belief, however, the entire state doesn't plunge into darkness come winter. On December 21, the shortest day of the year, the sun rises at 10:14 in the morning in Anchorage and sets at 3:42 in the afternoon – leaving you with nearly five and a half hours of daylight. After the winter solstice, daylight increases at a rate of about five minutes each day. In the far north, on the edge of the Arctic Ocean, Barrow enjoys two wonderful months of midnight sun during the summer. Come winter, it pays the price. The sun sets in the third week of November

An ice climber descends into a crevasse on Pika Glacier in Denali National Park, a favorite destination for mountaineers.

and doesn't rise again for 67 days. The shoulders of that season are filled with days of continual twilight.

So if you want to experience these exhilarating extremes of cold and dark, plan to come in December

or January. In February, the days are longer, though severe cold snaps are not uncommon. For sunny evenings and more spring-like skiing weather, March is unbeatable around the Anchorage area. If you're heading into the interior, be prepared for colder conditions but more sun.

Skiing to Sledding

The three major cities – Juneau, Anchorage, and Fairbanks – are your best jumping-off points for winter expeditions. Juneau has some fine opportunities for down-hill skiing and snowshoeing, but in the southeast, with its wet, slushy winters, the

snow can be undependable. For snowmobiling, dog-mushing, and the best cross-country skiing, you'll want to head farther north to Anchorage and Fairbanks. Ice-climbing devotees will find some of the best in the state outside Valdez on Prince William Sound, an hour's flight from Anchorage.

There is nothing like the exhilaration of schussing down a mountain slope in light powder snow, feeling like you're almost floating. Anchorage and Juneau are both within driving distance of popular downhill ski resorts with stunning views of mountains and sea. You can spend a day on the slopes and then soak your bones in a hot tub or enjoy drinks and dining at a four-star restaurant.

For cross-country skiing, it used to be that one set of skis was all you needed; indeed, only one kind was available. Today, you can get a different set of skis for each specialized kind of cross-country skiing, from telemark skiing to skate skiing. If you want to stay close to the city and on groomed and lighted trails, extensive networks throughout Anchorage and Fairbanks will take you through forests, over alpine meadows, and along the frozen inlet. The trails are often set for both skate and classic skiing. Check with ski clubs or sporting-goods stores for rental gear, maps, and directions.

You'll need a better pair of backcountry or touring skis for expeditions off groomed trails, because you may be breaking trail yourself with skis or snowshoes. Guides are available to take you on cross-country jaunts for a day or more, or you can plan your own adventure. Scattered throughout national forests and state parks are inexpensive public-use cabins. They are bare bones and rustic but a welcome respite in the wilderness. Frontier etiquette demands that you leave cabins in better condition than you found them. Chop firewood, clean up the place, and leave canned goods for the next occupants. Check with the Alaska

Division of Parks or the U.S. Forest Service for cabin locations and reservations.

For those who love dogs and speed, merely standing on a sled behind a leaping, barking, straining team of huskies can get your adrenaline pumping. Dog power is awesome, and the noise is deafening. Yet, an amazing quiet descends when you take off in a rush of speed along a frozen river or through the bobsled runs of a forest trail. The only sounds are a light panting of your team's breathing, the padding of paws on snow, the *whoosh* of sled runners, and the beating of your heart. Dog-mushing kennels abound around Anchorage and Fairbanks. They can take you on a dogsled adventure for an hour or a day or

whatever suits your spirit. The telephone directory or local visitor bureau can help with a list of mushers who offer tours. Many are veterans of such grueling long-distance races as the Iditarod Trail Sled Dog Race or the Yukon

Snow trekking (opposite, top) requires physical endurance as well as clothing that will wick moisture away from the skin.

The Iditarod Trail Sled Dog Race (opposite, bottom) each March begins with a mush down one of Anchorage's main streets.

Tours by dogsled (left) are popular in late February and in March, when the days get longer.

Snowboarders (below) are almost as common as skiers on the slopes of Mount Alyeska in the Chugach Mountains.

Treating Hypothermia

Hypothermia occurs when the body loses more heat than it produces. Cold, wind, and moisture can be a lethal combination. And, surprisingly, you can get the condition even if the air temperature is above freezing.

One of the first signs of hypothermia is violent and uncontrollable shivering. As the core body temperature drops, shivering diminishes and muscles become rigid. The chief symptoms at this stage are what one outdoor writer calls "the umbles": stumbling, mumbling, fumbling, bumbling. Speech is slurred, coordination poor, and comprehension dull. If not properly treated, the victim quickly becomes irrational, drifts into a stupor, and loses consciousness.

If you suspect a member of your party is suffering from hypothermia, immediately try to find shelter. Put the victim into dry clothes, wrap him in blankets or sleeping bags, keep him off the ground, and provide whatever heat may be available. If the condition worsens, put the victim in a sleeping bag with another person. Alone, the victim will be unable to produce enough heat to warm the bag much less his own body.

Sufferers of hypothermia often don't realize they're in danger and may even deny it. It only takes a few minutes to slip into the condition, and, if untreated, death can follow in less than two hours.

The best plan, of course, is prevention. Dressing properly can truly be a matter of life and death. Always bring extra clothing on outdoor adventures, and consider your options before you get into trouble.

Quest International Sled Dog Race. A visit to their dog lots is an adventure in itself: Dog mushers are notorious for their wild stories.

Snowmobiling is a big-time sport in Alaska – as

well as a practical mode of transportation – and it's easy to rent machines and find guides in the cities. Snowmachiners and cross-country skiers are not traditionally the best of friends. As one skier said, "Those snowmachines could drive you out of heaven." Indeed, the buzzing of snowmachines at popular backcountry sites can be relentless. While it's true that you can travel farther and faster on a snowmachine, you also can get yourself into more trouble. The best

advice is to go with a guide your first time. Be sure that you know how to operate the machine safely, heed all warning signs, mind your fuel gauge, and be careful of thin ice and overflow on rivers, lakes, and frozen ocean.

Getting Ready

"Be prepared" is advice that should be taken very seriously when traveling in Alaska in winter. Getting ready begins before you leave home. For activities like snowmachining, ice climbing, and dog mushing, and even cross-country skiing and snowshoeing, it's always best to engage the services of a guide or outfitter, especially if it's your first time in Alaska. Reputable outfitters can help you choose the expedition most suitable for your level of fitness and advise you on the kind of clothing and equipment you need. They can also provide you with information on local trail and weather conditions and how to avoid potential hazards such as avalanches.

As you array your travel wardrobe, remember that the aim of dressing for the Alaska winter is not only to stay comfortable but to guard against the dual threats of hypothermia and frostbite. The best choices are layers of garments made of wool or synthetics that protect you even when they're wet. You'll need a hat that covers your ears and a scarf or other type of covering that can protect

Frost is inevitable (opposite, top) when you breathe super-cooled air, but it's not a sign of hypothermia.

Winter camping (opposite, bottom) is challenging on Ruth Glacier.

Snowmobiles (left), known as "snowmachines" throughout Alaska, are limited to certain areas.

Virgin snow (bottom), like this expanse in the Ruth Amphitheater of Denali National Park, is irresistible.

your neck and face; gloves or mittens; and layers of socks. Even if you have sturdy winter boots, you may want to consider purchasing boots made especially for arctic weather. On days when the wind isn't blowing and snow isn't falling, and your head and hands feel toasty, your feet are still in contact with the frigid ground. Always pack more clothing than you think you'll need; it's essential to bring extra layers even if you're only going out for a few hours or a day.

Just when you think that all this preparation might be too much trouble – that heading south for the winter might be a better idea than braving the vast frozen North – imagine gliding through a silent landscape cloaked in white, or snow-shoeing alongside a massive river of ice, or standing outside on a cloudless night and seeing the northern lights drape the sky in swirling shades of blue, green, and purple. These are just some of the rewards of winter in this land of extremes.

◆

Wilderness Destinations

◆

Wander through the mists of Tongass National Forest, paddle the icy waters of Glacier Bay, fly between the walls of a granite gorge, or take a wild ride on a river through the high Arctic. The Alaskan wilderness offers a menu of adventures for your trip of a lifetime.

Misty Fiords National Monument

CHAPTER **6**

ountains rise like a giant amphitheater on all sides of your lake. And it is your lake this week; no other human will see it. Conifers blanket the slopes, but the angle is so steep that their roots don't always prevent mudslides. The residue of an old slide makes a gray streak down the mountain. Dead trees, their trunks bleached silver, lie convulsed at the water's edge like a pile of Tinker Toys. ◆ Something splashes on the far side of the brush pile. Trout? Bear? Neither. Six sleek forms wriggle off deadfall half in the water about 50 yards away. They are river otters. ◆ They slip into the water and swim effortlessly toward you. They move like porpoises, every so often popping up for air and maneuvering deftly through the jumble of logs. About 30 feet away, the lead otter veers your way and dives. And you think: Are otters dangerous? Do they bite? Then again, they're such small and playful creatures. What's the worst this one could do, gnaw on your boot?

Shrouded by rain-swollen clouds that tarry over forest and rock face, this spectacular beauty is a perfect match with its moniker.

The brown submarine pops his head out of the water and looks around. Whiskers, ebony eyes, tiny ears. Is he as thrilled by the encounter as you are? Probably not. In any case, he doesn't linger. He dives and joins his mates, and they wriggle down the lakeshore. ◆ Such encounters are not out of the ordinary at **Misty Fiords National Monument and Wilderness**. The park encompasses more than two million acres of granite cliffs, glaciers, coastal rain forest, and frigid mountain lakes in the Alaska panhandle about 22 miles from **Ketchikan**. No one is sure who named Misty Fiords, but everybody knows why: With about 160 inches

Granite walls rise majestically over a backcountry camp on Punchbowl Lake.

Previous pages: Canoeists ply the calm waters of Wonder Lake in Denali National Park.

Rangers say that you haven't really seen the monument if you visit on a sunny day. But then there's about as much chance of missing the mist at Misty Fiords as there is of missing sand in the Sahara. May and June offer the best chance for sun. Summer is the season of soft, dripping rain, when clouds seem close enough to touch. Hard rains usually don't come before September.

On overcast days, it's as if God threw away all the colors in his palette except green and gray. Moisture hovers around evergreens in sluggish, dreamy clouds. The forest feels cool and humid, and the vegetation looks like it's been splashed with Miracle-Gro. Devil's club and skunk cabbage grow to elephantine proportions. Moss covers the forest floor and climbs tree trunks like an emerald carpet.

of rain per year, this is the wettest part of America's largest rain forest. The heavy precipitation is due in part to the Kuroshio Drift, which flows across the North Pacific and spins off an eddy called the Alaska Current. It warms the panhandle in winter and cools it in summer, producing a thick blanket of clouds.

This expanse of old-growth forest will never be logged. In one of his last acts as president, in December 1978, Jimmy Carter showed that lame ducks have teeth. He declared this portion of Tongass National Forest a national monument, which protected it from logging and mining. Two years

later, Congress transformed most of the park into designated wilderness, giving it yet another layer of governmental protection.

Watery Vistas

The deep, narrow waterways known as fjords, which were gouged from the mountains by receding glaciers at the end of the last Ice Age, are the main attraction of the park. Since the park has no roads, you have to visit the fjords by air or sea. A lucky few bring their own boats or rent sea kayaks, but most visitors rely on tour operators. Arranging a trip is easy. Start with a phone call or a visit to the Visitor and Convention Bureau in downtown Ketchikan, just a few steps from the cruise-ship harbor. The bureau has information on dozens of companies that offer cruises and combination trips (fly/cruise or cruise/kayak) ranging from a few hours to a full day or longer.

Tour boats, especially the smaller ones that hold a hundred passengers or less, cruise out of Ketchikan right up **Behm Canal** to **Rudyerd Bay**, an 11-mile fjord that juts east from the canal. In some cases, Forest Service rangers paddle out to the boats and answer questions. Visitors risk neck spasms staring up at 3,150-foot vertical walls at the entrance. Many compare Rudyerd Bay to Yosemite Valley in California, except that there's seawater at the base of the cliffs. Within Rudyerd, just past the entrance to **Punchbowl Cove**, pigeon guillemots share a rock wall rookery with glaucous-winged gulls; the guillemots occupy the lower tier, the gulls the upper.

Floatplanes give visitors a close-up

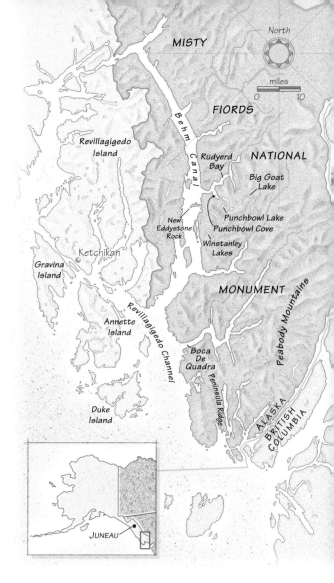

Snow clings to the shores of a lake (opposite, top) as spring arrives at Misty Fiords.

Sea otters (opposite, bottom) are found in abundance in the waters of the Inside Passage.

Skunk cabbage (right), as its name implies, has an unpleasant scent.

view of the granite walls. Flying over **Revillagigedo Island** just outside of Ketchikan, passengers see the fate of forests that have been heavily logged. Much of the island's west side has been clear-cut. Patches of slash remain, as do the twisting dirt roads that brought the trees to tidewater. Beyond the clear-cuts, the archipelago unfolds. Low tide reveals the granite edges of the islands, dark circles of rock that stick out like stubborn cases of ring-around-the-collar.

At Rudyerd Bay, the planes pass one rock face after another, getting close enough to see the grooves and striations cut by glaciers into the granite. Some flightseeing

priced and come with wood or oil stoves. Some cabins are on salt water, but most are on mountain lakes and have rowboats for fishing and exploring. While the cabins themselves are a great value, traveling to them can be expensive. Even a short hop by floatplane from Ketchikan will cost several hundred dollars.

Among the most scenic cabin sites are those at Big Goat and Punchbowl Lakes, but there's a drawback. These and several other lakes are on a main flight path, and you're likely to see and hear small aircraft throughout the summer.

What visitors sacrifice in scenery beyond the flight path they will make up for in serenity. A good alternative is the cabin at **Wynstanley Lake**, a crescent of clear water brimming with cutthroat trout and visited by herons and loons. A two-mile trail leads to tidewater, where you may spot bald eagles, harbor seals, and perhaps a pod of killer whales. Around the lake, 150-foot trees are arranged on the mountainsides like choirboys on risers. What from the air looks like a sea of green becomes a magnificent garden on the ground. There are hemlocks with drooping boughs, red and yellow cedars with flat needles, and stately Sitka spruce. Sculptors could never duplicate the shape of roots and knots. Perfumers could never match the thick conifer musk.

Across the lake from the cabin, halfway up the mountain, the ground flattens and the tops of the great trees form a bench where morning mist lingers like a fat gray

trips feature a landing at a mountain lake. Pilots may choose to set down in Punchbowl Lake, named for the steep rock walls and small islands that, from the air, resemble cakes of ice in a punch bowl. Another favorite landing site is **Big Goat Lake**, bordered on two sides by mountains that rise 2,500 feet above the water's surface and on the other two by a steep, 1,500-foot drop. From above, the lake looks as if it's suspended in midair. Farther south, **New Eddystone Rock** sticks out of a tiny island in the middle of Behm Canal. The formation is a magma plug that hardened in the throat of a volcano. The cone eroded away and left the plug jutting skyward.

Scenery and Serenity

There are no restrictions on camping or backpacking for those hardy souls who want to explore the park on the ground. Given the abundant rain, however, many people leave their tents at home and rent one of 14 public-use cabins. They are reasonably

cat on a green couch. To the east, near the inlet creek, mist from a hot spring curls back to the glassy surface. Puffy clouds the size of boats dawdle just above the lowest branches of the trees. They hang there, almost within reach, as if too lazy to climb any higher.

Even the walk to the outhouse is majestic. A narrow dirt path meanders between 300-year-old spruce rising from a blanket of moss. You almost expect Frodo Baggins and his Hobbit pals to come strolling down the trail.

There's an almost palpable silence here, and a kind of emptying takes place after just a single night's sleep. Deadlines and details drift away. When the air taxi pilot leaves, the place is yours for however long you wish to stay, maybe longer, given Misty's propensity for grounding small aircraft. The only human sounds are those you make yourself, and the hum of a distant airplane seems a roaring intrusion.

Few trails thread through the monument, but this one (opposite) connects Punchbowl Cove with Punchbowl Lake.

Floatplanes like this Beaver (above) provide easy access to mountain's lakes in the monument.

Wooded islets (below) dot the mountainous southeast coast.

TRAVEL TIPS

DETAILS

When to Go

May through August is the best time to visit. May and June usually have the most sun, but visitors to Alaska's panhandle should always expect heavy mist, fog, drizzle, even downpours, especially in September and October. Temperatures average 50° to 66°F in July. Winter temperatures are mild, averaging 40° to 30°F in January.

How to Get There

Arrange an air taxi or charter boat from Ketchikan, or take a ferry on the Alaska Marine Highway System. Numerous charter companies offer tours of the monument.

Getting Around

There are no roads in the park. Travel is by foot, powerboat, or kayak. Most visitors rely on tour operators. A list of operators is available through the Ketchikan Visitors Bureau or the U.S. Forest Service's Southeast Alaska Visitors Center.

Backcountry Travel

No permit is required for hiking or camping at Misty Fiords, although visitors should discuss their plans with rangers before arriving. For detailed information, call the U.S. Forest Service, 907-228-6214.

INFORMATION

Alaska Marine Highway (State Ferry System)

P.O. Box 25535; Juneau, AK 99802-5535; tel: 800-642-0066.

Alaska Public Lands Information Center

3031 Tongass Avenue; Ketchikan, AK 99901; tel: 907-228-6220.

Ketchikan Visitor Bureau

131 Front Street; Ketchikan, AK 99901; tel: 800-770-3300.

U.S. Forest Service

Southeast Alaska Visitor Center, 50 Main Street; Ketchikan, AK 99901; tel: 907-228-6214.

CAMPING

Camping is permitted within the park, but there are no established campsites. Cabins and three-sided shelters are available for rent and can be reserved by calling or writing the Forest Service. About 150 cabins are available for rent elsewhere in Tongass National Forest. To reserve a campsite or cabin, call 877-444-6777.

LODGING

PRICE GUIDE – double occupancy

$ = up to $49 $$ = $50–$99

$$$ = $100–$149 $$$$ = $150+

Blueberry Hill Bed and Breakfast

500 Front Street, P.O. Box 9508; Ketchikan, AK 99901; tel: 907-247-2583.

This spacious house, set on a quiet hill in downtown Ketchikan's historic district, has four guest rooms, including a suite. Simple but tasteful, the rooms are large, with queen-sized beds and private baths; some rooms have views of either the Tongass Narrows or Deer Mountain. Large homemade breakfasts are served. $$–$$$

Gilmore Hotel

326 Front Street, P.O. Box 6814; Ketchikan, AK 99901; tel: 800-275-9423 or 907-225-9423.

This 1927 hotel in downtown Ketchikan retains a period atmosphere. Guest rooms have private baths; some offer views of the bay and mountains. A restaurant is on the premises. A courtesy van transports guests anywhere within city limits. $$

Ingersoll Hotel

303 Mission Street; Ketchikan, AK 99901; tel: 800-478-2124 or 907-225-2124.

In the heart of downtown Ketchikan, the Ingersoll offers 58 modern guest rooms with private baths. The hotel serves complimentary tea and coffee in the lounge and provides a courtesy van. $$–$$$

Super 8 Motel

2151 Sea Level Drive; Ketchikan, AK 99901; tel: 800-800-8000 or 907-225-9088.

This four-story motel, built in 1983 and recently remodeled, has more than 80 spacious rooms and suites with queen-sized beds and private baths; some rooms have views of the Tongass Narrows. One and a half miles from downtown Ketchikan, the motel is situated next to a number of restaurants and a bowling alley. A laundry service is on the premises. Free shuttle service to and from the Airport Ferry, Alaska Marine Highway Ferry, and town are available. $$

Westmark Cape Fox Hotel

800 Venetia Way; Ketchikan, AK 99901; tel: 800-544-0970 or 907-225-8001.

Many of the 75 guest rooms offer sensational views of the Tongass Narrows. All rooms have private baths, décor with a Native Alaska theme, and either two double beds or one king-sized bed. The hotel is set on a hillside above town and is reached by a scenic tram. A restaurant and lounge are on the premises. $$$–$$$$

TOURS & OPERATORS

Alaska Cruises

P.O. Box 7814; Ketchikan, AK 99901; tel: 800-228-1905.

Passengers cruise Misty Fiords aboard a yacht and return by floatplane. Sights include waterfalls, pristine lakes, and 3,000-foot cliffs.

Island Wings Air Service

P.O. Box 733; Ketchikan, AK 99901; tel: 888-854-2444.

The service offers tours of Misty Fiords, glacier and wildlife viewing, charters, and drop-off service.

Ketchikan Kayaking Adventure

Southeast Sea Kayaks,1430 Millar Street; Ketchikan, AK 99901; tel: 800-287-1607.

Kayak rentals and a variety of tours are offered in the Ketchikan and Misty Fiords area.

Promech Air

1515 Tongass Highway; Ketchikan, AK 99901; tel: 907-225-3845.

The service provides charters, Misty Fiords tours, lake trips, and scheduled flights.

Southeast Exposure/Sea Kayakers of Alaska

P.O. Box 9143; Ketchikan, AK 99901; tel: 907-225-8829.

Day trips and extended journeys explore Misty Fiords. Rental equipment is available.

Taquan Air

1007 Water Street; Ketchikan, AK 99901; tel: 800-225-8800.

Flightseeing, charter flights, wilderness drop-offs, and scheduled passenger service are available.

MUSEUMS

Totem Heritage Center

601 Deermont Street; Ketchikan, AK 99901; tel: 907-225-5900.

Exhibits include a totem-pole collection and working carvers and weavers. A self-guided nature path explores rain-forest habitat.

Excursions

Ketchikan

Ketchikan Visitor Bureau, 131 Front Street; Ketchikan, AK 99901; tel: 800-770-3300.

Ketchikan is known to locals as "the First City" because of its location at the bottom of the Alaskan panhandle. But Ketchikan may just as aptly be called "Totemtown," for world travelers nowhere will find this city's rival in the category of totems. The Totem Heritage Center offers daily tours of these intriguing symbols in summer. Dolly's House, a brothel turned museum, examines the history of prostitution during the town's frontier days.

Tongass National Forest-Ketchikan District

U.S. Forest Service, Southeast Alaska Visitor Center, 50 Main Street; Ketchikan, AK 99901; tel: 907-228-6214.

An hour's flight west of Misty Fiords, this area makes up the southern third of the national forest and is roughly the size of New Jersey. Fourteen remote cabins, thirteen designated trails, five lakeside shelters, and four recreational sites are maintained by the Forest Service. The lush rain forest provides an idyllic backdrop for hiking, camping, fishing, canoeing, kayaking, and wildlife viewing beneath a fragrant canopy of towering cedars, spruce, and hemlocks.

Prince of Wales Island

U.S. Forest Service, Southeast Alaska Visitor Center, 50 Main Street; Ketchikan, AK 99901; tel: 907-228-6214.

Prince of Wales, the third-largest U.S. island, is 15 air miles west of Ketchikan. Kayaking, canoeing, sailing, water-skiing, backpacking, and camping are some of the island's popular activities. Wildlife includes black bears, bald eagles, Sitka black-tailed deer, and whales. A network of roads makes island travel easy. Of additional interest to spelunkers is the extensive limestone cave system. Prince of Wales is accessible by air charter or ferry.

Admiralty Island National Monument

CHAPTER **7**

On a clear, calm evening in July, as darkness settles softly over **Seymour Canal** in Southeast Alaska, two kayakers paddle toward the outlet of **Pack Creek** on **Admiralty Island**. A hundred yards from shore, they stop to watch and listen. All around them, barely visible now in the fading light, are the ghostly outlines of chum salmon coming to spawn in the creek's clear waters. These fish are jumpers, and their loud splashes have drawn two adolescent brown bears – the ursine equivalent of teenagers – to the stream's mouth. ◆ Both bears have spent much of their day on the mudflats, eating grass, chasing salmon, and napping. Now the adolescents come face to face, their growls carrying across the water. Tense moments pass before one bear backs away. The other rushes toward the water and does a belly flop among the salmon. It dives underwater and chases fish for several minutes but catches nothing. Playfulness, not hunger, seems to be the motivation. ◆ As darkness deepens,

Protection is the watchword on Admiralty Island, where the Fortress of Bears offers safety for wildlife and visitors alike.

another shadowy form emerges from the old-growth forest that borders the flats. It's a mature male weighing 1,000 pounds or more. He's larger than the others and a much better fisher. The big bear rarely comes to these tidal flats in daylight; he's learned to avoid humans, to hide in the forest. ◆ There are others like this male, fishers of the night. Pack Creek is theirs from dusk until dawn, when human visitors have departed and the mechanized roar of planes and boats has faded, when the only sounds are growls, splashes, and the screeches of eagles, or the rush of wind and the tapping of rain. This is when Admiralty Island more closely

Bald eagles are swift and sure hunters, sweeping down from the heights to pluck fish from the water. The monument protects one of the densest concentrations of nesting bald eagles in the world.

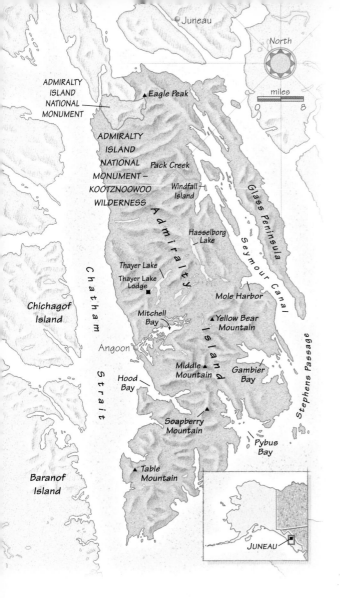

Map labels:

Juneau

North

miles

0   8

ADMIRALTY ISLAND NATIONAL MONUMENT

Eagle Peak

ADMIRALTY ISLAND NATIONAL MONUMENT – KOOTZNOOWOO WILDERNESS

Pack Creek

Windfall Island

Glass Peninsula

Hasselborg Lake

Thayer Lake

Thayer Lake Lodge

Mole Harbor

Admiralty Island

Seymour Canal

Chichagof Island

Chatham Strait

Mitchell Bay

Yellow Bear Mountain

Angoon

Middle Mountain

Gambier Bay

Hood Bay

Stephens Passage

Soapberry Mountain

Pybus Bay

Baranof Island

Table Mountain

JUNEAU

spotting scopes, and video gear. Fly-in visitors begin their day in **Juneau**, about 15 miles away; most stay only a few hours before returning to Alaska's capital and other sightseeing adventures. Other visitors, less focused on bears, come to Admiralty for days at a time to explore its beaches, kayak its coastal waters, fish for trout and salmon, or canoe a route that crosses the island from west to east.

Access to Admiralty Island is limited to boat or plane. No rental facilities are available on the island, so visitors must bring all their own gear and expect to be self-sufficient. Before heading out, it's a good idea to contact the U.S. Forest Service in Juneau, which manages most of the island and can provide details on recreational opportunities. Those seeking local expertise may also wish to arrange guided canoe excursions or bear-viewing trips in Juneau. Numerous wildlife-watching and sportfishing charters also are available. The Juneau Convention and Visitors Bureau can help with planning.

State and federal regulations restrict visitor numbers and access during the prime bear-viewing period in July and August, but Pack Creek nonetheless loses much of its wildness during visiting hours. From 9 A.M. to 9 P.M., up to 24 permit-holding visitors – plus two government staffers – walk along forest and beach trails in the hope of seeing Admiralty's famous brown bears, the coastal cousin of Alaska's inland-dwelling grizzlies. Visitors are greeted by either state or federal personnel. Following a short talk on Pack Creek's do's and don'ts, the permit-holders are turned loose, though the options of where to turn are limited. Bear watching is allowed only at a sand spit near the creek's

resembles its ancient roots – a forest kingdom ruled by bears.

With only a faint band of orange still lighting the horizon, the kayakers paddle back to their camp on **Windfall Island**, half a mile away. They'll return when Pack Creek reopens to humans.

Drop In for a Visit

Daylight changes everything. It's as though an alarm sounds at 8:45 A.M., signaling the start of another bear-viewing day. Planes and boats converge on Pack Creek, bringing people armed with cameras, tripods,

Cottongrass (left) is common around Freshwater Lake on Admiralty Island.

Island bears feed at Pack Creek (opposite, top), feasting on salmon and building fat to carry them through winter.

Distin Lake (opposite, bottom) is part of the Cross-Admiralty Canoe Route that connects several streams and lakes.

mouth and an upstream observation tower; clearly marked paths lead to both.

Anticipating this daily traffic, most of the bears escape into the forest before the tourists arrive. But a mix of adult females, cubs, and adolescents have become accustomed to the presence of humans, and on any given day when the salmon are running, from one to 20 bears may be seen here. The number of bears depends largely on the size of Pack Creek's salmon run, which can range between several hundred and several thousand fish. Weather also comes into play; sightings of brown bears tend to drop on warm, sunny days – but of course those are the exceptions in Southeast Alaska.

Although the viewing system is still being refined to minimize impact on the bears' environment, Pack Creek has a sparkling safety record. According to the Forest Service, no one has been injured by a Pack Creek bear since 1935, nor have any bears been harmed as a result of the viewing program. For this success, a ranger says, "We give most of the credit to the bears."

All visitors to Pack Creek must store and eat their food at a designated food cache and picnic site, and no camping is allowed in the immediate area except on nearby

Windfall Island. Because Windfall and Admiralty are separated by several hundred yards of salt water, campers need some sort of boat to cross the channel.

Otherwise, many overnight visitors stay at one of the 15 public-use cabins managed by the Forest Service. The cabins can accommodate four to eight people and must be reserved in advance; all but three

can be reached only by plane. Another, more luxurious, option is **Thayer Lake Lodge**, a small, rustic operation in the island's heavily forested interior; activities include fishing, boating, and guided bear-viewing.

A Safe Place for Wildlife

Admiralty Island has always been recognized as a refuge for brown bears. Tlingit Indians, the island's earliest human residents, called it *Kootznoowoo*, meaning "bear fort" or, as it's more commonly translated today, "fortress of bears." It's a fitting description for one of North America's richest habitats for brown bears and certainly more appropriate than the name chosen by Capt. George Vancouver in 1794 to honor the English admiralty.

The island is 96 miles long and up to 25 miles wide; it has nearly 700 miles of coastline, dozens of salmon streams, and forested mountains that rise to 4,650 feet. Some 1,500 to 1,700 bears inhabit the island, about one per square mile; few places in the world have a denser population of the animals.

The name Kootznoowoo is appropriate for reasons that go beyond rich habitat and high bear numbers. "Fortress" evokes images of a walled enclosure that affords special protection against attack – in other words, a stronghold. And in recent decades, as more and more of Southeast Alaska's coastal rain forest was clear-cut, crisscrossed with roads, and otherwise developed, that's exactly what Admiralty has become: a sanctuary for brown bears. More than 90 percent of the island is set aside as **Kootznoowoo Wilderness** – the second-largest block of designated wilderness in Alaska's 17-million-acre Tongass National Forest.

The creation of this sanctuary protects not only brown bears but a vast expanse of old-growth forest and the creatures that live in and around it. Once labeled "decadent and unproductive" by the U.S. Forest Service, old-growth forest is now recognized as a critical habitat for a variety of animals. On Admiralty these include Sitka black-tailed deer, minks, river otters, beavers, and five species of Pacific salmon.

The island supports a great variety of birds, too. Migratory

Glacier Walking

Standing on the frigid surface of **Mendenhall Glacier**, just outside of Juneau, you can't help but think: So this is how the Lilliputians felt as they tied down Gulliver. At any moment, it seems, the giant might stir and shake everyone loose. And yet, it's almost impossible to resist the grand scale of glaciers – the jumbled spires of ice, the mysterious fissures, the furrowed, snowy plains. Who wouldn't want to walk atop Gulliver for a while?

Mendenhall is just one of more than 40 glaciers that flow from the 1,500-square-mile **Juneau Icefield**. Several Juneau companies offer flightseeing tours of the ice cap; some set down on the surface and let you walk around for a while. Others supply a guide and all the necessary equipment – boots, crampons, ice axes, and so forth – for a two-hour trek and even a little ice climbing.

Less ambitious travelers can view Mendenhall close-up from a Forest Service information center about 13 miles north of town. The center is set on a lake filled with icebergs that have calved from the massive wall of ice. A short trail leads to the base of the glacier. – *Sherry Simpson*

Helicopter flightseeing (left) offers the benefits of a bird's-eye view and the ability to land precisely on a glacier.

Ancient Sitka spruce (opposite, top) can't be logged within the boundaries of the Kootznoowoo Wilderness, which makes up 90 percent of the island.

A pod of killer whales, or orcas (right), exhale moistly as they surface offshore.

birds such as the trumpeter swan and Canada goose stop at the island on their way to summer nesting grounds, as do ducks like the green-winged teal and northern pintail. Look in coastal waters for the beautiful harlequin duck, white-winged scoter, and arctic tern. Along the shore you'll see clownish black oystercatchers, with their pink legs and feet, and bright orange bills and eye rings. And you'll find such songbirds as the chestnut-backed chickadee, hermit thrush, and Townsend's warbler in muskeg meadows at the edge of the rain forest.

Admiralty also sustains thousands of bald eagles. The U.S. Fish and Wildlife Service has mapped more than 800 eagle nests along the coast, making it one of the densest concentrations of nesting bald eagles in the world. Eagles are frequently seen soaring over the island and its surrounding waters, perched in trees, or scavenging coastal flats, especially during the salmon runs. Though they are dependent on the forest for cover and nesting, they get most of their nourishment from the sea.

There are no long-distance trails on Admiralty, and walking through the rain forest can be extremely difficult, so most wildlife watchers tend to hike along the shore or explore the island by boat. Kayakers and canoeists can take a ferry from Juneau to the little Tlingit village of **Angoon** and then paddle to **Mitchell Bay**. From here, a system of seven lakes and portage trails runs across the island to **Mole Harbor**. The trip takes about 10 days and requires keen outdoor skills, but it offers the best prospect for exploring the interior of the island.

Experienced kayakers also may consider paddling around the island. This is a long and difficult trip with several open water crossings, but paddlers are likely to be rewarded with close-up encounters with humpback whales, orcas, sea lions, sea otters, and other marine mammals.

TRAVEL TIPS

DETAILS

When to Go

Peak bear-viewing is from mid-July to late August. Temperatures in July average from 47° to 64°F. Weather is normally cool and wet; rain gear and rubber boots are essential. Daily park visitation is limited to 24 people from July 5 to August 25. The Forest Service issues permits on a first-come, first-served basis beginning March 1. Applications may be submitted beginning February 20. Bear-viewing, permitted from 9 a.m. to 9 p.m. daily, is best in morning and evening.

How to Get There

The island is reached by boat or plane only. Most visitors arrive first at Juneau International Airport. Juneau, the gateway to the island, is less than 30 minutes from Pack Creek by air. During bear-viewing season, Juneau air-taxis make scheduled and charter flights to the island. For details about transportation, contact the Forest Service Information Center, 907-586-8751.

Getting Around

Island travel is by foot or boat. Collapsible kayaks, transportable by bush plane, are ideal, particularly for those who wish to camp at Windfall Island.

INFORMATION

Admiralty Island National Monument

8461 Old Dairy Road; Juneau, AK 99801; tel: 800-586-8790.

Alaska Public Lands Information Center

3031 Tongass Avenue; Ketchikan, AK 99901; tel: 907-228-6220.

Forest Service Information Center

101 Egan Drive; Juneau, AK 99801; tel: 907-586-8751.

Juneau Convention and Visitors Bureau

369 South Franklin Street; Juneau, AK 99801; tel: 907-586-1737.

CAMPING

The park has 15 public-use cabins, available through the Forest Service Information Center up to six months in advance. Camping is not permitted at Pack Creek. Visitors must have a boat to reach the Windfall Island campground, a half-mile from Pack Creek. Wilderness camping is permitted in most of the park.

LODGING

PRICE GUIDE – double occupancy

$ = up to $49 $$ = $50–$99

$$$ = $100–$149 $$$$ = $150+

Admiralty Island Wilderness Homestead

Four Crab Cove; Funter Bay, AK 99850; tel: 907-586-6243 (winter) or 907-789-4786 (summer).

Tucked into Funter Bay, on the north end of Admiralty Island, this five-acre homestead specializes in made-to-order nature adventures – beach-combing from open skiffs, cruises along Chatham and Icy Straits, nature hikes through rain forest and meadows. Two guest rooms in the main house offer private baths, hardwood floors, Persian rugs, and bay views. A private carriage house offers basic accommodations. Meals, included in packages, specialize in vegetables, salmon, and crab. Open May to September. $$$$

Breakwater Inn

1711 Glacier Avenue; Juneau, AK 99802; tel: 800-544-2250 or 907-586-6303.

The inn overlooks Aurora Harbor and the wild mountains of Douglas Island. The main building has 40 guest rooms, all with private baths, mountain views, and kitchenettes, some with balconies. Cabins offer spacious rooms, private baths, picture windows, and views of the harbor. The inn, a short walk from downtown Juneau, has a lounge and award-winning seafood restaurant. A free airport shuttle is available. $$–$$$

Pearson's Pond Luxury Inn and Garden Spa

4541 Sawa Circle; Juneau, AK 99801-8723; tel: 888-658-6328 or 907-789-3772.

A mile from Mendenhall Glacier, this resort offers both recreation and relaxation. Among the many activities are mountain biking, boating, and hiking on glacial trails. Unwinding can include massages, soaks in hot tubs, or strolls among the inn's lush gardens. Each of the inn's tastefully appointed guest rooms has a queen-sized bed, private bath, stocked kitchenette, electric fireplace, and deck. Forest and pond views are available. Open year-round. $$$–$$$$

Thayer Lake Lodge

Box 8897; Ketchikan, AK 99901; tel: 907-247-8897 or 907-225-3343.

This tranquil lodge, in the heart of Admiralty Island National Monument, has been operated by the same family since 1952. *Newsweek* called it "the kind of place Henry David Thoreau would have loved." Guests stay in private, lakeside cabins. Fishing, bear-watching, or float-trip packages include meals, air transportation to and from Juneau, guides, and the use of a skiff or canoe. $$$$

TOURS & OUTFITTERS

Alaska Discovery

5449 Shaune Drive, Suite 4; Juneau, AK 99801; tel: 800-586-1911.

Guides lead bear-viewing and

kayak trips to Admiralty Island. Excursions of a day, a week, or longer are available.

Coastal Wilderness Tours

c/o Alaska Coastal Airlines, 1873 Shell Simmons Drive; Juneau, AK 99801; tel: 800-556-8101.

Small, personal, eco-friendly flightseeing tours explore Admiralty Island and other wilderness areas in the Alaskan panhandle.

Deishu Expeditions & Alaska Kayak Supply

12 Portage Street, P.O. Box 1406; Haines, AK 99827; tel: 800-552-9257.

The company offers a variety of adventure packages in Southeast Alaska, including a seven-day kayak and hiking trip from Juneau to Admiralty Island and Tracy Arm-Fords Terror Wilderness.

MUSEUMS

Alaska State Museum

395 Whittier Street; Juneau, AK 99801-1718; tel: 907-465-2901.

The museum interprets the human and natural history of Alaska, with a special emphasis on wildlife, Native cultures, Russian trade and exploration, and the American period.

Juneau Douglas City Museum

155 South Seward; Juneau, AK 99801; tel: 907-586-3572.

Exhibits and video presentations concentrate on frontier life in early Juneau and the region's gold-mining history.

Excursions

Juneau

Juneau Convention and Visitors Bureau, 369 South Franklin Street; Juneau, AK 99801; tel: 907-586-1737.

Juneau, travel writer John Murray observes, is "the only state capital in the country where the governor's mansion is only nine blocks from prime grizzly bear habitat." Snowcapped peaks surround the city; a spawning creek flows through town. Originally a mining camp, Juneau retains some of its gold-rush-era hot spots, such as the Red Dog Saloon and Alaskan Hotel Bar. A must-see is the onion-domed, octagon-shaped St. Nicholas Russian Orthodox Church, built in 1894. The Alaska State Museum interprets Alaska's Native cultures and examines the state's natural history.

South Baranof Wilderness

U.S. Forest Service, Sitka Ranger District, 201 Katlian Street, Suite 109; Sitka, AK 99664; tel: 907-474-4220.

This spectacular 320,000-acre wilderness straddles the southern portion of Baranof Island. The area's western side is honeycombed with bays, inlets, estuaries, and spruce-canopied glades. The eastern side has hanging glaciers. Sheer mountains, two miles inland, exceed 4,000 feet; valleys end in steep basins resembling amphitheaters. Brown bears, Sitka black-tailed deer, beavers, seals, mink, and sea otters inhabit the island, which is reached only by boat or floatplane.

Tracy Arm-Fords Terror Wilderness

Forest Service Information Center, 101 Egan Drive; Juneau, AK 99801; tel: 907-586-8751.

A popular destination among kayakers, 50 miles south of Juneau, Tracy and Endicott Arms are long, glacier-carved fjords reaching into the heavily glaciated Coast Mountain Range. Active tidewater glaciers at the head of these fjords calve icebergs into the sea. Fords Terror, an area of sheer rock walls, forms a slender entrance into a small fjord. The wilderness, bordered on the east by Canada, is reached primarily by boat or floatplane from Juneau.

Glacier Bay National Park

CHAPTER 8

The essence of this place is ice, in every color, shape, and form imaginable: Icefields a thousand feet deep, and ice that flows in vast rivers 25 miles long. Icebergs with the opaque density of porcelain or the marbled grandeur of jade. Ice that appears black, thrown into deep shade by a passing cloud. Ice with the brilliance of a blue sapphire struck by a laser. Miniature ice crystals buried in tundra sphagnum, and massive rafts rushing down dark interior rivers. Cliff ice like a castle with columns and porches, amphitheaters and antechambers. ◆ In Glacier Bay, the geological clock has been turned back, allowing you to view, in the cold fjords and forests, the world as it was during the Pleistocene, when immense glaciers ruled the Northern Hemisphere. From such a wilderness of earth and sky, moss and mist, lumbering bears and howling wolves walked a creature that would one day erect the Parthenon, compose symphonies, and land a spacecraft on the moon. To visit Glacier Bay is to take a time machine into the

Take a kayak or tour boat into an icy wilderness of calving glaciers, breaching whales, and lumbering bears.

distant past and see the harsh but beautiful world from which the human race came – and, perhaps, if geological history is predictive, to visit the distant future and see the world as it one day will be again. ◆ Located 60 miles northwest of Juneau, Alaska's capital, **Glacier Bay National Park and Preserve** is one of the state's most visited parks. Declared a national monument in 1925 and a national park in 1980, the park protects nearly 3.3 million acres, an area larger than Yellowstone National Park and Great Smoky Mountains National Park combined. The park has five chief natural attractions: a 65-mile-long bay with a half-dozen major fjords; 12 tidewater

Icebergs lightly bump against a sea kayak exploring Johns Hopkins Inlet of Glacier Bay, an icy wonderland not far from Juneau.

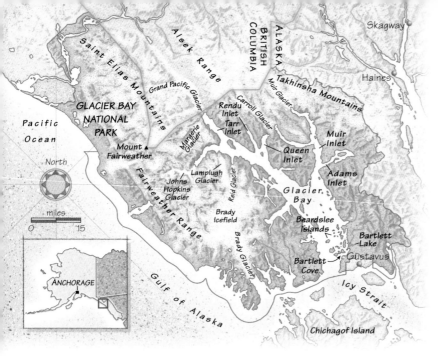

a thousand feet taller than California's Mount Whitney, the highest mountain in the Lower 48 states.

Getting Started

Glacier Bay National Park is most conveniently entered via **Gustavus**, near the southern mouth of the bay. Access to this friendly, compact village of about 300 year-round residents is by airplane and boat. The half-hour flight from Juneau is the most popular means of reaching the park. Many also visit the park by cruise ship. Park headquarters is

glaciers; a world-class abundance of wildlife, particularly marine mammals (whales, sea otters, and porpoises) and coastal seabirds; a little-known outer coast fronting the Pacific Ocean and extending more than 100 miles from north to south; and the high alpine mountains of the Fairweather Range. **Mount Fairweather**, which rises three miles above sea level and lords over Glacier Bay like a presiding spirit, is nearly

located at **Bartlett Cove**, about 10 miles west of the Gustavus airfield and quickly reached by shuttle bus. Both Gustavus and Bartlett Cove have cabins, but Bartlett Cove also has campgrounds.

Most visitors come between mid-May and mid-September, when the long summer days afford more time for outdoor activities and wildlife observation. Around the summer solstice in June, for example, there are only five hours of darkness, or twilight. Visitors earlier in the season (late April through June) generally will have more sunshine. September can be a rainy month throughout Southeast Alaska. Winter along the coast is famous for its seaborne storms reminiscent of those in Winslow Homer's paintings.

For the purpose of most recreational visits, Glacier Bay National Park can be divided into two distinct regions: the lower bay near Bartlett Cove and the two arms of the upper bay. Although the lower bay is 43 miles from the major tidewater glaciers, quite a lot can be done in the area. At Bartlett Cove, visitors will find a comfortable campground set among the trees and the popular Glacier Bay Lodge, which operates from mid-May to mid-September. Park naturalists conduct daily hikes from the lodge, and rangers present films, videos, talks, or slide shows nearly every evening.

Several good hiking trails around Bartlett Cove lead through the forests and meadows, and beachcombing and birding (gulls, terns, bald eagles, murrelets, cormorants, oyster-catchers) along the ample shorelines are always rewarding. Moose usually can be seen around nearby **Bartlett Lake**.

A special boating permit is required in advance to enter the park's waters because of the regulations protecting humpback whales. Kayakers will find good paddling in and around Bartlett Cove, where kayaks can be rented, and among the **Beardslee Islands**, just north of the cove. Kayak rentals and outfitters are also located in Gustavus. All boaters are encouraged to carry a portable radio; the Park Service monitors several radio frequencies.

World of Glaciers

A tour boat leaves Bartlett Cove dock every morning for the trip up the bay's **West Arm,** where several showy glaciers march down from the mountains and release ice-

Cruise ships (opposite) tour Tarr Inlet, along with smaller day boats and independent kayakers.

Moose (left), bears, wolves, and Sitka black-tailed deer all live in the park.

Freshly calved icebergs (below) from McBride Glacier are stranded by low tide in Muir Inlet.

bergs into the water. Some glaciers are more approachable than others. **Reid Glacier**, now in retreat, is set like a gem inside a cove, while **Lamplugh Glacier** drops directly into the broad inlet. **Johns Hopkins**, which discharges armies of icebergs, is tucked into a backdoor entrance to the Fairweather Range. Several other glaciers are stranded among the thousand-foot peaks that ring this stunning basin. Around the corner, **Margerie Glacier** and **Grand Pacific Glacier** meet at the head of **Tarr Inlet**, a stony chute. **Rendu Inlet** and **Tidal Inlet** are remarkable for their numerous water-

falls that cascade down barren cliffs. These fjords, as well as **Queen Inlet**, offer isolated eddies off the main thoroughfare of vessel traffic.

Muir Inlet in the **East Arm** is reachable only on multiday trips on tour boats that depart from towns on the **Inside Passage**, such as Ketchikan, Sitka, and Juneau.

A trip to the upper bay is a voyage back in botanical time. The forest at the mouth of the bay is a lush climax assemblage of spruce and hemlock. These trees gradually dwindle to stands of cottonwood, a hardier species, and then dense thickets of alder and willow. At the head of the bay, among the rubble and moraines, grow yellow-flowered dryas and dwarf fireweed, northern plants best suited to establish the first toehold of life on newly forming soils. These tough pioneers colonize areas left bare by the retreating glaciers and help to produce the soil on which other, more deeply rooted plant species eventually will live. The glaciers in the upper bay have retreated more than 80 miles since their discovery during the 1794 expedition by Captain George Vancouver. Such rapid retreat of major glaciers is unknown elsewhere in the world, and scientists are actively studying the phenomenon, hoping to gain fresh insights into the causes and effects of long-term climatic changes.

More adventuresome travelers, with more time, can arrange for boats operated by park concessionaires to drop them off in remote wilderness locations for camping, hiking, exploring, and sea kayaking. Air taxi services operating out of Gustavus also can take visitors flightseeing to view the seemingly endless miles of spectacular landscape. Another popular activity in the park is fishing; anglers should remember to obtain a fishing license and to review

An ice cave (left), beneath tons of ancient ice, reflects an eerie blue glow.

Cow parsnip (top) blooms among shoreline lyme grass at Icy Point on the less-traveled outer coast of Glacier Bay National Park.

An explorer (right) squeezes into the silent reaches of a crevasse that formed at the base of a glacier.

Rivers of Ice

Three factors are necessary for the formation of a glacier: abundant snowfall, deep basins in which snow can accumulate, and steadily cold temperatures. If just one of these criteria is missing, a glacier will not form.

As snow and ice pile up, the frozen mass becomes compacted into a dense, opaque slab as solid as rock. When ice accumulates to a depth of about 100 feet, the glacier begins to move downhill under its own weight. Over time its irresistible movement shapes the surrounding landscape, smoothing jagged rock formations, widening narrow valleys, bulldozing huge piles of rubble known as moraines, and picking up boulders, or erratics, and depositing them miles from their source.

Cracks or crevasses form when the glacier's heavy middle area moves faster than its shallow edges, resulting in a laceration or tearing of the ice sheet. Crevasses can be quite deep and are always a danger to hikers.

Harbor seals' fur is so dense that the animals (left) can easily tolerate lying directly on ice floes.

A black bear (below) prowls a rocky inlet intent on finding a meal.

Whales like this breaching humpback (opposite) are closely monitored to ensure that fishing, boating, and tourism don't negatively affect the population.

and observe the current regulations. Landscape photographers nearly always find the cloudy-bright conditions and frequent rain of Glacier Bay a challenge. Ansel Adams spent the better part of a week here in 1948 and only was able to take a handful of photographs of the rain forest at Bartlett Cove and of an iceberg grounded on the beach.

Watching for Whales

Glacier Bay is celebrated for its whales, which are plentiful in the area every summer. Two species, the humpback and minke, are

found in the bay. Humpbacks, the most acrobatic, often can be seen heaving their bodies – averaging 50 feet in length and weighing more than 40 tons – out of the water. Coastal feeders, they live on krill, shrimp, and various small fish. Humpbacks do not feed year-round; they store enough fat in the summer to survive the rest of the year. They are considered an endangered species because of overhunting and loss of habitat, especially their nursery habitat in Hawaii and Baja California. Minke whales, which are also migratory, are fast swimmers and can reach 20 miles per hour. They live primarily on cod and pollock, average around 26 feet in length, and, because of their protein-rich meat, are heavily hunted.

Orcas, commonly known as killer whales, also are found in the bay, often in extended family groups. In these pods, the whales use sonic communication to aid one another in times of distress, and work cooperatively while hunting. They prey on a wide variety of creatures, from birds to sea lions and other whales. Averaging 26 feet in length, orcas can accelerate to speeds of 34 miles per hour while attacking. When you are out on the waters of Glacier Bay, look for their prominent black-and-white dorsal fins, which may reach six feet high in adult males.

Special precautions need to be taken whenever traveling in the

Alaskan wilderness, especially in Glacier Bay. Of particular concern are the frequently calving tidewater glaciers and numerous unstable icebergs; brown bears and black bears concentrated along shorelines; dangerous stream and river crossings; powerful tides and waves; and breaching whales and large cruise ships in close proximity to kayaks and small boats. Hypothermia also is a worry whenever people find themselves on or around the water, particularly in rainy or snowy conditions. Park rangers can provide information about all of these subjects. Because of the wet maritime climate, travelers are well advised to bring knee-high rubber hiking boots and traditional backcountry rain gear such as ponchos and rain pants.

Astronauts who have made several trips into space have often observed that there is nothing quite as exciting and memorable as that first wild ride into orbit. So it will be with your first view of Glacier Bay, whether it is from the center of a 12-foot sea kayak or the side of a 10-story cruise ship. The spectacular beauty of the place will forever change your views of wild nature and the geographic diversity of the North American continent. When the naturalist John Muir visited Glacier Bay in 1879 after decades of climbing the high peaks of California's Sierra Nevada range, he was stunned by the place. "Beneath the frosty shadows of the fjord," he wrote, "we stood hushed and awe-stricken, gazing at the holy vision; and had we seen the heavens opened and God made manifest, our attention could not have been more tremendously strained."

Such is the power of Glacier Bay to stir the spirit. The coming and going of the tides, the sudden thunder of the calving glaciers, the crackling of icebergs, the changing sky, the quiet of the evergreen forests, the breaching whales, the flocking seabirds – they will remain with you forever. Glacier Bay is, as some old-timers are fond of saying, "comeback country."

TRAVEL TIPS

DETAILS

When to Go

The park is open year-round, the visitor center mid-May to mid-September. Visitation peaks in July. Average July temperatures range from 48° to 63°F; January, 26° to 16°F. Rain and cold weather are possible in any season. Pack a hat, gloves, rain gear, and waterproof boots.

How to Get There

Commercial airlines serve Juneau International Airport, 70 miles from Glacier Bay. There is no road to the park, which is reached only by charter boat and plane. Scheduled air service is available from Juneau to Gustavus; buses and taxis run the 10 miles between Gustavus and the park entrance. Contact the park office for a list of transportation services.

Getting Around

Kayaking is popular with independent travelers in the park. Kayak rentals and guides are available. The majority of travelers view Glacier Bay from cruise ships. Daily cruises depart from Glacier Bay Lodge, nine miles from Gustavus. Contact the park for details on boating permits and restrictions.

Backcountry Travel

Hiking and backpacking are allowed in the park; no fee or permit is required, but all backcountry travelers are advised to contact rangers before departing.

INFORMATION

Alaska Public Lands Information Center
605 West 4th Avenue, Suite 105; Anchorage, AK 99501; tel: 907-271-2737 or 3031 Tongass Avenue; Ketchikan, AK 99901; tel: 907-228-6220.

Glacier Bay National Park
P.O. Box 140; Gustavus, AK 99826-0140; tel: 907-697-2230.

Gustavus Visitor Association
P.O. Box 167; Gustavus, AK 99826; tel: 907-697-2475.

CAMPING

The park campground at Bartlett Cove is available on a first-come, first-served basis. Campers must attend a free camper orientation at the Visitor Information Station and check out a bear-resistant food canister. Bear-resistant food caches, firewood, and a warming hut are provided at the campground.

LODGING

PRICE GUIDE – double occupancy	
$ = up to $49	$$ = $50–$99
$$$ = $100–$149	$$$$ = $150+

Annie Mae Lodge

Grandpa's Farm Road, P.O. Box 80; Gustavus, AK 99826; tel: 800-478-2346 or 907-697-2346.

This two-story log lodge, about four miles from Gustavus Airport, has wrap-around porches and spectacular views of the rain forest, mountains, and Icy Strait. Eleven guest rooms offer private or shared baths. Two- to five-day packages include breakfast, packed lunches, and fresh seafood dinners served in the dining room. Also included are whale watching, sea kayaking, flightseeing, and hiking. Free ground transportation is provided. $$$$

Bear Track Inn

P.O. Box 255; Gustavus, AK 99826; tel: 888-697-2284 or 907-697-3017.

This handcrafted log lodge has 14 spacious guest rooms with private baths, two queen-sized beds, and down comforters. The lobby, whose ceiling rises 30 feet, has a walk-around fireplace, overstuffed suede couches, and moose-antler chandeliers. Packages include gourmet meals, ferry transportation from Juneau, and all ground transportation. Guests choose from activities such as whale watching, sea kayaking, and flightseeing. Open February 15 to October 1. $$$$

Glacier Bay Lodge

Glacier Bay Park Concessions, 520 Pike Street, Suite 1400; Seattle, WA 98101; tel: 800-451-5952 or 206-626-7110.

Striking views of the rain forest are available from the park's only lodge, set on Bartlett Cove, nine miles from the airport in Gustavus. More than 50 rooms, each with three bunk beds, are available in men's and women's dormitories. Guests share bath and shower facilities. Breakfast, lunch, and dinner are served in the dining room; patio dining is available in the evening. Boat tours, which leave from the dock below the lodge, and a camper drop-off service are available. Open May 15 to September 10. $

Gustavus Inn

P.O. Box 60; Gustavus, AK 99826 (May to September) or 7920 Outlook; Prairie Village, KS 66208 (October to April); tel: 800-649-5220 or 907-697-2254.

This cedar-sided, New-England-style house was built in 1925 and later expanded. Overlooking Icy Strait about eight miles from the park, the inn offers 13 rooms, each with a private bath, a queen-sized bed, and one twin bed. Included in the price are three daily meals, featuring fresh vegetable and seafood dishes. Boat tours, fishing charters, whale watching, and sea kayaking are offered. Open May 15 to September 15. $$$

Puffin's Bed and Breakfast

P.O. Box 3: Gustavus, AK 99826; tel: 907-697-2260.

The lodge is situated on a seven-acre homestead, surrounded by wildflowers and berries. It offers modern cottages with laundry facilities and private baths. Full country breakfasts are served each morning. Recreational opportunities include bicycling, fishing, kayaking, whale watching, and Glacier Bay tour packages. Open seasonally. $–$$

TOURS & OUTFITTERS

Alaska Discovery

5449 Shaune Drive, Suite 4; Juneau, AK 99801; tel: 800-586-1911.

Guided kayak trips range from evening paddles to expeditions lasting several days.

Coastal Wilderness Tours

c/o Alaska Coastal Airlines, 1873 Shell Simmons Drive; Juneau, AK 99801; tel: 800-556-8101.

Eco-friendly flightseeing tours specialize in the wilderness and wildlife of the Alaskan panhandle.

Glacier Bay Sea Kayaks

P.O. Box 26; Gustavus, AK 99826; tel: 907-697-2257.

The park concession offers sea-kayak rentals, outfitting, orientation and instruction, and can arrange drop-off and pick-up service on the park tour boat.

Northgate Tours & Cruises

P.O. Box 20613; Juneau, AK 99802; tel: 888-463-5321 or 907-463-5321.

Three- to five-night "active adventure" cruises aboard the 86-passenger M/V *Wilderness Discoverer* explore Glacier Bay and the Inside Passage. Passengers sleep on board and spend each day sea kayaking or hiking on shore.

Spirit Walker Expeditions

P.O. Box 240; Gustavus, AK 99826; tel: 907-697-2266.

Guided sea-kayaking and camping expeditions range from a half-day to a week or longer.

Excursions

Kluane National Park

P.O. Box 5495; Haines Junction, YT YOB 1L0, Canada; tel: 867-634-2251.

Situated in the southwest corner of the Yukon Territory about 100 air miles from Glacier Bay National Park and Preserve, Kluane is home to Canada's highest summit, Mount Logan. The Saint Elias Mountains sprawl across the park, containing some of the most expansive nonpolar icefields. Mountain lakes, tundra, alpine meadows, and rivers typify the park's landscape. One of the world's largest grizzly-bear populations is found here. Other species include ptarmigan, golden eagles, caribou, Dall sheep, mountain goats, wolves, and moose.

Tatshenshini-Alsek Provincial Park

Skeena District, 3790 Alfred Avenue, Bag 5000; Smithers BC V0J 2N0, Canada; tel: 250-847-7320.

This Canadian refuge, between the Yukon's Kluane National Park and Alaska's Glacier Bay National Park, was established in 1993 and declared a World Heritage Site the following year. The Tatshenshini River, one of the world's most picturesque waterways, flows into the Alsek River near the center of the park. Alpine tundra and towering glaciers are visible along the rivers, perfect for kayak or raft trips. Grizzly bears, mountain goats, bighorn sheep, moose, foxes, and wolves inhabit the refuge; peregrine falcons and numerous bald eagles patrol the sky.

West Chichagof-Yakobi Wilderness

U.S. Forest Service, Sitka Ranger District, 201 Katlian Street, Suite 109; Sitka, AK 99664; tel: 907-474-4220.

Encompassing the western region of Chichagof and Yakobi Islands, this 265,000-acre wilderness has a spectacular 65-mile-long coastline. In addition to fine views of the Pacific Ocean and rugged offshore islands, the area has old-growth rain forest and wild-shrub forests. Western hemlock and Sitka spruce cover about one third of the wilderness. Sheer mountains rise 3,600 feet above the ocean. Savanna glades are found along portions of the coast. Sitka black-tailed deer and brown bears inhabit the islands; seals are found on the shore.

Chilkoot Trail

C H A P T E R **9**

The second-biggest gold rush in American history began on August 17, 1896, when George Washington Carmack and a couple of fortune-seeking associates hit paydirt at a godforsaken place called Rabbit Creek in northwest Canada. Before you could say *Eureka!,* the word got out. And by January 1897, nearly 50 years after the strike at Sutter's Mill that turned California into the Golden State, the hot new place to be was the Yukon. ◆ Hordes of adventurers flocked to Alaska. Most of the fever-stricken headed for **Skagway**, a small port at the north end of the **Inside Passage**. Skagway was the jumping-off place en route to the Klondike region and Rabbit Creek, renamed **Bonanza Creek**. All through the fall of 1897, steamers out of Seattle and Vancouver packed with would-be millionaires arrived at Skagway. Its population surged from 10 to 10,000, most of the newcomers living in tents and shacks. ◆ Saloons and gambling houses sprang up along the muddy

Follow the route of gold-rush "stampeders" up the Golden Stairs and over the infamous Chilkoot Pass, where history lies underfoot.

streets, ladies of easy virtue plied their trade, and lawful behavior was the exception. For the better part of a year, Soapy Smith terrorized the town as gambler, outlaw, gang leader, swindler, and bully, until he met his reward in a dramatic shootout. Those who managed to get past him and his gang went on to cross the **Coast Mountains** as they embarked on the hazardous journey to the Klondike gold fields. ◆ One route, beginning in Skagway, was the **White Pass Trail**, dubbed Dead Horse Trail for the thousands of pack animals that died along the way. Although steeper, a parallel route first blazed by the Tlingit Indians was deemed a faster way to cross the

A mountain creek cascades into the Taiya River along the Chilkoot Trail.

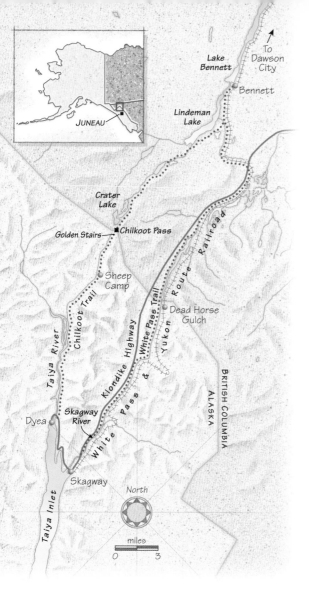

Lake
Bennett

To
Dawson
City

Bennett

Lindeman
Lake

JUNEAU

Crater
Lake

Golden Stairs — ■ Chilkoot Pass

White Pass & Yukon Route Railroad

Sheep
Camp

Dead Horse
Gulch

Chilkoot Trail

Taiya River

Klondike Highway

White Pass & Yukon Route Trail

ALASKA

BRITISH COLUMBIA

Dyea

Skagway
River

Skagway

White Pass

Taiya Inlet

North

miles

0   3

been staked. Some stayed to work for the luckier miners, while others moved on to more promising sites.

Gold Rush Outpost

Much of what remains of the period is preserved by **Klondike Gold Rush National Historical Park**, which administers the White Pass and Chilkoot Trails and visitor centers in Seattle and Skagway. The best way for backpackers to immerse themselves in the stampeder experience is to follow the Chilkoot Trail. Each year thousands of people make the 33-mile trek over the 3,525-foot pass into Canada, returning on the **White Pass & Yukon Railway**, which closely parallels the White Pass Trail.

The journey starts in Skagway, a diverse town with several museums, a restored historic district, and many hotels, motels, and restaurants. The National Park Service/Parks Canada **Trail Center** on Broadway, several blocks north of the harbor, provides information on hiking the trail and issues hiking permits (50 people per day are allowed to cross the pass). These permits allow use of the nine primitive campgrounds along the trail, the first located at **Mile 4.9**, the last in **Bennett**. Across the street at the National Park Service **Visitor Center** are fascinating exhibits on the gold rush, which hikers will want to view before they set out.

Walking the entire trail takes about three to five days. Although it can be traversed from either direction, park officials recommend that hikers start from the Skagway area. Because of the steep grade and many loose rocks at the pass, the trail is much safer to ascend than descend. The well-marked trailhead is nine miles northwest of Skagway just beyond the Dyea ranger station and campground. Those staying at hotels or motels in town can arrange an early-morning taxi to the trailhead.

mountains. This was the **Chilkoot Trail**, beginning in **Dyea**, a settlement three miles north of Skagway. Hazards abounded. Some men perished in icy crevasses, or froze to death, or fell victim to mundane illnesses. The worst incident occurred in April 1898 when an avalanche buried almost 100 prospectors at Chilkoot Pass.

The frenzy lasted only two years. Many gold diggers arrived in the Klondike only to discover that all the good claims had

Historic Footsteps

The Chilkoot Trail offers hikers a physically challenging and highly educational tour of the

southeastern Alaskan and Canadian wilderness, from coastal rain forest to alpine tundra to boreal forest. Hikers pass through a beautiful wilderness that resonates with lively associations from the recent past. It is a country full of lessons, both from natural and human history.

For the first eight miles, the trail runs parallel to the **Taiya River** through dense stands of hemlock, cottonwood, and spruce, with considerable deadfall and large standing trees cloaked in moss. Bald eagles often are spotted near the river, and spawning salmon can be seen in the side streams from midsummer through September. Hikers should pay particular attention to downed trees and snags. Both support an array of wildlife, from short-tailed weasels to red squirrels to hairy wood-peckers. Clearings permit a close-up view of local bird life, including the solitary vireo and the ubiquitous robin. Search the riverbank for beavers, muskrats, foxes, and coyotes. Lucky visitors may also spot the elusive northern lynx or reclusive wolverine on a distant gravel bar. Wolves can sometimes be "howled up." More

White Pass & Yukon Railway

The White Pass & Yukon (above) chugs across the Tunnel Mountain tressel.

Gold-rush artifacts (opposite) are strewn along the trail, but souvenir-seeking is banned.

Feverish for gold, men and women made temporary camp (top) in the canyon between Dyea and the Chilkoot Pass.

A lot of feathers were ruffled when railroad workers laid tracks for the White Pass & Yukon line. The project was begun in May 1898. The narrow-gauge railroad crossed White Pass and reached Whitehorse in the Yukon just over a year later, despite labor strikes and an unstable work force easily distracted by nearby gold discoveries, not to mention some very rough weather.

The railway ended the dominance of the Chilkoot Trail and those who controlled it by providing an easier route to the goldfields. By the spring of 1899, even before the last rails were laid, the population of once-booming Sheep Camp, a settlement on the Chilkoot Trail, had dwindled to 18. After crews forged ahead to Whitehorse, the town of Bennett was virtually deserted.

A Chicago newspaper editor declared, with hubris typical of the era, "The solitude of nature is forever undone, and the absolute reign of the monarchs is over." Though the mountain kings may have been conquered, the White Pass & Yukon Railway was a monarch in its own right, controlling local economies and leaving ghost towns in its wake.

By the time the last spike was hammered, the Klondike Gold Rush was over. The railroad prospered for years, carrying passengers and freight between Skagway, Alaska, and Whitehorse, Canada. It finally closed in 1982, but the train was reborn in 1988 as a popular tourist attraction granting visitors a chance to ride the rails of history in comfort. – *Andromeda Romano-Lax*

often, their distinctive five-toed tracks are seen along the river.

Beginning at **Mile 4**, hikers encounter artifacts left by the hopeful throngs that walked the trail a century ago: rusting stoves; sleds and wagons; pieces of clothing and shoes; plus pulleys and cables, the remnants of a freight-hauling aerial tramway. Canadian archaeologists working at the top of the pass in the early 1990s unearthed fragments of a newspaper dating from February 1898.

At **Mile 8**, the trail turns to the northeast and climbs away from the canyon floor for about three miles, following the bypass that stampeders took after the winter of 1897–98, when the frozen Taiya River began to melt. The forest remains thick through this stretch of trail, with occasional berry patches and rock slides; fantastic mountains and hanging glaciers are visible through the trees to the south and north. The trail becomes more scenic as it nears 3,525-foot **Chilkoot Pass**, and gradually the forest is left behind.

Soon encountered are the infamous **Golden Stairs**, once a series of 1,400 steps kicked into the snow and ice. Hundreds of historic photographs depict a solid, foot-to-heel line of overburdened prospectors inching up the snow-covered slope to the pass. Even for today's trekker, the final assault can be quite an ordeal, especially when carrying a heavy backpack.

Hikers early in the season climb mostly over snow. After mid-July, the climb is over rock. Many ascend the steep slope literally on all fours. It is not a place for those with an aversion to heights, but the view from the top rewards those who make the effort.

Chilkat Bald Eagle Preserve

Bald eagles are regarded as solitary birds, and spawning salmon are considered a summer-only phenomenon. Both notions are proven to be misconceptions when you visit the 48,000-acre **Chilkat Bald Eagle Preserve** north of **Haines**.

From October through January, 2,000 to 3,000 of the great raptors gather to dine on a late run of chum salmon. Warm-water springs ensure that a three- to five-mile stretch of shoreline near the junction of the **Chilkat** and **Tsirku Rivers** remains free of ice. This draws the spawning salmon and, in turn, the wintering eagles, which fill the air with their screeching calls.

When the birds aren't feeding on dead and dying salmon, they wait their turn in the river flats and conserve their energy during winter's chill. Or they

roost in the cottonwood trees along the river, engage in mock battles, or soar overhead, spreading their seven-foot wingspan. The eagles' banquet is visible from the **Haines Highway** beginning at Milepost 17.
– *Adromeda Romano-Lax*

Stampeders (top) trod a steep, single-file trail along the Golden Stairs.

Bald eagles (left and above) congregate at the salmon-filled Chilkat River.

Hikers (opposite, top) near the trail's summit.

The Slide Cemetery (right) in Dyea recalls the deadly avalanche of 1898.

Throughout this region the Chilkoot Trail passes through sub-alpine and alpine ecosystems – areas that are vastly different from the lush forests and meadows near the trailhead. Above timberline, plants and animals live in an extremely harsh environment. Winter weather persists through mid-June and begins again in mid-August. The wind constantly blows, and sun-shine is more intense than at lower elevations. Hikers will notice that plants – blueberry, crowberry, reindeer moss, dwarf birch, and willow – hug the ground, where they find relatively protected places to live and reproduce. Birds are plentiful despite the severe condi-tions. Look for such ground-nesting species as long-tailed jaegers, rock ptarmigan, and Lapland longspur as well as golden eagles, ravens, and others that nest on rock escarpments and cliffs. Mammals also are present in surprising numbers and are easy to spot as there are no trees to block your view. Expect to see the hamster-like collared pikas (listen for their distinct warning chirps), white-bearded mountain goats, and black-tailed deer, which range in the uplands in summer. Moose also are occasionally spotted above timberline.

On the other side of the pass, in far northwest British Columbia, **Crater Lake** appears below. Surrounded by vast tracts of tundra, the scene evokes the beautiful lochs of the Scottish highlands. Beyond Crater Lake, several smaller lakes can be seen as the trail gradually descends into a forested region. The trail then follows the east shore of picturesque **Lindeman Lake** and finally reaches the south end of **Lake Bennett** and the town of **Bennett**, where hikers can board the White Pass & Yukon Railway for the 41-mile return to Skagway.

Although a trek on the Chilkoot Trail is normally safe, some precautions are necessary. This is grizzly and black-bear country, so all of the standard practices should be followed: Make noise when traveling through brushy areas, and don't camp near the same area where food is prepared. The final ascent of Chilkoot Pass is up a 35- to 45-degree slope over boulder slides and scree. Those in poor physical condition should think twice before attempting the climb, particularly if they customarily live at or near sea level.

G.LEON
USA
DIED
1898
CHILKOOT
TRAIL

APRIL.3.

TRAVEL TIPS

DETAILS

When to Go

Peak visitation along the trail occurs in July and August. Summer is cool and dry but often windy; rain is common in September. Mid- to late June is drier and less crowded.

How to Get There

Most visitors arrive in Skagway by cruise ship, although the town may be reached by small plane, car, train or bus (in summer), and by ferry (on the Alaska Marine Highway System). Dyea, nine miles from Skagway, is reached by foot, bicycle, or taxi.

Backcountry Travel

Backcountry travelers must clear Canadian customs and pay a reservation fee for trail use in Canada before leaving Skagway. Parks Canada permits 50 people per day to cross the summit. A Canadian permit also covers use of the trail in Alaska. Reservations and permits are available through the Trail Center, 907-983-2046. Hikers should purchase return train tickets to Skagway before setting out. For train information, call 800-343-7373. Hypothermia is a trail hazard; pack rain gear and layers of warm, water-resistant clothing.

INFORMATION

Alaska Public Lands Information Center

605 West 4th Avenue, Suite 105; Anchorage, AK 99501; tel: 907-271-2737.

Haines Convention and Visitors Bureau

P.O. Box 530; Haines, AK 99827; tel: 800-458-3579.

Klondike Gold Rush National Historic Park

P.O. Box 517; Skagway, AK 99840; tel: 907-983-2046 or 907-983-2921.

Skagway Convention and Visitors Bureau

P.O. Box 415; Skagway, AK 99840; tel: 907-983-2854.

CAMPING

Tent sites are available seasonally in Dyea; reservations are not required. For information, call the park at 907-983-2046. Hikers may not camp outside of established sites.

LODGING

PRICE GUIDE – double occupancy

$ = up to $49 $$ = $50–$99

$$$ = $100–$149 $$$$ = $150+

Captain's Choice Motel

P.O. Box 392; Haines, AK 99827; tel: 800-247-7153 or 907-766-3111.

The motel, within walking distance of shops and restaurants, has 40 spacious guest rooms and suites. All rooms have private baths; many have balconies and ocean views. The motel's furnished outdoor patio offers panoramic views of Lynn Fjord, Portage Cove, and the Coast Range. A restaurant, tour desk, room service, and complimentary transportation to the ferry terminal are available. $$–$$$

Hotel Halsingland

P.O. Box 1589; Haines, AK 99827; tel: 800-542-6363 or 907-766-2000.

Situated between the Chilkat Range and Lynn Fjord, this building once lodged Fort Seward's officers. The Victorian-style hotel offers modern amenities with historic atmosphere. Fifty-five guest rooms have private baths, many with original decorative Belgian tiles, claw-foot tubs, and ocean or mountain views. Five economy rooms share bath facilities. A seafood restaurant and lounge are on the premises. Open seasonally. $$–$$$

Skagway Inn

P.O. Box 500; Skagway, AK 99840; tel: 907-983-2289.

Established as a brothel in 1897, this gold-rush-era bed-and-breakfast now offers gracious hospitality, comfortable rooms, and hearty breakfasts. Each of the 12 guest rooms has individually-styled Victorian decor. Other offerings include a fine restaurant, tour desk, courtesy shuttles, and transportation to the Chilkoot Trail. Open year-round. $–$$$

Westmark Inn

Third and Spring Streets, P.O. Box 515; Skagway, AK 99840; tel: 800-544-0970 or 907-983-6000.

This inn next to Skagway's historic and retail districts offers more than 200 guest rooms with private baths and turn-of-the-century style. Common areas are decorated with period furniture, brass trim, and historic photographs. A lounge and two fine restaurants, one seafood and one Italian, are on the premises. A gift shop, travel agency, and free airport and ferry pick-ups also are available. Open May to September. $$–$$$

The White House

P.O. Box 4; Skagway, AK 99840; tel: 907-983-9000.

Built in 1902 and listed on the National Historic Register, this bed-and-breakfast is two blocks from downtown Skagway. The inn offers attractive rooms with private baths, handmade quilts, queen-sized beds, and ceiling fans. The first floor features French doors, a striking wood staircase, and a large parlor stocked with books, games, and an entertainment center. Laundry facilities are available. Open year-round. $$–$$$

TOURS & OUTFITTERS

Alaska Nature Tours

P.O. Box 491; Haines, AK 99827; tel: 907-766-2876.

Guides lead year-round bus tours, hikes, birding, and wildlife-viewing excursions in and around Chilkat Bald Eagle Preserve.

Chilkat Cruises

P.O. Box 509; Haines, AK 99827; tel: 888-766-2103.

The ferry service runs between Haines and Skagway. Native-owned, the company offers on-board narration of Native lore and culture.

Chilkat Guides/Chilkat Bald Eagle Preserve

P.O. Box 170; Haines, AK 99827; tel: 907-766-2491.

Guided raft trips venture through the Chilkat Bald Eagle Preserve.

L.A.B. Flying Service

P.O. Box 272; Haines AK 99827; tel: 800-426-0543 or 907-766-2222.

The service offers scheduled flights and flightseeing tours of gold-rush trails, Glacier Bay National Park, and the Juneau Ice Cap.

Skagway Walking Tours

Klondike Gold Rush National Historic Park, P.O. Box 517; Skagway, AK 99840; tel: 907-983-2046 or 907-983-2921.

The Park Service offers 45-minute walking tours of Skagway's historic district. Tours depart four times a day from the visitor center at 2nd Street and Broadway.

White Pass & Yukon Railway

P.O. Box 435; Skagway, AK 99840; tel: 800-343-7373 or 907-983-2217.

Several itineraries are available on this vintage, narrow-gauge railroad, built in 1898 to serve mines in the Klondike.

Excursions

Chilkat State Park

Alaska Division of Parks, 400 Willoughby Avenue; Juneau, AK 99801; tel: 907-465-4563.

The park, about 10 miles south of Haines on the Chilkat Peninsula, is an excellent destination for those in search of a wilderness setting with developed campground facilities. Moose, brown bears, black bears, deer, and bald eagles are commonly seen in the park, while whales, seals, and sea otters frequent Lynn Canal. A coastal trail grants fine views of marine life and of glaciers across Chilkat Inlet in Glacier Bay National Park. Beachcombing, picnicking, and hiking are popular activities.

Endicott River Wilderness

U. S. Forest Service Information Center, 101 Egan Drive; Juneau, AK 99801; tel: 907-586-8751.

About 30 miles south of Haines, this wilderness area occupies 99,000 acres of the glacially-carved Chilkat Peninsula west of Lynn Canal. The area is typified by scenic, undeveloped spruce-and-hemlock rain forest. Seldom visited, the wilderness offers prime backcountry hiking, camping, and wildlife-watching. Hundreds of bald eagles and many brown and black bears fish the Endicott River during the annual salmon run. Mountain goats and moose also inhabit the wilderness, which is reached only by boat or floatplane.

Point Bridget State Park

Alaska Department of Natural Resources, Division of Parks and Outdoor Recreation, Southeast Area Office, 400 Willoughby; Juneau, AK 99801; tel: 907-465-4563.

Visitors to this park often see humpback whales and sea lions from vantages along rocky beaches and ocean cliffs. Situated on Lynn Canal, about 50 air miles south of Skagway, the park is forested with western hemlock and Sitka spruce. Meadowlands of high-tide marsh are blanketed by wildflowers in spring and summer. Wildlife includes black-tailed deer, brown bears, black bears, moose, and mountain goats. The park has two public cabins. There are no developed campgrounds.

Wrangell-St. Elias National Park

The storm passes, the wind dies, and now, by delicate degrees, the silence returns, a silence so deep and distant it stretches all the way to Canada. For a hundred miles, not a sound. Everything is black and white, positive and negative, rock and ice and snow. A January sunrise, veiled by swollen clouds, leaks a brooding gray across the southeastern sky, revealing peak after peak of the **Chugach Mountains**, the volcanic **Wrangells**, and the mighty **St. Elias**, the highest coastal mountains in the world. Who would come here? And having come, who would stay? ◆ "I expected to see a comparatively low, forested country," wrote Israel C. Russell, leader of an expedition attempting to climb Mount St. Elias in 1891. "What met my astonished gaze was a vast snow-covered region, limitless in expanse, through which hundreds, perhaps thousands, of bare, angular mountain peaks projected. There was not a stream, not a lake, and not a vestige of vegetation of any kind in sight. A more desolate and utterly lifeless

Dominated by glaciers and snowcapped mountains, Alaska's stronghold of winter invites travelers searching for adventure.

land one never beheld." Russell failed to reach the summit of Mount St. Elias. But he succeeded in defining the region. ◆ **Wrangell-St. Elias National Park and Preserve** is the imperial palace of mountainous Alaska, a birthplace of massive glaciers, a topography of confusion where rivers flow in every direction. Nine peaks reach over 14,000 feet, four above 16,000 feet, and crowning them all is **Mount St. Elias** at 18,008 feet, the second highest mountain in the state. ◆ The park's ruggedness is surpassed only by its size. At 13.2 million acres, Wrangell-St. Elias is the largest unit in the U.S. National Park System. And together with

Guyot Glacier is the largest of three glaciers that spill into Icy Bay in Wrangell-St. Elias National Park and Preserve.

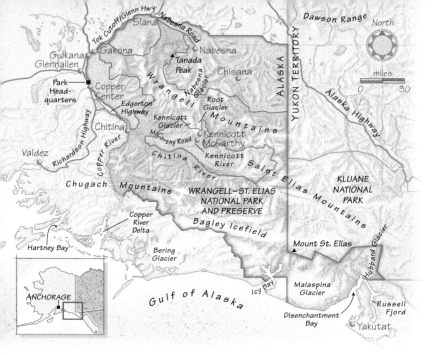

trackless battlements of ice and rock make their own weather. If any place in North America truly can boast having mountains without handrails, this is it.

Wrangell-St. Elias was first established as a national monument in 1978 and upgraded to a national park in 1980. Many "don't-tread-on-me" Alaskans opposed the creation of the park, and many still do. Rangers were vilified. Government property was destroyed. But in time the new park has come to symbolize something more meaningful than parochial complaints about handcuffed freedoms. It is a grand and sweeping promise that in a world driven by progress and profit a rugged corner of Alaska will remain as it has been since time began: wild and primitive. The commerce of men will not take precedence over the liberties of bears, the musings of rivers, the journeys of wolverines and wolves.

neighboring parks in Canada and Alaska, it forms a 24-million-acre World Heritage Site – the largest international preserve in the world.

It snows every month of the year here, as fierce storms blow west to east across the **Gulf of Alaska** and hit these walls of granite. The air rises, cools, and drops its moisture from bruised and burdened clouds. January or July, it doesn't matter. These

Pleistocene Now

Early explorers like Israel Russell had good reason to be daunted by the landscape. The topographic maps are white with glaciers and icefields that cover nearly a third of the park. The **Bering** and **Nabesna Glaciers** are among the longest in the world, and the **Malaspina Glacier**, spilling onto the forelands below Mount St. Elias, is one of the largest piedmont glaciers in the world. Beyond the ice, contour lines merge in tight-fisted vertical relief that bespeak ceaseless erosion and entropy. Such are the defining elements of Wrangell-St. Elias, where the Ice Age isn't something of the past; it's here and now, alive and kicking.

"High above the valley I could see a jet drifting westward," author Ned Gillette wrote during a trek through the park. "It would cover in 20 minutes distance that it had taken our party 32 days to get over.

Nowhere on earth, I reflected, could a man find contrasts more dramatic or more difficult to understand and assimilate. At that moment my feeling was that of a primitive man, mouth agape, gazing with amazement at the 20th century."

Though winter is the truth about this region, and summer a little lie, summer does indeed bring warmth and melting. Serrated fins of rock emerge from beneath snow and ice. Glaciers unveil yawning blue crevasses. Rivers swell with meltwater. Beavers emerge from their dens and get to work chewing and building. Moose feed in thickets of willow. Birds chatter and sing from boughs of spruce. A pair of ravens fly overhead and suddenly flip onto their backs in mid-flight, croak loudly, then spin back upright and croak again as if amused at their own antics.

Another remarkable bird, the water pipit, has been called an acrobat of the high alpine zone. It flies with great agility, sometimes diving off cliffs with flashing velocity, other times hovering in fierce headwinds to regard hikers with a curious dark eye. Present, too, are gray-crowned rosy finches, rock ptarmigan, golden eagles, and sharp-shinned hawks. Despite the animals that make their homes here, this is not known primarily as a wildlife park. It's a landscape park, a place more noteworthy for its size and geologic features

than for its birds and bears.

Still, alpine tundra turns green with summer grasses, mosses, and dozens of wildflower species. On mountain slopes above the **Chitina River**, Dall sheep and mountain goats – two animals that occupy the same ecological niche in different parts of Alaska – graze together, for here their ranges collide like the mountains themselves.

Climbers and Miners

Summer also brings people. Wrangell-St. Elias may be a mountain fortress, but it's not an impregnable one. Only six years after

Beneath Kennicott Glacier (opposite), dramatic light reveals the beautiful contours of an ice cave.

Dall sheep (top) are abundant on inland mountains; goats are more common on coastal mountains.

Mount Sanford, at 16,327 feet (right), stands among a backbone of heavily glaciated volcanoes and peaks.

When Copper Was King

One of the world's richest copper deposits was discovered in 1900 when prospectors Clarence Warner and Jack Smith stumbled across green cliffs of malachite in the Wrangell Mountains while looking for a place to graze their horses.

Mining engineer Stephen Birch acquired the claims and arranged the backing of the Guggenheim brothers and J. P. Morgan. Known collectively as the Alaska Syndicate, the investors formed (and misspelled) the Kennecott Mines Co., later the Kennecott Copper Corp.

The ore was remarkably pure. While mineral-bearing rocks in the southwestern United States averaged about two percent copper, those at Kennecott, when first assayed, averaged 76 percent.

An immense mining complex sprouted like fireweed. A 200-mile rail line between Kennicott and Cordova was completed in 1911. And by 1916 production of copper ore in Alaska had surpassed that of gold, with annual profits exceeding $8 million. At its peak, the town of Kennicott was occupied by 600 people and included a school, hospital, post office, and dozens of houses. A smaller community, McCarthy, sprang up nearby, and offered a predictable choice of saloons, gambling halls, and back-alley brothels.

But every boom has its bust, and in 1938 the mine closed. In 27 years it had yielded more than one billion pounds of copper and nearly 10 million ounces of silver worth $300 million. Today, the red mine buildings are listed in the National Register of Historic Places and are among the most attractive historical structures in Alaska.

Ruins of the Kennecott Mines (above and below) are testament to the once-thriving copper-mining industry.

Experienced climbers (opposite, top) will find unparalleled views when the weather is clear.

Wilderness lodges such as the McCarthy Lodge (opposite, bottom) offer rooms and meals for travelers who arrive by road and air.

Israel Russell failed to reach the summit of Mount St. Elias, it was climbed by the most unlikely of suitors: Luigi Amedeo of Savoy, Duke of Abruzzi, a 24-year-old Italian millionaire who was accompanied by a team of skilled alpinists.

Not all early travelers were so fortunate, however. The following year, in 1898, a party of 19 New Yorkers set out across the 50-mile-wide Malaspina Glacier to reach the Klondike goldfields. Forsaking the more popular routes over the White and Chilkoot Passes, this party of greenhorns followed a pious but ignorant leader into disaster. Frigid temperatures, snow blindness, avalanches, fatigue, scurvy, insanity, and starvation, they suffered it all. Only four of the men returned alive, and two of them were permanently blinded by the snow and ice.

The region did indeed hold mineral wealth, but it was copper rather than gold that turned out to be the most profitable. In fact, the Ahtna Indians, or "Ice People," had long fashioned spearheads out of local copper. Archaeological sites at **Taral**, **Cross Creek**, and **Batzulnetas** suggest that people had found the metal

around their summer subsistence camps for many generations.

The establishment of mining camps after the turn of the century boosted mineral production and employed pioneering aviators like Bob Reeve, the original "glacier pilot," who flew miners, supplies, and occasional adventurers to remote sites. When Reeve was asked by mountaineer Bradford Washburn if he could transport a team of climbers into the St. Elias Mountains, the pilot responded with a single laconic line: "Anywhere you'll ride, I'll fly." And so he did, taking Washburn and another climber deep into the mountains. But the landing and takeoff were so treacherous that Reeve couldn't return. After Washburn and his companion reached the summit of their target mountain, they had to walk out.

Entering the Park

Today, two unpaved roads penetrate the park. The northern entry is **Nabesna Road**, which leads 43 miles from **Slana** on the **Tok Cutoff** of the **Glenn Highway** to the tiny community of **Nabesna**. Caribou, moose, and grizzly bears are occasionally spotted in the open country along the road, and Dall sheep inhabit the hills around 9,358-foot **Tanada Peak** about 15 miles southwest of Nabesna.

The more popular route is **McCarthy Road**, which leads 61 miles from **Chitina** on the park's western border to **McCarthy** and then dead-ends at the ghost town of **Kennicott**. Lodging may be arranged in

McCarthy, **Cordova**, or **Glennallen**. A wilderness lodge in Kennicott is accessible by road, and there's a fly-in lodge in the park itself.

Both Nabesna and McCarthy are historic mining towns that attracted few travelers until the national park was established. For many years a hand-pulled tram across the **Kennicott River** was the only way to enter McCarthy, but a more "efficient" footbridge has now been built in its place. Waves of mountain bikers peddle five miles up a graded road from McCarthy to the historic **Kennecott Mine** and spend the day exploring the bright red buildings and their equally colorful past. Visitors also hike up nearby **Bonanza Ridge** or walk to **Kennicott** and **Root Glaciers** with their catacombs of ice caves.

River rafting provides adventure in the park, but beware that the glacier-fed, boulder-strewn rivers are anything but subdued, and the water is very cold. The **Copper** and **Chitina Rivers** are both popular choices. The 77-mile run down the Copper River from Chitina to the **Gulf of Alaska** passes through rugged terrain along the park's western boundary.

Flightseeing can be arranged with air taxis in McCarthy and outside the park in **Valdez**, Glennallen, **Gulkana**, and **Gakona**. "Where the roads end the real Alaska begins," bush pilots like to say. Indeed, it is exciting to fly in a small, nimble plane over such big country and to be dropped off or picked up in remote terrain as a growing number of hikers do. But with this growth comes increased noise and a diminution of the silence that makes Alaska special.

On the coast, kayakers can explore the

waters of **Icy Bay**, an inner sanctum of erosion and deposition rimmed by tidewater glaciers that calve ice into the sea. Unlike the drier interior regions of the park, the coast is beset with maritime influences, ebbing and flooding tides, strong currents, and unbridled glacial dynamics. Wilderness is more than a political designation here, it's an essential truth. Trails are scarce, rivers powerful, and glaciers unpredictable.

In 1986, **Hubbard Glacier**, a large tidewater glacier that spills from the mountains into **Disenchantment Bay** near **Yakutat**, surged forward and closed off **Russell Fiord**. For six months the glacier dam held, and the water level in the fjord climbed 30 feet. When the

The Wrangell Mountains (left) rise above boreal forest and a beaver pond in the park's northern uplands.

A sandhill crane chick (right) nestles in wild geraniums.

Spring migration (below) on this major flyway near Cordova fills the sky with western sandpipers and dunlins.

glacier dam finally broke on a rainy October night, a massive wall of water burst into the bay. Its volume was estimated to be 35 times greater than that of Niagara Falls.

Geologic evidence suggests that this sort of episode has happened before and will no doubt happen again. If there is a unifying theme at Wrangell-St. Elias, it is the dynamics of ice, water, and rock that make these mountains among the wildest in the world.

Copper River Birding

The western sandpiper is a small, unassuming bird. Until, that is, it takes flight with 10,000 other western sandpipers. The entire flock darts this way and that, snapping in the air like a sheet in the wind until – *whoosh* – they all alight at once to feed on a tidal flat. Then suddenly they're up again, airborne, moving to choreography only they can understand. Their presence along the **Copper River Delta** lasts only a few days each spring (usually in early May), but for those who have seen the spectacle of their flight, the memory can last a lifetime.

An annual shorebird festival in nearby **Cordova** celebrates the arrival of the sandpipers, and it grows in popularity each year, offering some of the best birding in Alaska. Having left winter homes in California only a few days earlier, the sandpipers fly to the Copper River Delta and **Hartney Bay** to rest and feed before continuing north to breeding grounds on the Arctic tundra.

A few days after they depart, a second wave arrives, this one composed of ducks, geese, and swans that descend on the vast constellations of lakes and ponds

that are scattered throughout the delta. They, too, are on their way north. By the thousands they arrive, rest, and depart, eager to begin mating and raising a family.

Dozens of species pass through the region. They come from every state in the Union, plus Central and South America, yet recognize no political boundaries, only the etchings of rivers, the sweep of shores, the refrain of mountain passes, and other geographic features that lead them from one home to another. Many of the same species pass through on their return journey in fall but aren't quite as colorful, having exchanged their bright breeding plumage for less brilliant winter feathers.

TRAVEL TIPS

DETAILS

When to Go

The park is open year-round, but peak visitation is in August. Summer temperatures range from the 40s to the 70s, cooler at high elevations. Wildflowers (and mosquitoes) peak in June and July. The prime mountaineering season is from mid-March to early June. Snow is possibile at any season in the high country. Warm weatherproof clothing is necessary year-round.

How to Get There

Major airlines serve Anchorage International Airport. The park's western boundary is about 200 miles from Anchorage on the Glenn Highway. The park's main entrance is on the Edgerton Highway at Chitina, about 100 miles south of Glennallen.

Getting Around

The park has two maintained roads – McCarthy and Nabesna – both passable in summer. The remaining portions of the park are reached by air. Charter flights to the park's central region are available from airports in Gulkana and Tok. Charter flights to the park's southern coastal region are available from airports in Yakatat, Cordova, and Valdez.

Backcountry Travel

Backcountry visitors must be self-sufficient and carry enough food to cover unexpected delays in air service. No fee or permit is required for backcountry travel, but visitors are encouraged to fill out a backcountry itinerary, available at the park office. Glacial travel and mountain ascents should be discussed with a ranger beforehand.

INFORMATION

Alaska Public Lands Information Center

605 West 4th Avenue, Suite 105; Anchorage, AK 99501; tel: 907-271-2737.

Greater Copper Valley Chamber of Commerce

P.O. Box 469; Glennallen, AK 99588; tel: 907-822-5555.

Wrangell-St. Elias National Park and Preserve

P.O. Box 439; Copper Center, AK 99573; tel: 907-822-5234.

CAMPING

The park has no maintained campgrounds, but backcountry camping is permitted. State campgrounds are available outside the park at Liberty Creek, near Chitina, and along major highways. Cabins and bunkhouses are available for rent along the McCarthy and Nabesna Roads. Contact the park for information.

LODGING

PRICE GUIDE – double occupancy	
$ = up to $49	$$ = $50–$99
$$$ = $100–$149	$$$$ = $150+

Caribou Hotel

P.O. Box 329; Glennallen, AK 99588; tel: 800-478-3302 or 907-822-3302.

Built in 1990, this downtown Glennallen hotel has 45 guest rooms with private baths and custom-made furniture. Six rooms have two-person whirlpool baths; some suites have two bedrooms and a kitchen. Airport transportation, a restaurant, gift shop, and an information/tour desk are available. $$–$$$

Cleft of the Rock Bed-and-Breakfast

Sundog Trail, P.O. Box 122; Tok, AK 99780; tel: 800-478-5646 or 907-883-4219.

This bed-and-breakfast, three miles west of Tok, offers neat accommodations in both the main house and three new log cabins. Most rooms have private baths and king- or queen-sized beds. Two rooms share a bath with a Jacuzzi tub and full shower. Rates include a home-cooked hot breakfast. Mountain-bike rentals, for use on Tok's 15 miles of paved bicycle paths, are available. The inn also offers guided wilderness bike tours, which include drop-off, pick-up, and meals. Open all year. $–$$

McCarthy Lodge

P.O. Box MXY; Glennallen, AK 99588; tel: 907-554-4402.

Located in the old mining town of McCarthy (population 28), this lodge was opened by aviator "Mud Hole" Smith in 1954. Built in 1921 and renovated in 1987, the lodge has 16 double rooms with turn-of-the-century decor. Hiking, rafting, and sightseeing adventures can be arranged. Gourmet meals, including Alaska salmon, are available. A saloon is on the premises. $$–$$$

Ultima Thule Outfitters

P.O. Box 109; Chitina, AK 99566; tel: 907-256-0636.

This extraordinary wilderness lodge, 100 miles from the village of Chitina on the Chitina River, offers deluxe in-park accommodations. Guest cabins have two or three bedrooms, a wood stove, and a private bathroom. A wood-fire sauna is available. Meals include a variety of fruits, vegetables, fresh breads, pastries, and local fish and game. Flightseeing, glacier exploration, rafting, wildlife viewing, and trekking are available. Access is by aircraft only. Open year-round. $$$$

Winter Cabin

P.O. Box 61 TR; Tok, AK 99780; tel: 907-883-5655.

This wilderness lodge offers three log cabins with one or two rooms each and various bed arrangements. Each cabin has a picnic table, barbecue, porch, and refrigerator stocked with breakfast goods. Guests share a large modern bathhouse. Horseshoe pits and gold panning are available. $$

TOURS & OUTFITTERS

Alaska Discovery

5449 Shaune Drive, Suite 4; Juneau, AK 99801; tel: 800-586-1911.

The group offers guided kayak tours of Icy Bay.

Alaska River Rafters

P.O. Box 2233; Cordova, AK 99574-2233; tel: 800-776-1864 or 907-424-7238.

Float trips on the Sheridan and Copper Rivers run from three hours to 10 days.

Alaska Wilderness Journeys

World Wide Adventures, P.O. Box 220204; Anchorage, AK 99522; tel: 800- 349-0064.

Fully outfitted hiking, kayaking, trekking, rafting, and sailing tours in Wrangell-St. Elias and throughout Alaska are available.

St. Elias Alpine Guides

1327 H Street; Anchorage, AK 99501; tel: 888-933-5427 or 907-277-6867.

Guides lead a wide range of customized adventure tours, including glacier hiking, ice climbing, mountain climbing, backpacking, and kayaking.

MUSEUMS

George Ashby Memorial Museum/Copper Valley Historical Society

Mile 101 Old Richardson Highway, P.O. Box 84; Copper Center, AK 99573; tel: 907-822-5285.

Exhibits trace the history of the Copper River Valley, concentrating on gold and copper mining and early Russian settlers.

Excursions

Icy Bay

Wrangell-St. Elias National Park and Preserve (Yakutat Office), P.O. Box 439; Copper Center, AK 99573; tel: 907-784-3295.

This relatively unknown sea-kayakers' paradise lies just south of Wrangell-St. Elias. Here paddlers take in mesmerizing views of the highest coastal range in the world, including the 18,000-foot-high Mount St. Elias, and behold Malaspina, a glacier the size of Rhode Island. Not for the novice, this kayak adventure requires careful planning and coordination with the park office at Yakutat.

Russell Fiord Wilderness

Tongass National Forest, Sitka Ranger District, 204 Siginaka Way; Sitka, AK 99835; tel: 907-747-6671.

Ice towers as tall as 30-story buildings creak, crumble, and crash into the sea at Hubbard Glacier, the gateway to Russell Fiord. Forested river channels and alpine meadows surround the glacier-carved Russell and Nantak Fiords. Both Situk Lake and the headwaters of the Situk Wild and Scenic River are in this 349,000-acre wilderness, whose wildlife include mountain goats, wolves, brown bears, harbor seals, and sea lions. The park is reached by floatplane from Yakatat or Juneau, or by guided tour.

Tetlin National Wildlife Refuge

P.O. Box 779; Tok, AK 99780; tel: 907-883-5312.

North of Wrangell-St. Elias National Park, just west of the Canadian border on the Alaska Highway, this 900,000-acre refuge shelters thousands of birds. More than 100 species nest here; an additional 68 species migrate to the refuge. Tetlin's abundant waterfowl include cranes, ducks, and geese. Among the refuge's featherless creatures are red foxes, snowshoe hares, wolves, black bears, brown bears, lynx, moose, and Dall sheep. There are seven scenic pullouts on the highway and two lakeshore campgrounds.

Prince William Sound

Orcas cruise just beneath the surface, their long dorsal fins slicing effortlessly through the water. Humpback whales rise from the depths and expel a plume of salty mist. Sea otters munch on shellfish or doze in a tangle of seaweed. Eagles perch on treetops along the shore. And icebergs the size of houses break apart with thunderous cracks.   ◆   These are the images of **Prince William Sound**. And whether you visit for a day, a week, or longer, they will be etched in your memory forever.   ◆   Named in 1778 by Captain James Cook for the English monarch's third son, this area of south-central Alaska lives up to its regal name, offering scenes of unparalleled beauty even in the steady drizzle that often greets visitors. Measuring roughly 70 by 30 miles, the sound is bordered by pristine wilderness and about 3,500 miles of tidewater glaciers. Two imposing islands stand guard where the sound meets the **Gulf of Alaska**. Like two giant

Out on the water is where you want to be, among the otters and whales, islands and icebergs.

arms folded over a watery chest, **Montague** and **Hinchinbrook Islands** keep the brunt of the severest Pacific Ocean storms at bay. Other rugged islands, small and large, dot the sound. Some are merely rock piles with no easy anchorage, but others have protected coves that are easily explored by small boat or sea kayak.   ◆   Entering these coves is like walking into a quiet room and shutting the door behind you. The waves outside continue their never-ending march, but inside the surface is calm and glassy. You almost feel the need to whisper, as if speaking in a normal tone would somehow desecrate this magical place.   ◆   Three far-flung communities provide easy access to Prince William Sound. All may be reached by air

Serpentine Glacier descends from the Chugach Mountains into Harriman Fjord, where paddlers can maneuver around bits of icebergs, large and small.

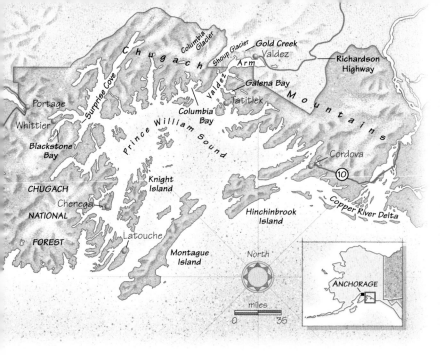

three communities, it is often the busiest because of its proximity to Anchorage. Visitors traveling by car to Whittier usually drive to **Portage**, an hour southeast of Anchorage, then put their cars on the Alaska Railroad for the last leg of the trip, a half-hour ride that includes passage through two long tunnels. Soon work will be completed on an extension of the road from Portage through a two-mile tunnel to Whittier, which will inevitably make this town of several hundred permanent residents an even more popular destination for visitors who want to explore the sound. Travelers without cars can take the train from Anchorage all the way to Whittier.

or by the state ferry, and all have, in varying quantities, hotels, bed-and-breakfast inns, restaurants, stores, guides, and outfitters. The two primary starting points for exploring the sound are situated at the dead-end of Alaska's road system, and the third community is entirely apart from it. The latter, **Cordova**, is a fishing village of about 3,000 people in the eastern part of the sound, near the mouth of the **Copper River Delta**. **Whittier** lies at the western side of the sound, and though it is the smallest of the

Valdez, terminus of the 800-mile Trans-Alaska Pipeline, is a modern town of about 4,000 and the jumping-off point for many who want to be ferried out of the port and through **Valdez Arm** to explore the main part of the sound. The 305-mile drive from Anchorage to Valdez is a spectacular excursion that follows the **Glenn Highway** between the Talkeetna and **Chugach Mountains**. It then winds south on the **Richardson Highway** past the icy arms of **Worthington Glacier**, through panoramic **Thompson Pass**, and along lush **Keystone Canyon** to road's end in Valdez.

Travel Options

Though the sound is protected somewhat by its twin island sentinels, clouds moving into the area are halted by the Chugach Mountains.

When not draping the peaks with their somber, moody veils, the clouds are dropping rain and snow. The 2,771-foot Thompson Pass, known for its record snowfalls, has sustained more than 81 feet in a single winter, over 24 feet in a single month. The average annual snowfall in Valdez is much less: a mere 20 feet! Fortunately, in late spring and summer, prime time for visitors, the monthly rainfall in the sound is less than five inches, and average daytime temperatures are in the 60s, falling to the mid-40s at night. Near glaciers and in waters filled with icebergs, the daytime temperature, especially in the presence of wind and rain, seldom rises above the 40s.

As long as you're prepared, even a day

Kayakers (left) paddle through water choked with ice from Cascade and Barry Glaciers.

Mount Muir is reflected in a pond (opposite) on Point Doran across from Harriman Fjord.

A small harbor in Cordova (below). The town relies heavily on the rich fisheries of Prince William Sound.

of light rain and mist should not stop you from getting out on the water. Options for exploring the sound vary in price and comfort. Full- or half-day glacier cruises depart from Whittier and Valdez, and some Whittier packages, arranged in advance, include transportation from Anchorage. Luxury cruises on comfortable vessels serving gourmet meals range from two to five days. Or you can hop aboard a 40-foot

The Big Spill

If you're concerned about the environment, you probably still shudder over the *Exxon Valdez* disaster of 1989. The first reports were sobering: A supertanker, filled to the brim with crude oil, had grounded on Bligh Reef in Prince William Sound and was steadily disgorging its cargo into the pristine waters. Recovery teams could only watch helplessly as the oil was carried by strong ocean currents into the Gulf of Alaska as far as Kenai Fjord National Park near Seward and Kodiak Island National Wildlife Refuge on Kodiak Island. More than 1,300 miles of shoreline were fouled, and thousands of seabirds and marine mammals perished.

More than a decade later, the sound's delicate ecosystems and wildlife are still recovering. What the oil most disrupted were the vital phytoplankton, the small one-celled plants on which other ocean life ultimately depends. As a result, salmon fishermen are still experiencing poor harvests in many areas. Biologists have also noted continued impacts on sea otters, seals, and killer whales, as well as on terrestrial mammals such as brown bears, black bears, and mink, which sometimes feed on contaminated saltwater fish. Though it is unlikely that visitors will see remnants of the spill, pockets of oil have been found beneath the surface of remote shorelines. – *John Murray*

might consider a flight-seeing tour from Valdez to get a grand view of the sound, its glaciers, and the surrounding mountains.

The Joys of Kayaking

Another option for getting around on the water is to go out in a sea kayak with a guide or on your own if you are more experienced. Outfitters in Whittier, Valdez, and Cordova can escort you for all or part of a day, as well as provide all necessary equipment and give you an introductory lesson. They can also guide you on multiday trips, following one of their scheduled itineraries or tailoring a trip to suit your interests and the current weather conditions. Other trips, like those to **Columbia Glacier** from Valdez, use water taxis to take paddlers and their craft to a kayak departure point.

sloop for a day of sailing, then relax at a remote camp for a few days. If you prefer, you can easily charter a boat and guide to get you where you want to go. Some captains are happy to drop you off at the designated shore of your choice for the day, or with your camping gear for an extended stay, and pick you up later at a prearranged time. If you're unsure about which part of the sound to target, you

A small bay just outside of Whittier offers a perfect introductory kayak trip. An easy one-day paddle from town, **Shotgun Cove** is a pristine place with just enough boat traffic outside the cove to keep you company. You can camp at the head of the bay, where salmon spawn in late summer and lush eel grass grows along a clear,

Crystalline icebergs (right), calved from Columbia Glacier, lie near the shore of Heather Island in Prince William Sound.

An oil-soaked pigeon guillemot (opposite, top) was among the victims of the *Exxon Valdez* oil spill; recovery workers (opposite, middle) cleaned rocky beaches.

The harbor seal (opposite, bottom) is one of eight seal species in Alaska, all protected.

Orcas (bottom) are the largest member of the dolphin family.

cold stream. If you want to go farther, stay out longer, and enjoy more solitude and adventure, follow the coastline around the point and paddle to the head of **Blackstone Bay**, 13 miles from Whittier. Active glaciers fill the head of the bay, and icebergs float lazily by. Although this trip can be done in two days, relax and make it a four-day excursion, which gives you time to hike in the area and take in some spectacular views. For a truly magical two- or three-day trip, cross Blackstone Bay and paddle into **Surprise Cove**, a state marine park tucked in among towering hills and trees. Here, winds and seas are calm. So enchanting is this spot that it may be busy as well, especially on weekends, when powerboats cruise in for safe anchorage.

For a good beginning kayak trip out of Valdez, head west from the dock for three miles to **Gold Creek**. Along the way, you'll see waterfalls tumbling from the rain forest down sheer granite slopes. A beach at the mouth of the creek is ideal for a picnic. A groomed trail just up the creek leads west across a bridge and into a dense forest with waist-high ferns. Longer day trips from Valdez go to **Galena Bay**, a glacial fjord, and to **Shoup Glacier**, at the head of a bay filled

with wildlife, including a seabird colony.

Whether you paddle your own craft or explore the sound via tour boat, you are certain to see wildlife out on the sound and in the secluded bays and coves. The black heads of seals, wet and shiny, emerge from the water. Their round eyes seem to widen in surprise as they scrutinize passing boaters. With a twitch of their whiskers, they disappear beneath the surface. Sea

lions surface with loud snorts, as if clearing the water from their nostrils. Clumsy and lumbering on shore, these marine mammals are surprisingly quick and agile in the water. Their curiosity can be alarming when they approach a sea kayak and nudge it from below. Humpback whales break the surface, then dive again to feed after showing their flukes. Bald eagles, cormorants, and gulls perch on icebergs between meals. Flocks of harlequin ducks, resembling precisely painted decoys, let you get close enough to appreciate their beauty before they fly away.

Snap, Crackle, Pop

Dozens of glaciers flow into the sound, but the best known is probably Columbia Glacier in **Columbia Bay**, named by the 1899 Harriman expedition under the auspices of Columbia University. Forty-one miles long and four miles wide at its face, this river of ice rises 300 feet above the water. It has receded drastically in recent years, often clogging the bay with giant icebergs. This is an ideal place for spotting seals that haul out on icebergs to soak up the summer sun. In addition to tour boats and kayak outfitters that take visitors to the glacier, the *Bartlett*, an Alaska Marine Highway ferry, passes by the bay on its scheduled run between Whittier and Valdez. Passengers enjoy a comfortable day-long journey with a crew that knows this part of the sound intimately. The captain routinely points out whales, bald eagles, and other wildlife; on some trips, a state park naturalist is on board. Conditions permitting, the ferry creeps into Columbia Bay for a close-up look at jostling icebergs.

The Columbia, like most tidewater glaciers, calves icebergs of all sizes into the sea. They clank against boat hulls as captains try to sneak through the icy soup to get closer to the source. Passengers can trust the captains to stay a safe distance from the face of the glacier and the falling icebergs. Much of the floating ice is translucent,

Prime hiking (opposite) can be found near coastal communities.

Mountain goats (left) may be seen in the coastal mountains around Prince William Sound.

Black-legged kittiwakes (below) nest near waterfalls on the north side of Passage Canal.

with a characteristic blue tinge. All around is the sound of crinkling and crackling, making you feel as if you're sitting in a giant bowl of icy Rice Krispies. An occasional roar and *whoomph* announce the falling of more ice. The bulk of an iceberg hangs underwater, and it rolls restlessly as chunks of ice break off or melt.

Being in the presence of a glacier in Prince William Sound is an experience that will remain with you long after you leave. Don't be surprised if you hear the crashing of calving icebergs in your dreams. It's a sound that you won't be able to forget.

TRAVEL TIPS

DETAILS

When to Go

Peak visitation is from mid-May to September. Summer temperatures average 61° to 46°F. Early summer is best for kayaking; late summer, which tends to be windy, is best for sailing.

How to Get There

Three communities serve as entry points for Prince William Sound: Whittier, Valdez, and Cordova. Both Valdez and Cordova have regularly scheduled air service; Whittier can be reached via road from Anchorage. State ferries operate between the three communities.

Getting Around

The best way to explore Prince William Sound is by small boat. Tour boats, kayaking and sailing tours, and kayak rentals are available at Whittier, Valdez, and Cordova.

Backcountry Travel

A network of backcountry trails for hiking and mountain biking is maintained in Chugach National Forest around Prince William Sound. For trail information, contact the Alaska Public Lands Information Center in Anchorage or the Cordova Ranger Station.

INFORMATION

Alaska Public Lands Information Center

605 West 4th Avenue, Suite 105; Anchorage, AK 99501; tel: 907-271-2737.

Cordova Chamber of Commerce

P.O Box 99; Cordova, AK 99574; tel: 907-424-7260.

Cordova Ranger District

U.S. Forest Service; P.O. Box 280; Cordova, AK 99574; tel: 907-424-7661.

Valdez Convention and Visitors Bureau

P.O. Box 1603; Valdez, AK 99686; tel: 800-770-5954.

CAMPING

Backcountry camping in the coastal areas of Prince William Sound can be challenging. Late snowmelt in the area creates deceptively spongy meadows. Pitch your tent on grassy knolls or on the upper portions of tidal meadows. Backcountry camping is permitted almost everywhere in Chugach National Forest. Contact the Cordova Chamber of Commerce and the Valdez Convention and Visitors Bureau for a list of developed campgrounds in the area.

LODGING

Blueberry Mary's

P.O. Box 1244; Valdez, AK 99686; tel: 907-835-5015.

Set on a hillside one mile from downtown Valdez, this bed-and-breakfast offers exquisite views of the bay and snowcapped mountains. Guest rooms, decorated in either Victorian or log-cabin style, have private baths and queen-sized featherbeds. A sauna and kitchenette are available. Breakfasts often include waffles smothered with hand-picked blueberries. Open from June to October. $$

Cordova Rose Lodge

1315 Whitshed, Box 1494; Cordova, AK 99574; tel: 907-424-7673.

Housed in a 1924 barge towed to its present site in 1964, this bed-and-breakfast has five guest rooms, some with private baths, each with views of Hawkins and Spike Islands, Cordova, and the snowcapped Wrangell Mountains. Full breakfasts include sourdough pancakes and Alaskan reindeer sausages. A cedar-lined sauna is on the premises. $$

Emerald Cove Lodges

P.O. Box 2053; Elamar, AK 99686; tel: 907-835-4734.

These lodges, which accommodate up to eight guests each, are situated on the secluded beaches of Elamar, on the east side of Prince William Sound, and surrounded by glacial mountains and scenic islands. Guided fishing, and wildlife- and whale-watching excursions are offered daily. Gourmet meals are served. $$$$

Keystone Hotel

P.O. Box 2148; Valdez, AK 99686; tel: 888-835-0665 or 907-835-3851.

Within walking distance of Port Valdez and the ferry terminal, the Keystone offers 107 rooms with private baths. The Keystone Seafood Grill, the hotel's restaurant, specializes in salmon and halibut dishes. A laundry facility is on the premises. $$

Thompson Pass Mountain Chalet

Mile 19, Richardson Highway, P.O. Box 1540; Valdez, AK 99686; tel: 907-835-4817.

Wooded peaks tower over this remote chalet, 19 miles north of Valdez. The chalet accommodates up to four people and has a living/kitchen area, sleeping loft, reading loft, spiral staircase, and bathroom. Breakfast is included. $$$

A Touch O' Old Town

1465 Richardson Highway, P.O. Box 1264; Valdez, AK 99686; tel: 800-830-4302.

Built in the 1890s, the inn is set on a salmon stream with magnificent mountain views about two miles from downtown Valdez.

Two rooms and a suite have private baths. Pastries are served each afternoon. A hiking and bicycling trail is on the property. $$–$$$

TOURS & OUTFITTERS

Alaska River Rafters

P.O. Box 2233; Cordova, AK 99574-2233; tel: 800-776-1866 or 907-424-7238.

Three- to 10-day rafting trips explore the Copper and Sheridan Rivers.

Alaska Sea Kayakers

P.O. Box 1129; Chickaloon, AK 99674; tel: 800-746-5753.

Services include single and multi-day kayak tours, instruction, gear, and rentals.

Alaskan Wilderness Sailing and Kayaking

P.O. Box 1313; Valdez, AK 99686; tel: 907-835-5175.

Sailing, kayaking, and backcountry camping are offered around Prince William Sound.

Auklet Charter Services

P.O. Box 498; Cordova, AK 99574-0498; tel: 907-424-3428.

Tours emphasize wildlife viewing, hiking, photography, and birding, and offer kayak trip support and drop-off services.

Era Aviation

Valdez Airport Terminal, 6160 Carl Brady Drive; Anchorage, AK 99502; tel: 907-248-4422.

Helicopter sightseeing tours and combined helicopter and hiking tours are provided.

Ketchum Air Service

237 North Harbor Drive, P.O. Box 670; Valdez, AK 99686; tel: 907-835-3789.

Services include Columbia Glacier tours, flightseeing, and drop-off service.

Excursions

Chugach National Forest

3301 C Street, Suite 300; Anchorage, AK 99503; tel: 907-271-2500.

Roughly the size of New Hampshire, Chugach National Forest stretches from the Kenai Peninsula to the Copper River delta. Myriad land mammals – including moose, bear, Dall sheep, and mountain goats – roam the forest. Dall porpoises, harbor seals, sea otters, sea lions, and whales thrive in the coastal waters. Camping, backcountry hiking, kayaking, river running, and mountaineering are popular activities.

Kayak Island

Cordova Ranger District, P.O. Box 280; Cordova, AK 99574; tel: 907-424-7661.

About 62 miles southeast of Cordova, this narrow, 22-mile-long island was the first North American landing of naturalist Georg Stellar and Commander Vitus Bering, who came ashore here in 1741. Excellent opportunities abound for camping, beachcombing, berry picking, and backcountry exploration. Self-sufficiency and careful planning are essential in this highly remote area. Be prepared for weather-related delays. Boat travel to the island from Cordova takes 12 to 16 hours.

Whale Bay

Chugach National Forest, 3301 C Street, Suite 300; Anchorage, AK 99503; tel: 907-271-2500.

Southwest of Chenega Island on the edge of Prince William Sound is Whale Bay, an area of extraordinary beauty perfectly suited for kayak touring. Open meadows filled with wildflowers lie in sharp contrast to sheer rock cliffs. Icebergs, some gigantic, bob offshore. The source of the ice floes is due west in Icy Bay, which has three active tidewater glaciers: Tiger, Princeton, and the mighty Chenega.

Kenai Peninsula

CHAPTER 12

At Gwin's Lodge, a rustic roadhouse in **Cooper Landing** across the highway from the **Kenai River**, a distracted waitress slides burgers and bowls of salmon chowder onto picnic tables crowded with customers. The door swings open and bright sunlight streams into the dark log-cabin lodge. Three more people cram into the shadows, grabbing menus. The waitress winces. ◆ This roadside restaurant, bursting with customers wearing rubber rain gear and heavy fleece jackets, could be located in any resort town. But there's no real "town" here – just a few businesses and homes along the highway, a churning blue-green river beyond, and mountains rising in all directions. ◆ The conversation is different, too. "I kept backing away, down the trail, but that bear just kept following," a young, sunburned guy crows. At another table, a woman still wearing a thick wool hat half-whispers, "The plane climbed and banked, and suddenly we were back in the Ice Age." ◆ Three hours ago, the

> **What it may lack in size, the Kenai makes up in bounty, long attracting seekers of gold, great beauty, big fish, or complete silence.**

woman eating chili was shivering in front of a calving glacier. The man was sweating on a riverbank as he tugged on a salmon that weighed nearly twice as much as the mountain bike he rode in on. The shy-looking elderly couple across the room were screaming their lungs out on a white-water rafting trip on the Kenai River. And an hour from now, this whole crowd will be dispersed again to the bays and trails of this double-lobed peninsula like a ball of mercury shattered into dozens of quicksilver specks. They will be absorbed back into a landscape wild and large enough to engulf them all. The **Kenai Peninsula** has a mixed reputation: part crowded

Homer's harbor on Kachemak Bay is the home port for recreational boaters and charter operators as well as commercial fishermen.

Floatplane travel to the Kenai Peninsula (left) from Anchorage shaves hours off a trip that can take three to five hours by road.

Arctic terns (opposite, right) are fierce defenders of their nests, often diving to attack a trespasser.

Harding Icefield (opposite, bottom) in Kenai Fjords National Park was created when several large valley glaciers connected and formed a thick sheet.

Kenai Peninsula long enough to do much damage ("Soldotna, 50 years old!" a highway sign proclaims). Surprisingly, given the area's gas, oil, and timber wealth, only about 46,000 residents live here year-round, and they are clustered in four small towns, several Native villages, and a dozen tiny outposts.

Just south of the state's biggest city, the Kenai is known as Anchorage's playground. But playground doesn't capture half of it. Stick to the scenic route that forks to the coastal towns of **Seward** and **Homer**, and you'll get

carnival – as at Gwin's Lodge and at some campgrounds and road-accessible riverbanks – and part pristine wilderness. The peninsula is heavily traveled by Alaskan standards, but there's still more than enough wilderness to go around. Most of it is undeveloped public land, and much is unvisited in any season. You could slip Vermont into the Kenai's interior and overlap only one major road. You could lose sprawling Chicago and all its suburbs in the Harding and Sargent Icefields.

There are a few strip malls here and there, spaced about a hundred miles apart. But white settlers just haven't been on the

stuck behind a few RVs, rub shoulders with other tourists (about 100,000 a month in summer), and generally keep your head dry and your hands clean. But wander a mile or two off the **Seward** and **Sterling Highways** – mere threads across an oriental carpet of multitextured wilderness – and you'll experience a microcosm of Alaska: dark forests, deep fjords, wildflower meadows, and mile-high icefields.

You can drive five hours along a scenic, winding highway to the end of the road (Homer claims that honor, but the asphalt meets breaking waves at Seward, too). And

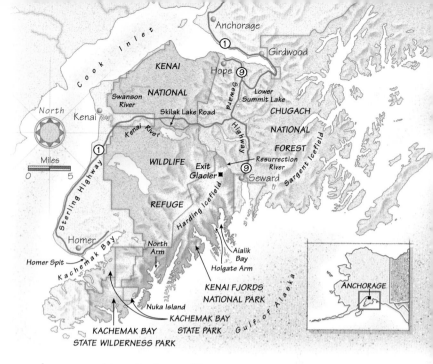

if that's too confining, you can go even farther – to coastal hamlets with no roads at all. Or you can go to a glacier-capped coastline without any coastal hamlets or to the open ocean, where giant halibut are hauled from the depths and where honeycomb-shaped islets blur under the frantic, beating wings of tens of thousands of seabirds.

Kenai People

Almost everyone who has settled on the Kenai was attracted here by the abundance of land or the promise of seclusion. Athabascan and Alutiiq Natives were joined by Russian fur traders, gold prospectors, and homesteaders who came after World War II. Today's residents tend to wear many hats. In Homer, a person might fish for salmon in summer, paint with watercolors in winter, sell gourmet jam to tourists, work a little construction, and volunteer at a public radio station spinning old jazz records.

The variety of lifestyles is matched only by the diversity of the wildlife. For nearly a century the Peninsula has been a mecca for hunters and fishermen attracted by its large moose population and gem-colored rivers and lakes brimming with the world's

biggest salmon. It's not uncommon to see anglers standing shoulder to shoulder along some rivers, a practice known as "combat fishing" because they're constantly dodging hooks, poles, and flopping fish.

But in recent years, wildlife watchers have become as numerous as wildlife stalkers. Cameras easily out-number guns here – especially on the coast or at roadside lakes, where animals are easiest to spot. At the end of **Homer Spit** in winter, quick-snapping tourists line up next to professional photographers aiming cannon-sized lenses at the dozens of bald eagles that congregate on drift-wood-covered beaches framed by the wide, indigo sweep of **Kachemak Bay**. By some estimates, 90 percent of the eagle photographs an American will see were shot at close range from the end of Homer Spit.

In fall, a man photographing graceful trumpeter swans on **Lower Summit Lake**, just off the Seward Highway, may be on vacation, or he may be working for a national magazine. He, too, is joined by other photo-snappers.

Alaska SeaLife Center

Seward has seen its share of hard times. First there was the disastrous earthquake and tidal wave on Good Friday in March 1964 that obliterated the harbor and downtown area. Next was the *Exxon Valdez* oil spill on Good Friday in March 1989 that nearly destroyed the region's fishing industry and depressed tourism. After each calamity, the local people pulled together and rebuilt their community. With financial assistance from the *Exxon Valdez* Restoration Settlement funds, Seward built the Alaska SeaLife Center.

Situated on Resurrection Bay, the center is a state-of-the-art facility dedicated to educating the public about the Alaskan marine ecosystem and to wildlife research and rehabilitation. Within the 115,000-square-foot center, three large, two-story tanks re-create habitats for harbor seals, Steller sea lions, and seabirds, including tufted puffins, common murres, and pigeon guillemots. Aquariums along one wall show the complete spectrum of local marine life, from creatures on the ocean floor to those in the tidal zone. Visitors can peer through scopes on the observation deck for a look at wild sea otters, harbor seals, and other marine life. In late spring and early summer, humpback whales some-times enter the bay and can be seen from the center.

Accessible by highway from Anchorage, the Alaska SeaLife Center serves as a fascinating introduction to the plants and animals you might see on a guided boat trip in the waters of nearby Kenai Fjords National Park.

Steller sea lions (left and below) are game for a playful meeting at Seward's Alaska SeaLife Center, a newly built facility funded by a portion of oil-spill restoration dollars.

Horseback riders (bottom) find paradise exploring the tidal zone of Kachemak Bay near Homer.

Bald eagles (opposite) are easy to spot in the highest places: solitary trees or promontories.

"I've never seen so many in one place," a woman says, digging into a pocket for more film as a flock of the once-endangered birds glides past. The whiteness of the swans' feathers is echoed by the first fresh snow on the mountains and by cottony tufts of fireweed, now gone to seed. Like the others who have pulled onto the road's shoulder to watch the swans, she is part of a new trend – tourists visiting the Kenai in

the "shoulder seasons" of spring or fall, when the days are shorter but the crowds smaller, and when the wildlife is still plentiful.

Trails and Cruises

The tundra landscape of some other parts of Alaska, like Denali National Park, allows easy, distant viewing of moose, bears, and caribou. On the Kenai, dense forests of spruce, aspen, and alder limit viewing of most big game. To find terrestrial wildlife, you usually have to step out of the car and into the woods. Luckily, there's no shortage of trails. The **Skilak Lake Loop**, a side trip off the Sterling Highway past Cooper Landing, has camp-grounds and several short trails. Located in a restricted hunting zone and away from the buzz of major highway traffic, the loop is like a miniature wildlife refuge. Moose and eagles are easily spotted in areas burned decades ago by two major wildfires.

The Peninsula's most popular multiday traverse, the **Resurrection Pass Trail**, extends 39 miles from **Hope** to Cooper Landing along a turn-of-the-century prospector's route. Hikers, mountain bikers, cross-country skiers, anglers, and hunters share the trail, which climbs from 500 to 3,400 feet and passes forested lakes, alpine tundra, and countless creeks still glimmering with the promise of gold. Hikers arriving at the Sterling Highway with few blisters can keep on heading south for another 32 miles on the **Russian Lakes** and **Resurrection River Trails**. Along the way, some travelers rest their feet at rustic Forest Service cabins (reservations required) spaced every three to seven miles.

Trekkers typically cover the well-maintained Resurrection Pass Trail in three to five days; the Russian Lakes Trail in another two to three; and the often-flooded, bear-infested Resurrection River Trail in a final day or so.

The Resurrection Pass traverse slices through the western edge of **Chugach National Forest**, which, at nearly six million acres, is the nation's second-largest and just one piece of the parkland puzzle that makes up the Kenai. The two-million-acre **Kenai National Wildlife Refuge** to the west encompasses lake-dotted flatlands connected by the **Swanson River** and **Swan Lake** canoe trails, mountainous ridges, and forests laced with more

than 200 miles of little-known hiking trails. Along the jagged coast to the south, national and state parklands preserve vast marine areas between Homer and Seward.

Kenai Fjords National Park, near Seward, is one of the country's less-visited national parks but one of its most fascinating. Like the Peninsula itself, the national park is a bizarre hybrid: easy to reach but nearly

impossible to penetrate. You can drive less than three hours south of Anchorage, enter the park, and stroll an easy half-mile to the massive, crevassed face of **Exit Glacier**, one of 35 that flow off the mile-high **Harding Icefield**. But you can't drive or walk anywhere else. The rest of the park is bordered, and often battered, by ocean. The interior is an otherworldly landscape of 700 frozen square miles – a remnant of the last Ice Age, and one of only four major icefields in the United States.

In downtown Seward, a friendly port town squeezed into the head of a steep fjord, two women pore over maps in the Kenai Fjords National Park visitor center. They're well prepared – rain gear tied around their waists, binoculars slung around their necks – but a little confused. "We've done Exit Glacier. But how do we get here?" they ask, pointing to the center of the map. Like nearly all Seward visitors, they don't have crampons or mountaineering experience. Flightseeing is a possibility, but they want to be outside – to smell the air and feel the dissonant shiver of a cool, icy wind blowing off a glacier while the mid-summer sun beats down on their heads.

"We could handle a kayak," one offers gamely. But the coastal boundary to the national park – and the most dramatic Ice Age scenery – starts more than a day's paddle south along the shore in rough, exposed waters. A charter drop-off to a more sheltered fjord, followed by a week of backcountry camping or a stay at a remote public cabin, is one option. The Park Service maintains rustic cedar cabins at

Aialik Bay, **Holgate Arm**, **North Arm**, and **Delight Creek**. Of the quarter-million people who visit Kenai Fjords each year, only about a hundred use the public cabin in North Arm, the most isolated of the four.

But the easiest and most popular way to see the park is to join one of the small cruise ships that make daylong loops beyond the bay and into the deep, crenelated fjords that echo with the sounds of calving ice and shrieking birds. Shorter tours stay within the bay.

Along the way, you'll see seals, sea otters, giant Steller sea lions, perhaps orcas or humpback whales, and at least a dozen of the 100 bird species that are found in the park. The name of one offshore islet, **Beehive Island**, refers to its raucous and teeming wildlife. From the rocky islet, tens of thousands of puffins, kittiwakes, and murres swoop and dive like a swarm of angry bees. At

another island, endangered male Steller sea lions bellow, while the smaller females nurse dark-furred pups.

It's almost worth forsaking a little solitude to share the experience with others, all "oohing" and "aahing" in unison on the tour boat. Back home, no photo will capture the density of the birds, the size of the tidewater glaciers, or the tension that mounts as a vertical ice sheet fractures and plunges into the dark ocean depths, emitting a delayed boom that sends nearby seabirds flapping for safety.

Quiet, Please

Sixty-five miles west, in **Kachemak Bay**, kayakers can choose quiet seclusion over panicked seabirds and crashing ice. The

McCarthy Glacier (opposite, top) spills downward from the Harding Icefield in a slow-moving river of ice.

Calving icebergs (opposite, bottom) and the wakes they cause can be troublesome for kayakers or other small boaters who fail to keep a respectable distance.

Steller sea lions (above) haul out on rocky islands to take some sun.

Red salmon (below and right), or sockeye, migrate into peninsula freshwater streams during summer runs.

Running Wild

If there are Seven Wildlife Wonders of the World, the annual migration of Alaska's salmon is surely one of them. The five species of wild Pacific salmon that thrive here – king, silver, red, pink, and chum – swim thousands of miles and fight their way past innumerable barriers (commercial fishing nets, eagle talons, and grizzly-bear paws) to return from the ocean to the fresh-water streams where they first hatched and ultimately will die.

Along the way, salmon stay oriented by following an internal magnetic map and using a remarkable sense of smell that leads each fish to the exact place of its birth. Upon entering freshwater, their colors change, males develop hooked snouts, and their bodies begin to disintegrate, even as they continue to struggle upstream. Reaching home, the salmon spawn. Finally, they die, leaving streambeds covered by ragged, gaping carcasses that quickly dissolve and filter down the food chain to the next piscine generation. Amid a racket of screeching birds, splashing bears, and rushing current, the cycle begins again.

Sea kayaking (left) the Kenai Fjords can be arranged in a group charter with rental kayaks, with a private guide, or undertaken on your own.

Horned puffins (bottom) gather fish in their large, colorful bills as they "fly" underwater.

The Kenai Mountains (right) are easily accessed by road in the Portage Glacier Recreation Area, Chugach National Forest.

state park across the bay from Homer is a pastoral landscape of emerald coves, moss-dripping old-growth spruce forest, and steep, rocky shores. Dropped off by water taxi at the head of Halibut Cove Lagoon, you can paddle away from a handful of sportfishing boats, listen to an eagle's high-pitched screech mimic a piece of chalk skipping over a blackboard, and watch king salmon cruise in schools around the cove. Their torpedo-shaped bodies rise near the translucent water's surface, visible as rotund, rose-colored outlines shimmering under green water. Sea otters appear so regularly in the distance, feeding, swimming and rolling on their backs, that it's difficult to imagine they were once at risk of extinction.

Kachemak Bay State Park is Alaska's oldest state park, and one that has

continued evolving thanks to the proceeds from the settlement in the *Exxon Valdez* oil spill. Small campgrounds, public cabins, and a ranger station attract visitors to the park's western edge, and a network of trails loops through primeval forest and leads to **Grewingk Glacier** and **Poot Peak**. But as always on the Kenai, what you see, and what you can easily reach by trail, is only a fraction of what exists. An eastern branch of the park, which encompasses **Nuka Island** and faces the **Gulf of Alaska**, can be reached only by boat or floatplane. The southern portion, which is actually called **Kachemak Bay State Wilderness Park**, is equally remote.

Across Kachemak Bay, on five-mile-long Homer Spit, campers, dog walkers, kite flyers, birders, and anglers strut the beaches, boardwalks, and harbor. Up the highway, the Cooper Landing waitress serves another mob of customers, and RVs form a conga line past the roadside lodge through narrow valleys back to Anchorage.

But on the secluded eastern side of Kachemak Bay, kayakers can hear only the rhythmic dunk and dripping of their paddles and the cries of an eagle, luring them farther on, farther on.

The Kenai may not be Alaska at its emptiest or most remote. But it is Alaska in miniature: beautiful, diverse, and wild.

TRAVEL TIPS

DETAILS

When to Go

Visitation on the peninsula picks up around mid-May, when snow gives way to wildflowers, and peaks from June to August. Summer temperatures average 49° to 63°F. Always prepare for rain and cooler temperatures, especially if you plan to explore the coast.

Getting There

Commercial airlines serve Anchorage International Airport, about 130 miles north of Kenai Fjords National Park. Bus, plane, and rail transportation are available year-round between Anchorage and Seward.

Getting Around

Car rentals are available at the airport. Air taxis offer charter service to wilderness destinations and between peninsula communities. Charter flights and cruises can be arranged in Anchorage, Seward, and Homer.

Backcountry Travel

No permits are required for hiking and camping on the public lands of the Kenai Peninsula. For information, call the Alaska Public Lands Information Center, 907-271-2737, which provides information on outfitters, cabins, trails, camping, canoeing, and other resources.

INFORMATION

Kenai/Prince William Sound Area State Parks Office

Mile 85 Sterling Highway, P.O. Box 1247; Soldotna, AK 99669; tel: 907-262-5581.

Kenai Visitors & Convention Bureau

11471 Kenai Spur Highway; Kenai, AK 99611; tel: 907-283-1991.

Seward Chamber of Commerce & Convention and Visitors Bureau

P.O. Box 749; Seward, AK 99664; tel: 907-224-8051.

CAMPING

Kenai Peninsula's numerous campsites range from maintained grounds with utility hookups to wilderness or beach camping. To request a list of campgrounds, contact the Kenai Visitors and Convention Bureau. Public cabins without plumbing or electricity are available in a number of remote areas, including Resurrection Pass Trail, Kenai Fjords, and Resurrection and Kachemak Bays. Rental fees are inexpensive, but reaching a cabin can be costly, often requiring a charter boat or plane. For information, call the Alaska Public Lands Information Center.

LODGING

PRICE GUIDE – double occupancy

$ = up to $49 $$ = $50–$99

$$$ = $100–$149 $$$$ = $150+

Across the Bay Tent & Breakfast

P.O. Box 112054; Anchorage, AK 99511; tel: 907-345-2571 (September to May) or P.O. Box 81; Seldovia, AK 99663; tel: 907-235-3633 (June to August).

This popular stopping place, about 10 miles from Seldovia, is set on Kasitsna Bay, with views of Herring and Yukon Islands. Guests stay in six "cabin tents" (shelters with carpeted platforms, four-foot-high walls, and tent roofs) and share a bathroom and shower facility. The lodge's many extras include a sauna, mountain-bike rentals, sea-kayak tours, and volleyball courts. Seafood meals are served at extra cost. Open late May to mid-September. $–$$

Driftwood Inn

135 West Bunnell Avenue; Homer, AK 99603; tel: 800-478-8019 or 907-235-8019.

A section of this inn, a stone's throw from Bishop's Beach, was a one-room schoolhouse in the 1920s. The Driftwood's 21 cozy guest rooms include a variety of styles and sizes, some with private baths and either two queen-sized or two double beds, many with ocean, mountain, or glacier views. A large stone fireplace warms the inn's sitting room. $$

Kachemak Bay Wilderness Lodge

P.O. Box 956; Homer, AK. 99603; tel: 907-235-8910.

The lodge offers private cabins surrounded by towering spruce trees on the shore of Kachemak Bay. Gourmet meals, included in the package, are served in the spacious log lodge. Modern cabins are cozy, with private, tile-and-cedar baths, fine art, homemade quilts, and picture windows. Guide service, sea kayaks, canoes, hiking trails, a solarium, sauna, and outdoor hot tub are available. A three- to five-day minimum stay is required. $$$$

Kenai Princess Lodge

P.O. Box 676; Cooper Landing, AK 99572; tel: 800-426-0500 or 907-595-1425.

Located in the center of the Kenai Peninsula, this wilderness retreat offers a panoramic view of the Kenai River valley and surrounding mountains. The lodge's 70 bungalows, reached by forest paths, have sun porches, wood-burning stoves, and private baths. The log lodge has a restaurant, gift shop, and tour desk. Open year-round. $$–$$$$

Seward Windsong Lodge

Mile 6, Exit Glacier Road, P.O. Box 2301; Seward, AK 99664; tel: 800-208-0200 or 907-224-7116.

This log-sided lodge, built in 1996, is in a quiet forest setting overlooking the Resurrection River three miles from Seward. The lodge has more than four dozen rooms, each with two queen-sized beds, natural log furniture, and a full bath. A restaurant, bar, and free transportation within the Seward area are available. Open from mid-April to the end of September. $$–$$$$

TOURS & OUTFITTERS

Alaska River Company

P.O. Box 827; Cooper Landing, AK 99572; tel: 907-595-1226.

Raft trips and guided hikes on the upper Kenai River are offered.

Alaskan Wildland Adventures

P.O. Box 389; Girdwood, AK 99587; tel: 800-478-4100.

The company specializes in five- to 12-day natural-history tours of the Kenai Peninsula

The Center for Alaskan Coastal Studies

P.O. Box 225; Homer, AK 99603; tel: 907-235-6667.

Guides lead natural-history tours of Kachemak Bay aboard the MV *Rainbow Connection*.

Renown Charters and Tours

507 East Street, Suite 201; Anchorage, AK 99501; tel: 800-655-3806 or 907-272-1961.

Take narrated tours of Kenai Fjords and the Alaska SeaLife Center.

True North Kayaking Adventures

P.O. Box 2319; Homer, AK 99603; tel: 907-235-0708.

Single- or multiday kayak tours can be customized to meet individual needs and interests.

MUSEUMS

Alaska SeaLife Center

Mile 0, Seward Highway, P.O. Box 1329; Seward, AK 99664; tel: 800-224-2525 or 907-224-3080.

This $52-million facility on Resurrection Bay serves as the gateway to Kenai Fjords National Park and re-creates the habitats of Alaska's marine life in three-story tanks.

Excursions

Caines Head State Recreation Area

3601 C Street, Suite 200; Anchorage, AK 99503-5929; tel: 907-269-8400.

This striking headland towers 650 feet above Resurrection Bay. The 6,000-acre recreation area, site of an abandoned World War II fort, fronts alpine meadowland and the Kenai Mountains and overlooks Blying Sound. Visitors can explore both Fort McGilvray and the South Beach Garrison. The park's beaches are scattered with shale and lined with forest. Fine sightseeing is available along former military roads now used as hiking trails. Picnic shelters, campsites, a public-use cabin, and latrines are on the grounds.

Deep Creek and Ninilchick State Recreation Areas

P.O. Box 1247; Soldotna, AK 99669; tel: 907-262-5581.

Popular among birders, these recreation areas cover a combined 257 acres on Cook Inlet, about 40 miles south of Soldotna on the Kenai Peninsula. Bald eagles inhabit the region year-round; sandhill cranes occupy the saltwater marsh each May. Visitors often see whales, otters, and seals offshore. Moose occasionally are observed in the forest. Scenic overlooks, trails, and both primitive and developed campgrounds are available. Anglers frequent Deep Creek for its celebrated king salmon and halibut runs.

Kachemak Bay State Park and State Wilderness Park

P.O. Box 1247; Soldotna, AK 99669; tel: 907-262-5581.

These parks, situated at the tip of the Kenai Peninsula, encompass rain forests, rugged mountains, fjords, and coves. Both brown and black bears roam the parks, joined by moose, wolves, wolverines, and coyotes. Commonly seen marine life include seals, porpoises, whales, and sea otters. Among the many species of birds are bald eagles and puffins. Primitive campsites, cabins, and trails to mountain lakes and glaciers are available. The area is reached by plane or boat from Homer.

Chugach
State Park

CHAPTER 13

When Anchorage residents say they like living in the city because it's only ten minutes from Alaska, they're referring to **Chugach State Park**, a half-million acres of alpine wilderness set in the city's backyard. Chugach is the third-largest state park in the nation. It sweeps north to the **Knik River** in the **Matanuska-Susitna Valley** and south to **Turnagain Arm**, a breathtaking, fjord-like coastline with Dall sheep on the craggy cliffs above and beluga whales and bore tides in the gray, silty waters below. ◆ Dominating the landscape are the peaks and valleys of the **Chugach Mountains**, the highest coastal range in the world. Some 50 glaciers grip the park's higher elevations, covering about 10 percent of its total area. The erosive effects of these glaciers date back a million years. The great sheets of ice have deposited large boulders known as erratics high on hillsides, braided milky run-off streams, and gouged out 15 valleys and nearly 70 lakes. **Eklutna**, the largest natural lake in the park, is seven miles long and a mile wide. ◆ Numerous waterfalls add sparkle to the park, especially during "breakup," when rivers are swollen with snowmelt and flowing chunks of ice. **Thunderbird Falls** is the most spectacular and frequently visited waterfall. The gushing veils of water crash and bellow into a deep gorge in summer and freeze into glorious ice formations in winter. ◆ While the peaks of the Chugach Mountains hardly rival Mount McKinley, they are formidable. The range soars to more than 8,000 feet and offers plenty of rugged trekking. More than 90 percent of the park's terrain is mountainous, leaving only about 40,000 acres for skiing,

A vast mountain wilderness sprawls at the back door of Alaska's biggest city.

Winter sun illuminates ice floes that have been stacked along Cook Inlet's Knik Arm by the retreating tide.

plant community is alpine tundra with margins of boreal forest. Six evergreen conifers grow here – black, white, and Sitka spruce, western and mountain hemlock, and common juniper. Balsam poplar, black cottonwood, quaking aspen, paper birch, and 16 types of willow shrubs also grow in the park.

Wildflowers – both above treeline and below – enliven the scene each spring. Common types include mountain and bell heather, forget-me-nots, moss campion, and cinquefoil. Berries are abundant, too; blueberries and high and low bush cranberries attract bucket-toting pickers each fall.

Wildlife thrives here. The park is home to 47 species of mammals, including more than a thousand moose, 30 to 40 grizzly bears, 70 to 80 black bears, at least one pack of wolves, and some 2,000 Dall sheep. Elusive lynx, brown bats, coyotes, beavers, foxes, river otters, and weasels also find safe haven here.

Alaska is a magnet for migrating birds, and Chugach State Park is situated at the crossroads of two major migration paths – the Coastal and Pacific flyways. More than a hundred species have been spotted in the park, but only about 20 brave the winter. Year-round inhabitants include northern pintails, common mergansers,

snowmobiling, biking, and horseback riding. One of the range's smallest peaks, **Flattop**, at 3,550 feet, attracts up to 8,000 climbers annually. This little mountain is such a social place that musical concerts have taken place atop its summit. To celebrate a local outdoor club's anniversary some years ago, eight men hauled a tuba, a bass drum, and a few cornets and trombones to the top to play German polkas and waltzes.

Natural Abundance

Such a massive expanse of wilderness offers pristine habitat for plants and animals, and the park has many of both. Most of the region is above timberline, and its dominant

A Bird Ridge hiker (left) takes a rest and is rewarded with the panorama of the Chugach Mountains.

Black bears (opposite, top) are found in high densities throughout the region.

Glacial ice (right) of the Matanuska Glacier is sculpted into fantastic shapes by sun, wind, and rain.

Barrow's and common goldeneye, European starlings, and Bohemian waxwings. Chickadees and redpolls shiver to create body heat, and chickadees go into a state of torpor to reduce body temperature and save energy.

While birds are abundant, fish are not. The area supports only nine species of fish, but up to 11 creeks and streams invite anglers for a try at pink, red, king and silver salmon, Dolly Varden, and rainbow trout. **Bird Creek** and **Eagle River** are salmon spawning streams. **Rabbit Lake** is stocked with grayling and Eagle River with red salmon.

Visitors are attracted by the variety of plants, opportunities to observe wildlife, rich geologic features, and a chance to romp and roam in beautiful, open spaces. Park officials report that more than a million visitors enter the park every year.

First-timers should stop in at either the **visitor center** at Mile 12 of **Eagle River Road** or **park headquarters** at the Potter Section House at Mile 115 of the **Seward Highway** along Turnagain Arm. Headquarters is a good source of hiking information and the place to buy annual permits for parking, boat launching, and camping.

On the Trail

Getting into Chugach State Park for a day hike is no problem; 16 entry points provide access to more than 25 major trails. The **Glen Alps** entrance is by far the most popular, offering a short, easy walk to a spectacular view of the city or the two-mile hike up Flattop Mountain, with vistas stretching from the **Alaska Range** to **Cook Inlet**. Berry picking on **Blueberry Hill** and other sections of the park near this entrance is popular in August. Mountain bikers and

Lily pads (left) thrive in a Chugach Mountains lake.

Poisonous toadstools, brilliant in orange (below), are fall perennials in the Matanuska Valley.

Llamas do the heavy work (opposite, top) for packers and hikers enjoying autumn in Chugach State Park.

Moose (opposite, bottom) look benign, but be sure to give them a wide berth.

Opportunities abound for those in the mood for more adventure. **Bird Ridge Trail** climbs 2,000 feet up a short, steep, but well-marked route to a magnificent view of Turnagain Arm. Southern exposure makes this one of the earliest snow-free trails in spring. The trailhead is at Mile 102 of the Seward Highway.

Crow Pass Trail, also reached via the Seward Highway, is an excellent choice for close-up views of a glacier. The trail is a little more than four miles long and climbs about 2,000 feet over a short stretch of the historic Iditarod Trail to the nose of **Raven**

cross-country skiers relish this area for easy access to the 11-mile **Powerline Trail**, a wide, rocky "road" extending south to **Indian Creek Valley**.

An even easier stroll for the casual visitor is the short trail to **Thunderbird Falls** at Mile 25 of the Glenn Highway. It's a mile to the water, with an elevation gain of only 200 feet. The nearby **Eklutna Lakeside Trail** is an old roadbed offering a 28-mile round-trip to the base of **Eklutna Glacier**. The path is popular with mountain bikers, skiers, and hikers, and it leads to more ambitious trails like **Twin Peaks**, **Bold Ridge**, and **East Fork**.

Glacier. Along the way, you'll pass ruins and refuse left by miners. Gold was discovered at Crow Creek in 1896 and mined until 1940. Today, **Crow Creek Mining Company** is a summer tourist attraction just outside **Girdwood** that offers gold-panning and overnight camping.

Hiking isn't the only way to get around this vast park. Horseback riding is permitted year-round in many areas; nearby stables rent horses and can advise you on the best trails.

Mountain bikers have discovered the park and mainly use the Powerline and Eklutna Lake trails, or the **Gasline Trail** near the Glen Alps entrance.

Snowmobile use is restricted to assigned areas at Eklutna Lake, **Peters Creek**, Eagle River, **South Fork Campbell Creek**, and Bird Creek. Snowmobilers should consult with park personnel about snow conditions and to confirm which days the machines are permitted.

Boaters have their own brand of fun in Chugach State Park. Eklutna Lake is an excellent spot for canoes, kayaks, and windsurfers in summer, although weather changes rapidly in the mountains, and winds come up suddenly. Whitewater enthusiasts paddle the Eagle River. The best stretch runs from Mile 9 of Eagle River Road to the Eagle River Campground above Campground Rapids. The water here is cold and silty, and some stretches are for expert paddlers only. Campground Rapids is especially dangerous; novices should avoid it.

The park also has some excellent spots for ice-climbing, including road cuts between **Indian** and the **Potter Creek Weigh Station** on the Seward Highway; the icefalls on the north side of **O'Malley Peak**;

Thunder Gorge and **Heritage Falls** in the Eagle River Valley; Thunderbird Falls in Eklutna Canyon; and the Eklutna Lake area.

If a single day isn't enough, you may want to consider staying at one of the park's three camping areas: Bird Creek, Eagle River, and Eklutna Lake. There are also six public-use cabins, including a few near **Eklutna** and **Whiteout Glaciers**. The cabins are simple but warm and offer a safe way to prolong your visit. Reservations can be made through Alaska State Parks or the Alaska Public Lands Information Center in Anchorage.

If you have time for only one wilderness excursion in Alaska, Chugach State Park won't disappoint you.

Moose Manners

Moose may not look fierce, but they can be extremely dangerous, especially at certain times of the year. To play it safe, stay about 100 yards away, and keep a few tips in mind:

● Male moose, which stand about six feet tall and can weigh over 1,200 pounds, are highly aggressive from mid-September through mid-October. This is when they gather harems of cows in heat and actively defend them from other bulls. During this period, they have been known to attack humans.

● Cow moose can be as formidable as bulls, particularly when they have spring calves. In the predator-filled Alaska wilderness, they must exercise continual vigilance to protect their young from bears, wolves, coyotes, wolverines, and eagles until the calves have acquired full running strength.

● Moose can be aggressive when the air temperature is extremely cold, the snow is deep, and food is scarce. The animals have been known to behave unpredictably when stressed by harsh conditions.

● Wanting to get a clear, frame-filling picture is not a legitimate reason for crowding wildlife. Photographers should use a powerful telephoto lens instead of approaching moose at close range.
– John Murray

TRAVEL TIPS

DETAILS

When to Go

The park is open year-round. Summer temperatures range from 40° to 70°F; winter is relatively mild, with February temperatures averaging about 30°F.

How to Get There

Enter the park by road from the Anchorage Hillside area and along the Seward and Glenn Highways. Anchorage city buses service Hillside routes. Intercity bus companies provide drop-off service at trailheads. Air taxis are available in Anchorage. Call the Alaska Public Lands Information Center, 907-271-2737, for transport information.

Getting Around

With the exception of highway-access points, there are no roads within the park. Travel is by foot, canoe, skis, and, in some areas, horses, bikes, and motorboats. Aircraft access is limited to Eklutna Lake and a nearby landing strip.

Backcountry Travel

The park has many developed hiking and cross-country skiing trails, ranging from leisurely walks to arduous ascents. Backcountry hiking is unrestricted. Camping is permitted within one mile of developed hiking trails. Contact the park office for maps, access points, and conditions.

INFORMATION

Alaska Public Lands Information Center

605 West 4th Avenue; Anchorage, AK 99501; tel: 907-271-2737.

Anchorage Convention and Visitors Bureau

524 4th Avenue; Anchorage, AK 99501; tel: 907-276-4118.

Chugach State Park

HC 52, Box 8999; Indian, AK 99540; tel: 907-345-5014.

Eagle River Nature Center

Mile 12.7, Eagle River Road; Eagle River, AK 99738; tel: 907-694-2108.

CAMPING

The park has three public campgrounds, with picnic tables, fire pits, potable water, and latrines. Two public-use cabins also are available. For details and reservations, call the Alaska Public Lands Information Center, 907-271-2737.

LODGING

PRICE GUIDE – double occupancy

$ = up to $49 $$ = $50–$99
$$$ = $100–$149 $$$$ = $150+

Colony Inn

606 South Alaska Street; Palmer, AK 99645-6342; tel: 907-745-3330.

This Victorian-style inn, built in 1935 and lovingly restored in 1994, is situated in the small town of Palmer, site of the Alaska State Fair in August. Twelve guest rooms have mountain views, handmade quilts, antique reproductions, and whirlpool tubs. A large sitting room has cozy wing-backed chairs and a bay window. $$

Days Inn Anchorage

321 East 5th Avenue; Anchorage, AK 99501; tel: 907-276-7226.

The hotel, within walking distance of Anchorage's entertainment district and the train station, offers quality rooms and amenities at affordable rates. Twelve minutes from Anchorage International Airport and five minutes from Merrill Field, Days Inn has 130 guest rooms with private baths, most with two double beds. Extras include a restaurant, fitness center, spa, tour desk, car rental service and airport shuttle. $$–$$$$

Hotel Captain Cook

5th Avenue and K Street, P.O. Box 102280; Anchorage, AK 99501; tel: 800-843-1950 or 907-276-6000.

This downtown Anchorage hotel has views of Cook Inlet and the Chugach Mountains. Deluxe accommodations, including teak-wood and brass interiors, are available in the hotel's 562 guest rooms and 77 suites. Three restaurants, several shops, and an indoor pool are on the premises. $$$$

Sheep Mountain Lodge

HC 03, P.O. Box 8490; Palmer, AK 99645; tel: 907-745-5121.

The lodge is set between Palmer and Glennallen on the scenic Glenn Highway, 12 miles from Matanuska Glacier. Ten log cabins have private baths, double beds, and fine linens. Two dorm-style rooms share a bathhouse. Home-cooked meals are served in a spacious lodge, surrounded by decks, flower gardens, and mountain views. Guests watch Dall sheep through a telescope and hike the lodge's 12 miles of trails. A sauna and hot tub are available. $–$$

Westin Alyeska Prince Hotel

1000 Arlberg Road, P.O. Box 249; Girdwood, AK 99587; tel: 800-880-3880 or 907-754-1111.

Near the Mount Alyeska ski resort, this eight-story luxury hotel has 307 guest rooms and suites with private baths, cherry-wood furnishings, and views of the Chugach Mountains. Charming stone bridges and patios are on the grounds. Two dining rooms and three restaurants, including the elegant Seven Glaciers, are available. A tram transports guests to the hotel, located atop a mountain. $$$$

TOURS & OUTFITTERS

Alaska Backpackers Shuttle

P.O. Box 232493; Anchorage, AK 99523-2493; tel: 907-344-8775.

Shuttle service provides pick-up and drop-off for backpackers.

Alaska Railroad

422 West 4th Avenue, P.O. Box 107500; Anchorage, AK 99510; tel: 800-544-0552 or 907-265-2494.

Scenic rail tours run between Seward, Denali Park, and Fairbanks.

Klondike Mike Adventures

P.O. 232586; Anchorage, AK 99523-2586; tel: 800-781-2737.

One- to 10-day snowmobile excursions are offered in Chugach State Park.

Midnight Sun River Runners

P.O. Box 211561; Anchorage, AK 99521; tel: 907-338-7238.

Guides lead raft and kayak tours of Eagle River.

MUSEUMS

Anchorage Museum of History and Art

121 West 7th Avenue; Anchorage, AK 99501; tel: 907-343-4326.

Exhibits at the state's cultural center illustrate the art and history of Alaska and the polar North.

Crow Creek Mine

P.O. Box 113; Girdwood, AK 99587; tel: 907-278-8060.

Crow Creek camp, built in 1898, is preserved here in the form of a mess hall, blacksmith's shop, bunkhouse, barn, ice house, and meat cache. Tours and gold-panning activities are available.

Potter Section House and Historical Site

HC 52 Box 8999; Indian, AK 99540; tel: 907-345-5014.

This historic Alaska Railroad site, now state park headquarters, has an interpretive display and old railroad cars.

Excursions

Independence Mine State Historical Park

Alaska Division of Parks, HC 32, Box 6706; Wasilla, AK 99687-9719; tel: 907-745-3975.

High above tree level, encircled by the craggy peaks of the Talkeetna Mountains, is a green bowl filled with wildflowers. Here toiled prospectors during the gold boom of the 1930s and 1940s. The park, 19 miles north of Palmer, preserves mines and old buildings, including bunkhouses, warehouses, and mess halls. A museum and visitor center examine the mine's history. Berry picking, hiking, picnicking, and hang-gliding are popular summer activities. Just beyond the park is Hatcher Pass, with about 240,000 acres of backcountry recreation. Camping is permitted throughout the area.

Matanuska Glacier Recreation Site

Alaska Division of Parks, Mat/Su Area Office, HC 32, Box 6706; Wasilla, AK 99687; tel: 907-745-3975.

Matanuska Glacier, only a quarter-mile from the road, is one of the most accessible glaciers in Alaska. Travelers can not only hike to but hike on this natural landmark. The 229-acre recreation site is set in a birch-and-spruce forest surrounded by 8,000- to 9,000-foot peaks. A ridgeline trail and observation deck offer stunning views of the glacier and Matanuska River. Also available are primitive campsites, latrine facilities, and an interpretive kiosk. Moose and Dall sheep are regularly seen by visitors.

Nancy Lake State Recreational Area

Mile 0.7 Bogard Road, HC 32, Box 6706; Wasilla, AK 99654; tel: 907-745-3975.

This recreational area about 65 miles north of Anchorage is peppered with more than 130 lakes and ponds. Countless beavers, loons, grebes, ducks, geese, and sandhill cranes avail themselves of the park's waters. Moose and black bears are prominent residents; lynx, wolves, coyotes, and brown bears are less conspicuous, tending toward the remote regions of the park. Camping areas, public cabins, hiking, skiing, and canoe trails are available.

Lake Clark National Park

A party of hikers sets out shortly after sunrise and follows a moose trail up through dense alders and willows. Now and then they pause in grassy clearings as they press toward the distant heights. Two hours of steady climbing bring them to timberline, where the last of the scattered spruce, dwarfed and wind-flagged, abruptly gives way to thousands of acres of open tundra. Above them soar steep, knife-edged peaks dusted with early snow. ◆ It is early autumn, and the highlands are filled with the muted tones of the spent earth: rusted stalks of alpine fireweed, burgundy clumps of blueberry, dull orange streaks of dwarf birch, and, under it all, the grayish cream of reindeer moss. Peering through binoculars, they spot a herd of Dall sheep, a scattering of bright white dots against a broken shelf of schist. After moving steadily toward them for another hour, the hikers stop to observe the gentle animals feeding peacefully on grass and sedge, the young ones always near their mothers, gazing curiously at these intruders. Far below is a turquoise lake, and all around are mountains and valleys without end. ◆ This is **Lake Clark National Park and Preserve**, one of the largest and most beautiful of the many national parks established in Alaska in 1980. Situated about 150 miles southwest of Anchorage, the park protects more than four million acres that include virtually every feature one would choose for a major national park – volcanoes, glaciers, mountains, forests, rivers, waterfalls, canyons, sandy beaches, rocky coastlines. Indeed, many people choose to visit the park because it is a veritable cross-section of Alaska, both

Across Cook Inlet lies a wilderness with rugged coastlines, 10,000-foot volcanoes, scenic rivers and waterfalls, and, at its heart, a 40-mile-long lake.

The Chigmit Mountains, dusted with autumn snow, form a ridge between the interior of the park and Cook Inlet to the east.

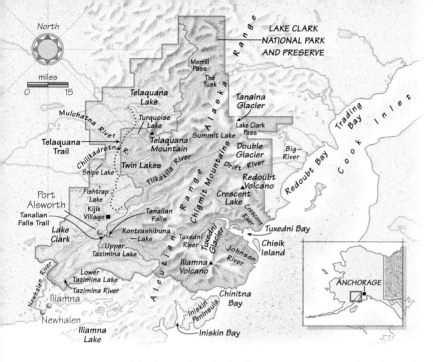

Map labels

North

miles
0 — 15

Mulchatna River

Telaquana Trail

Port Alsworth
Tanalian Falls Trail

Lake Clark

Newhalen River

Iliamna

Newhalen

Iliamna Lake

Telaquana Lake

Turquoise Lake

Telaquana Mountain

Twin Lakes

Snipe Lake

Chilikadrotna R.

Fishtrap Lake

Kijik Village

Tanalian Falls

Kontrashibuna Lake

Upper Tazimina Lake

Lower Tazimina Lake

Tazimina River

Merrill Pass

The Tusk

Summit Lake

Lake Clark Pass

Tanaina Glacier

Tanaina Glacier

Lake Clark Pass

Double Glacier

Drift River

Redoubt Volcano

Crescent Lake

Tuxedni River

Tuxedni Glacier

Iliamna Volcano

Johnson River

Iniskin Peninsula

Iniskin Bay

Chinitna Bay

Chisik Island

Tuxedni Bay

Crescent River

Big River

Trading Bay

Redoubt Bay

Cook Inlet

LAKE CLARK NATIONAL PARK AND PRESERVE

Alaska Range

Chigmit Mountains

Aleutian Range

Tlikakila River

ANCHORAGE

---

chocolate, these swift, cold rivers plunge into **Cook Inlet**.

The ancestral home of fishing-based Indian communities, the Lake Clark region was first visited by Europeans about 200 years ago, when Russian missionaries penetrated to Lake Iliamna. In 1897, John Clark, an agent for the Alaska Commercial Company, made his way to the interior lake that now bears his name. This was 30 years after the United States purchased Alaska from Russia. It says something about the remoteness of the area that it took a full generation after the land was acquired for the first American explorers to reach Lake Clark.

geographically and ecologically.

On the surface, the mountain country seems serene, but it is a work in progress. The surrounding ranges are born of eons of geological action, collisions of tectonic plates, and erupting volcanoes. The great valleys and convolutions are carved by glaciers; among the largest are **Tuxedni**, **Double**, and **Tanaina**, though there are scores of smaller, unnamed ones. Silty, glacier-fed streams polish the valleys of the eastern slopes. Colored like milk

Remote Wilderness

Most people see Lake Clark National Park for the first time while driving the coastal road, the Sterling Highway, on the Kenai Peninsula south of Anchorage. En route to Homer, you look across Cook Inlet and see two enormous volcanoes only 40 miles to the west. Lovely and symmetrical, **Redoubt** (10,197 feet) and **Iliamna** (10,016 feet) rise like twin Mount Fujis across the sparkling blue water.

There is no highway leading to the park – nor will there ever be, given its location – so access is almost exclusively by air-

A bush plane soars above an expanse of boreal forest east of the Alaska Range.

Arctic willow (opposite, top) grows among blackish oxytrope on Tanalian Mountain.

Tanalian Falls (right) is just a few miles on foot from Port Alsworth.

craft, though small boats sometimes make the passage across Cook Inlet. Wheeled planes land on open beaches, gravel bars, flat stretches of upland tundra, or private airstrips in or near the park. Floatplanes take visitors to the many lakes and rivers throughout the area. A one- to two-hour flight from Anchorage, Kenai, or Homer provides access to most points within the park and preserve. Scheduled commercial flights between Anchorage and Iliamna, 30 miles outside the park boundary, are another way to get there. From Iliamna, visitors can then charter small aircraft.

Trips to Lake Clark generally fall into one of two categories: those to the eastern coast along Cook Inlet for fishing and viewing wildlife, and those across the rugged mountains to the interior lakes for rafting, camping, hiking, wildlife observation, and fishing. If you choose the former, you will have a shorter and less expensive plane trip, especially if you depart from airfields in Kenai or Homer instead of the more distant Anchorage. Popular areas include **Tuxedni Bay** near **Chisik Island** and **Chinitna Bay** just north of the **Iniskin Peninsula**, as well as the major waterways: **Crescent River**, **Johnson River**, and **Tuxedni River**.

Brown bears gather along these rivers during the summer and autumn salmon runs, when they can be observed feeding on the fish much as they can at Brooks Camp in Katmai National Park but without the

large crowds of people (or the comfort of a viewing stand). Seabirds nest and feed along the beaches, on rocky wave-worn bluffs, and among the region's scattered islands. Kittiwakes, gulls, puffins, murres, and auklets gather in colonies where they find food sources and nesting opportunities. Thousands of shorebirds, ducks, and geese occupy the coastal mudflats and marshes each spring and fall, and some of the park's 250 harbor seals haul out on the beaches and inner islands.

Taking Flight

Almost all trips into the western side of Lake Clark National Park are funneled through two high mountain passes, **Lake Clark Pass** above **Summit Lake** and **Merrill Pass** (where air travelers can view the famous "Tusk" formation). Inclement weather sometimes prevents passage for many days, but once travelers are through the passes, a wonderful wild country opens up beneath the airplane. To the north is the tail end of the mammoth **Alaska Range**, a chain of peaks that stretches east all the way to Canada. To the south is the **Aleutian Range**, which extends west through the islands nearly to Russia. Ahead is a trackless landscape

that stretches to the **Bering Sea** some 500 miles away.

In such a wild land, the only practical way of getting around other than by air is by boat. Visitors typically are flown into the headwaters of a river, or to the upper stretches of a lake, and then are picked up days or weeks later after rafting or canoeing to a downstream site. One of the most popular trips begins at **Turquoise Lake** beneath **Telaquana Mountain** and then proceeds down the magnificent **Mulchatna River** to a predetermined pickup point. The scenery along the river is superb, and the fishing is world-class. In addition, the Mulchatna caribou herd, currently more than 200,000 animals strong, is one of the largest in Alaska, and large bands of the animals can be seen during the spring migration. Commercially guided trips are available for running the park's major rivers.

Around the Lake

Many visitors also choose to spend their time boating, camping, and hiking on and around **Lake Clark**. More than 40 miles long, the lake offers excellent opportunities

Glacial studies are conducted from the Glacial Research Base Camp (left) in Summit Crater of Mount Redoubt Volcano.

Setting up camp (top) above timberline, campers need cold-weather clothing as well as rain gear.

Flat-water kayaking (right) makes for easy going on Lower Twin Lake.

for solitude while being relatively close to other wilderness camps. The high country around the lake is famous for its Dall sheep, caribou, moose, and grizzly bears. Backpacking trips are possible into the surrounding mountains, but hikers will find that there is only one maintained trail, the 3.5-mile **Tanalian Falls**, leading from **Port Alsworth**, on the south side of the lake, to the falls and then to **Kontrashibuna Lake**.

Hikers also can seek out the rugged and difficult **Telaquana Trail**, a historic route on the north side of Lake Clark blazed by the region's first human residents. The 50-mile route begins near **Kijik Village** (now abandoned) on the lake and runs north along the Alaska Range to **Telaquana Lake** after crossing numerous rivers and streams along the way. Be aware that much of the footpath is poorly marked and overgrown. Instead of hiking the entire route, most trekkers choose to bypass the difficult sections by starting at **Snipe Lake** or **Fishtrap Lake**, accessible by floatplane.

Lake Clark attracts a steady stream of visitors from Anchorage. Many Alaskans prefer Lake Clark National Park to Denali National Park because the latter has become fairly crowded in recent years, at least by Alaskan standards. Outsiders find it attractive for much the same reason. Still, visitation at Lake Clark is low compared with national parks in the Lower 48, and visitors, particularly those who are not familiar with the Alaskan bush, should exercise care.

As with all parks

Tie One On

Sport fishing is extraordinary in the lakes and streams of Lake Clark National Park thanks largely to the abundance of rainbow trout, Dolly Varden, arctic grayling, whitefish, lake trout, northern pike, and, particularly in the Cook Inlet drainage, silver and king salmon.

The Chilikadrotna and Mulchatna Rivers offer some of the park's best prospects. Many anglers arrange to be dropped off in the upper reaches of one of these rivers and, after inflating a raft, drift and cast their way downstream for a few days. There's also good fishing in Kontrashibuna, Telaquana, and Turquoise Lakes and in the streams that flow in and out of them. Lake Clark itself has given up trout larger than 50 pounds.

It takes years for the region's trout, grayling, and char to reach trophy size, so most anglers practice catch-and-release fishing. For many, that means fly-fishing. Spinning gear works well, too, particularly if anglers use single, barbless hooks, rather than treble hooks on spinners and spoons. Fish taken on bait tend to swallow hooks, damaging delicate gill tissue and internal organs, which leads to bleeding and, ultimately, death.

When fishing catch-and-release, play a fish as briefly as possible and avoid removing it from the water. Use forceps or needle-nose pliers to grasp the hook and gently slip it from the fish's mouth. If the fish must be handled, make sure that your hands are wet. Dry hands are more likely to remove the slimy coating on the fish's body, leaving it prone to deadly fungal infections. Cradle the fish underwater for as long as necessary until it recovers and swims away under its own power. – *Ken Marsh*

Dick Proenneke (top, left), famed for his memoir of a year in the Lake Clark region, joins friend Cheryl Bloethe on an alpine slope overlooking Upper Twin Lake.

A red salmon (left) must regain equilibrium before the angler releases the fish.

Launching into the Chilikadrotna River (opposite, top) a group prepares to continue a float trip.

Paddlers (opposite, bottom) seek a shortcut through a narrow waterway in Lake Clark National Park.

in the Alaskan outback, self-sufficiency tempered by a bit of common sense is the rule. This means carrying enough provisions to live in the bush for a few days longer than expected should your departure by air or boat be delayed by bad weather or mechanical problems. Two-way radios and emergency signal flares are often included among camp supplies. A head-net and repellent are necessary throughout the summer bug season.

Wilderness travel in the winter is recommended only for those traveling with experienced local guides. Both bears and moose are plentiful in Lake Clark and should always be avoided; park rangers can provide detailed information on how to deal safely with wildlife.

Local Dena'ina Indians and rural residents still pursue their subsistence way of life within the park and should not be disturbed as they carry out their hunting and fishing activities.

Perhaps the best preparation for

a trip to Lake Clark is to read Richard Proenneke's classic memoir *One Man's Wilderness: An Alaskan Odyssey*. The author spent a year living in a cabin in the area, recording his encounters with wolves and grizzly bears and reflecting on the sometimes harsh beauty of the Alaskan bush. "This is as close as I hope to get to heaven," he wrote. "How can heaven be any better than this?"

TRAVEL TIPS

DETAILS

When to Go

The park is open year-round, but most travelers visit from mid-June to early September, when temperatures average from 60° to 75°F. Coastal areas are about 10° cooler and are rainier and windier. Expect snowfall as early as September. Winter temperatures dip well below zero.

How to Get There

The park is not accessible by road. Most visitors charter a flight from Anchorage, about 90 minutes from Lake Clark. Charter flights also are available from the Kenai Peninsula. Commercial airlines fly between Anchorage and Iliamna, from which many charter outfits fly into the park.

Getting Around

Because of the virtual absence of roads within the park, back-country travel is on foot or by small plane, kayak, or canoe.

Backcountry Travel

Backcountry travel in some wilderness areas requires a permit. Contact the park for information. Voluntary registration at park headquarters is advised for the safety of backcountry hikers.

INFORMATION

Alaska Public Lands Information Center

605 West 4th Avenue, Suite 105; Anchorage, AK 99501; tel: 907-271-2737.

Lake Clark National Park and Preserve

4230 University Drive, Suite 311; Anchorage, AK 99508; tel: 907-271-3751 or General Delivery; Port Alsworth, AK 99653; tel: 907-781-2218 (field headquarters).

CAMPING

The park has no developed campgrounds. Primitive camp-grounds require no fee or permit. Travelers must be completely self-sufficient; warm clothing, rain gear, and extra food are essential. Limited food and supplies may be purchased in the park seasonally.

LODGING

PRICE GUIDE – double occupancy	
$ = up to $49	$$ = $50–$99
$$$ = $100–$149	$$$$ = $150+

Alaska's Lake Clark Inn

General Delivery; Port Alsworth, AK 99653; tel: 800-781-2224 or 907-781-2224.

Magnificent views of Lake Clark and the Alaska Range are available from this modern, wood-sided inn. The main house has three tastefully appointed guest rooms with private baths; five cabins offer deluxe accom-modations, with private baths, kitchens, decks, and forced-air heat. A solarium, outdoor hot tub, and country store are on the premises. Large meals, guided excursions, boat rentals, charter flights, and travel planning are available. The inn is reached only by plane; the inn offers round-trip flights from Anchorage, 180 air miles northeast of Port Alsworth. Open year-round. $–$$

Alaska Wilderness Lodge

General Delivery; Port Alsworth, AK 99653; tel: 800-835-8032 or 907-781-2223 (summer only).

This remote fishing lodge, built in 1981, has seven lakeside cabins with private baths, all with views of Lake Clark and the Alaska and Aleutian Ranges. Gourmet meals are served in the cedar lodge, which has a cathedral ceiling, sitting room with fireplace, and a recreation center. A minimum stay of one week is required. The lodge is designed for anglers, who select from a number of first-rate fishing opportunities. Open from the first weekend in June to the first weekend in October. $$$$

The Farm Lodge

General Delivery; Port Alsworth, AK 99653; tel: 800-662-7661 or 907-278-2054.

This cedar-sided lodge is set on Lake Clark's Hardenberg Bay. Four wood-paneled guest rooms, decorated in rustic colors, have bunk-style single and double beds, private baths, and views of the bay and surrounding mountains. Prices include three meals per day; the menu features prime rib, turkey, fresh fish and vegetables, and homemade pastries. Among the lodge's many recreational opportunities are fishing, flightseeing, boat and plane charters, and bear-watching. Laundry and babysitting services are available. Flower and vegetable gardens are on the premises. $$

Wilder House

3323 Dry Creek, General Delivery; Port Alsworth, AK 99653; tel: 907-781-2228.

Built in 1982, this cedar inn occupies a remote wooded setting, with mountain views. Two lovely guest rooms, fur-nished with antiques, share a bath in the main house; a nearby rustic cabin has a private bath and kitchenette. Round-trip air-taxi service is available, as are flightseeing, bear-watching, and other wilderness adventures. An outdoor hot tub is on the premises. Open year-round. $$

TOURS & OUTFITTERS

Airborne Scientific

64999 Easterday Road; Homer, Alaska 99603; tel: 907-399-1755.

Multiday bush plane adventures explore Lake Clark National Park, with natural-history interpretation. Activities include kayaking, flight-seeing, fishing, and hiking.

Alaska Ecotours/High Adventure Air Charter, Guides, and Outfitters

P.O. Box 486; Soldotna, AK 99669; tel: 907-262-5237.

Guided three-day back-packing tours commence with a one-hour float-plane flight through Lake Clark National Park and a landing at Twin Lakes.

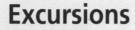

Natron Air

619 Funny River Road; Soldotna, AK 99669; tel: 907-262-8440.

Day flights into the park touch down at Tuxedni Bay and other beaches. Passengers picnic, hike, and photograph wildlife.

St. Elias Alpine Guides

1327 H Street; Anchorage, AK 99501; tel: 888-933-5427 or 907-277-6867.

Guides lead a wide range of customized adventure tours, including glacier hiking, ice climbing, mountain climbing, backpacking, and kayaking.

Talon Air Service

P.O. Box 1109; Soldotna, AK 99669; tel: 907-262-8899.

Tours of Lake Clark offer plenty of time for hiking, picnicking, and photographing wildlife. Remote drop-off service is available.

Windsong Wilderness Retreat

P.O. Box 513, Sterling, AK 99672; tel: 907-260-5410.

Guided fishing, hiking, photography, and rafting adventures on the Chilikadrotna River range from three days to a week. Some trips include a two-night stay at a remote log cabin in the Twin Lakes area.

Excursions

Togiak National Wildlife Refuge and Wilderness

P.O. Box 270; Dillingham, AK 99576; tel: 907-842-1063.

The refuge is situated between Kuskokwim and Bristol Bays just west of Dillingham, about 150 air miles southwest of Lake Clark. About 80 percent of the refuge is occupied by the Ahklun Mountains; the remaining topography is richly varied, with swift rivers, deep lakes, marshy lowlands, coastal lagoons, sea bluffs, and ponds. Waterfowl and shore-birds breed and rest here. Brown bears, moose, and caribou range the wilderness. Seven species of whales, along with spotted seals and walruses, frequent Togiak's coastal waters.

Walrus Island State Game Sanctuary

Alaska Department of Fish and Game, P.O. Box 230; Dillingham, AK 99576; tel: 907-842-5227.

This Round Island sanctuary, about 70 miles southwest of Dillingham, supports between 10,000 and 15,000 walruses each summer. Joining these mammoth migrators – male walruses can weigh over 2,700 pounds – are about 1,000 Steller sea lions, who lounge on the southern tip, and untold numbers of auklets, kittiwakes, puffins, cormorants, and murres. Red foxes den on the island's grassy slopes. Isolated and wind-swept, the sanctuary is reached by air taxi or charter from Dillingham. Camping is allowed in the island's designated areas; a permit is required.

Wood-Tikchik State Park

Alaska Department of Natural Resources, 3601 C Street; Anchorage, AK 99503; tel: 907-269-8698.

One of the largest state parks in the nation, Wood-Tikchik has six large clear-water lakes connected by rivers and streams. Spired mountain peaks and high alpine valleys typify the western edges; sand beaches and tundra stretch east of the lakes. A variety of waterfowl nest here; moose, caribou, and grizzly bears are readily observed. The park also is inhabited by wolves, lynx, foxes, and martens. Visitors should be self-reliant and prepared for harsh conditions.

Katmai National Park

CHAPTER 15

Exploring an unnamed valley at the base of the Alaska Peninsula in 1916, botanist Robert Griggs encountered "one of the most amazing visions ever beheld by mortal eye. The whole valley as far as the eye could reach was full of hundreds, no, thousands – literally tens of thousands – of smokes curling up from its fissured floor." ◆ The steaming volcanic vents that so impressed Griggs are largely quiet now; most stopped "smoking" decades ago. But the **Valley of Ten Thousand Smokes** in **Katmai National Park** remains an eerie, otherworldly place. Rimmed in part by lush vegetation, and walled in by ice- and snowcapped mountains, this Alaska valley evokes images of lunar landscapes or southwestern deserts. Vegetation is sparse here, wildlife even rarer. But this 40-square-mile volcanic plain 300 miles southwest of Anchorage doesn't have a desert's aridity or heat. Summer temperatures rarely rise above 65°F, rain may last for

A volcanic hot spot on the Pacific Ring of Fire is a world-class destination for fishing and bear watching.

days, and turbulent, gravy-colored streams erode the starkly beautiful landscape. ◆ Here, hypothermia and smothering dust storms are the chief dangers. With no warning, winds born in the **Gulf of Alaska** blast over **Katmai Pass** and into the valley. Gale-force gusts create dust clouds thousands of feet high. Visibility drops to near zero, and anything exposed to the wind's fury is likely to get sandblasted by volcanic grit or choked by dust. ◆ The valley's rock- and ash-covered bottom is a pastel blend of pink, orange, yellow, and brown. Hundreds of feet thick, the ash was deposited over lush green lands in 1912 by the eruption of **Novarupta Volcano**, the 20th century's largest volcanic explosion,

A sunrise dip for a brown bear isn't for bathing purposes so much as for snatching salmon in Naknek Lake.

Mount Cerberus, named after the three-headed dog that guards the gates of the underworld.

The Making of a Park

Impressed by expedition reports, President Woodrow Wilson proclaimed the Valley of Ten Thousand Smokes a national monument in 1918. The boundaries were extended over the years, and in 1980 an area of some four million acres was designated a national park and preserve. This sprawling parkland encompasses enormous lakes, lush forested lowlands,

ten times more forceful than Mount St. Helens. In two and a half days, volcanoes on the Alaska Peninsula spewed forth more than 33 billion tons of incandescent ash and debris.

Lured by reports of this incredible event, several scientific expeditions visited the region between 1912 and 1919, including four led by Robert Griggs, who named the Valley of Ten Thousand Smokes in 1916. The landscape's fiery desolation prompted Griggs and his colleagues to call one stream the **River Lethe**, which in Greek mythology flows through the center of Hades. For a peak at the head of the valley they chose

several rich salmon-producing streams (including the **Alagnak Wild River**), glacier-covered mountains, and rugged fjord-like coastal areas.

An estimated one million salmon spawn in the park's waters, and their eggs and decaying bodies provide food for predators: rainbow trout, char, bald eagles, gulls, wolves, otters, mink, and bears. No place in North America is more densely populated with brown bears, the coastal cousins of grizzlies. Other inhabitants of the region include moose, caribou, tundra swans, ptarmigan, and more than 40 songbird species. Coastal areas are home to sea lions, sea otters, seals, whales, and many species of shore birds.

People come here to float Katmai's rivers, climb its

World-class fly-fishing (left) attracts anglers, who can enjoy top-dollar packages at remote lodges with gourmet cooking.

The red fox (opposite, top) is found throughout most of Alaska. It's an omnivore, feeding on everything from plants and insects to small mammals.

The River Lethe (right) in the Valley of 10,000 Smokes takes its name from the mythological river that flows through Hades.

mountains, paddle its coastline, see its wildlife, fish for salmon and rainbow trout. Nearly all start their journey in Anchorage, where they catch a daily commuter flight to **King Salmon**, a small Alaska Peninsula town that serves as "gateway" to Katmai. From King Salmon, most visitors fly into the park using local air-taxi operators, though it's also possible to arrange boat rides to some destinations, most notably **Brooks Camp**. Those staying at sportfishing lodges usually have their transportation arranged for them.

Except for Brooks Camp and a few scattered lodges, Katmai's facilities are minimal. It's possible to arrange a bus ride from Brooks Camp to the edge of the Valley of Ten Thousand Smokes, but once you leave the road, you're on your own. Most of the park has no developed trails, no signposts, no campgrounds. And both the terrain and weather are challenging. Backcountry explorers must be self-sufficient and experienced in wilderness camping and travel.

Volcanic Landscape

Novarupta's eruption began on June 6, 1912, with a violent explosion that rocketed debris 25 miles into the atmosphere. Soon gas-rich magma spilled from fissures to produce a steamy mix of ash, pumice, and molten rock that rushed 13 miles down the

valley, destroying everything in its path. Much of the magma came from a chamber beneath neighboring **Mount Katmai**. Its reservoir emptied, Katmai collapsed to produce a caldera one and a half miles deep, three miles wide. When things finally quieted, ash and rock covered the valley to depths of 700 feet, and thousands of fumaroles vented steam as vaporized snow and water escaped through cracks in the land's new surface.

At Kaflia Bay, 30 miles from the blast, Ivan Orloff wrote to his wife Tania, "A mountain has burst near here, so that we are covered with ashes, in some places ten feet and six feet deep… We cannot see the daylight. In a word it is terrible, and we are expecting death at any moment."

On Kodiak Island, 60 miles away, ash fell so thickly it blotted out the sun for two days. The explosion was heard as far away as Juneau, 750 miles to the east. Volcanic dust fell in Puget Sound, 1,500 miles to the south, and ash blown into the upper atmosphere

River of Bears

Bears have always come first at Alaska's **McNeil River State Game Sanctuary**. Created in 1967 by the Alaska Legislature and managed by the state's Division of Wildlife Conservation, this Alaska Peninsula site 200 miles southwest of Anchorage protects the world's largest gathering of brown bears.

The sanctuary's centerpiece is **McNeil Falls**, where bears come to feed on chum salmon. Dozens of brown bears congregate here during the peak of the salmon run in July and August, and more than 140 individual bears have been observed in a single season.

To preserve this extraordinary gathering, human use of the sanctuary has been restricted since 1973. No more than 10 people a day – accompanied by one or two state biologists – are allowed to visit McNeil's bear-viewing sites from early June through late August. Because demand is so high, the state conducts an annual drawing to determine permit winners.

Since the permit system was put in place, the number of bears sighted at McNeil Falls has increased dramatically. Even more significantly, no sanctuary bears have been killed in self-defense and no humans have been injured by bears.

"It's widely assumed that bears and people don't mix," says Larry Aumiller, the sanctuary's manager since 1976. "Here we've shown they can mix if you do the right things. To me, that's McNeil's most important message: Humans can peacefully coexist with bears."

Bear viewing within the sanctuary begins in June at **Mikfik Creek**, but the falls are the primary focus in July and August. Lucky visitors not only will see a great number of bears, they'll see the animals at very close range. It's not uncommon for McNeil's most tolerant bears to eat salmon, take naps, or even nurse cubs within 15 feet of the viewing pads.

Fishing bears (top) possess unique personalities and fishing styles, ranging from slashing and leaping at fish to submarine fish-watching.

Visitors to the McNeil River (left) are allowed in limited number and selected through a lottery system.

Layers of volcanic ash (right) are visible evidence of volatile geologic history in the Valley of 10,000 Smokes.

Park Service built a 23-mile road connecting it to Brooks Camp, a popular tourist destination. Nowadays dozens of travelers come here daily in summer and walk a short trail along its western edge. Far fewer venture into the valley itself. Those who do will find a wealth of extraordinary geologic features. Among them are the churning River Lethe, which in places cuts steep-walled chasms narrow enough to jump across, and elsewhere forms broad, shallow, and turbulent channels that can be dangerous to cross; the milky blue **Mageik Lakes**, formed when hot ash landed on Mount Mageik's glaciers; Novarupta's half-mile-wide caldera and neighboring lava dome, with active fumaroles and warm springs; and triple-

remained there several months, producing spectacular sunsets around the world.

Over time the ash cooled and nearly all the "smokes" disappeared. Today only a few fumaroles continue to steam, a potent reminder that this area is an active volcanic center on the **Pacific Ring of Fire**.

Few people besides scientists entered the valley until 1963, when the National

Siberian asters (right) are tough little wildflowers, able to endure the most severe conditions in winter.

Gyrfalcons (bottom) prey on other birds such as ptarmigan and waterfowl.

Lynx (opposite, top) are well-adapted to walking on snow, with broad, furry pads that serve as "snowshoes."

Brooks Falls (opposite, bottom) brown bears can catch salmon in midair as the fish try to scale the falls.

peaked Mount Katmai, with its glacier-rimmed caldera, now partly filled with turquoise **Crater Lake**.

Look closely and you'll notice that pioneering plants – mosses, grasses, willows, and hardy wildflowers like dwarf fireweed – are restoring life to the valley. You may also see brown-bear tracks, a reminder that this seemingly barren landscape is part of Katmai's bear habitat.

Bear Country

Only a short distance from Katmai's desolate Valley of Ten Thousand Smokes is a river drainage teeming with life. Each July, thousands of silvery salmon push their way up the **Brooks River**, a clearwater stream nearly 12 miles long that connects **Brooks** and **Naknek Lakes**. As they approach their spawning grounds, the salmon are faced with one final obstacle: six-foot-high **Brooks Falls**. Every few seconds salmon leap from the water, attempting to scale the cascade.

Following the fish to the falls are brown bears. Solitary creatures by nature, they've learned to tolerate each other's company in the presence of an abundant, easy-to-catch, and high-energy food source. At the peak of the salmon run in July, it's not unusual to see a dozen or more bears at Brooks Falls. They grab sockeyes from atop the falls, snorkel in plunge pools below it, and watch from stream banks. Also watching are two to three dozen people, squeezed together on an elevated platform along the river's south shore. By summer's end, more than 14,000 people make the pilgrimage to **Brooks Falls**. Many have never seen a wild bear; this is their once-in-a-lifetime opportunity.

This ursine gathering puts Brooks Falls in a class with the world's most famous wildlife spectacles. Bears often fish within 50 feet of the viewing stand and sometimes pass much closer when approaching or leaving the falls. Visitors also can see bears from a second platform along the lower river or even when walking through Brooks Camp.

Only since the mid-1980s has this area become renowned for its bears. Previously the Brooks was best known as a fishing spot. Aleut and Yup'ik people came here for thousands of years to net salmon from the river and nearby lakes. Fishing is also what brought tourism and the present-day Brooks Camp to the river.

Brooks was the largest of five remote camps established at Katmai in the 1950s. The original tent camp, the forerunner of Brooks Lodge, accommodated up to 30 guests, who came either to fish or to visit the Valley of Ten Thousand Smokes. Those who preferred fishing discovered that Brooks

River was an angler's paradise, with plentiful grayling, salmon, and rainbow trout.

In the camp's early days, visitors saw few bears. Most were probably chased away or killed by fishermen or Native hunters. A dramatic change occurred when the Park Service began actively to manage the area in the late 1950s. Instead of harassing bears, park officials welcomed them. And as their tolerance of bears increased, so too did the number of animals. Within three decades, the Brooks River was transformed from an exclusive fishermen's paradise into a world-renowned bear-watcher's haven (though the stream remains popular with anglers).

Visitation has increased dramatically. In fact, some people fly in for only a few hours, have a look at the bears, and then leave. The booming day-use business is partly driven by Brooks Camp's limited overnight facilities. The lodge, with 16 cabins, and the Park Service campground each have a limit of about 60 people.

Visitors must obey a series of safety rules and are given a "Welcome to Brooks" bear talk upon their arrival from King Salmon, which is about 35 miles, or a 20-

minute plane ride, away. But for the most part, they are free to roam.

From a safety perspective, the system has worked almost perfectly. Since 1970, only one person has been injured by a bear at Brooks, and no bears have been killed here in "defense of life and property" since 1983. Meanwhile, the river's summer bear population is at or near historic highs. Brooks, in short, has demonstrated that humans and brown bears can coexist, if certain precautions are taken. Yet many people, both within the Park Service and outside it, worry that the growing number of travelers has adversely affected the bears and their habitat and the quality of the visitor experience.

The Park Service is considering some changes to minimize the impact of tourism on the bears and maximize safety. A limitation on the number of tourists is being reviewed, and visitor facilities may someday be moved to another location. But Katmai's world-famous midsummer ritual will remain largely the same. Salmon scaling Brooks Falls. Brown bears catching salmon. People watching bears.

TRAVEL TIPS

DETAILS

When to Go

Katmai National Park is open to visitors year-round, but July and September are the best bear-viewing months. Summer temperatures average 60°F. Expect cool and rainy days interspersed with warm and sunny ones. Spring and fall bring cool days and cold nights.

How to Get There

There is no road access to the park. Nearly all visitors take commercial flights to Anchorage International, then regional air service to King Salmon. Air taxis also are available from Soldotna, Homer, and Kodiak. Scheduled floatplane and boat services operate between King Salmon and Brooks Camp.

Getting Around

A 23-mile dirt road winds through the park from Brooks Camp to the Valley of Ten Thousand Smokes. Daily bus tours are offered at Brooks Camp. Otherwise, travel within the park is limited to foot, boat, or floatplane. Contact the park for information about Brooks Camp use permits. Permits for the McNeil River State Game Sanctuary are awarded by lottery. Application forms are available from the Alaska Department of Fish and Game in January, and permit holders are chosen in March.

Backcountry travel

The park has only two identified hiking trails: Dumpling Mountain (beginning at Brooks Camp) and Ukak Falls (beginning at Three Forks cabin). Backcountry permits, though not required, are helpful for determining park use and for notifying rangers of your approximate location. Required bear-resistant food canisters are available at the park office.

INFORMATION

Alaska Department of Fish and Game (McNeil River Information)

Wildlife Conservation Division, 333 Raspberry Road; Anchorage, AK 99518-1599; tel: 907-267-2182.

Alaska Public Lands Information Center

605 West 4th Avenue, Suite 105; Anchorage, AK 99501; tel: 907-271-2737.

Katmai National Park and Preserve

P.O. Box 7; King Salmon, AK 99613; tel: 907-246-3305 (King Salmon Office) or 907-486-6730 (Coastal Unit Office).

CAMPING

The Brooks Campground is limited to 60 people. Reservations are required, and visitors must attend the campground's Bear Etiquette School. Visitors at McNeil River stay in a designated camping area with nearby latrines. A wooden shack provides space for cooking, eating, and storage.

LODGING

PRICE GUIDE – double occupancy

$ = up to $49	$$ = $50–$99
$$$ = $100–$149	$$$$ = $150+

Brooks Lodge

4550 Aircraft Drive; Anchorage, AK 99502; tel: 800-544-0551 or 907-243-5448.

The lodge, set in Katmai National Park, offers nine guest rooms and seven cabins, all with private baths. One- to four-night packages include park access fees and round-trip air transportation between Anchorage and either King Salmon or the lodge. Buffet-style meals are served three times a day at additional cost. Bus and flight-seeing tours are available. $$$$

Grosvenor Lodge

4550 Aircraft Drive; Anchorage, AK 99502; tel: 800-544-0551 or 907-243-5448.

This lodge, in the secluded center of Katmai National Park, is surrounded by streams and rivers. Three guest cabins share a modern bathhouse. The dining area affords a fabulous view of Grosvenor Lake. Also included in the three- to seven-day packages are round-trip air transportation between Anchorage and the lodge, meals, open bar, boat and guide service, and fishing gear and license. Open late May to late September. $$$$

King Ko Inn

3340 Arctic Boulevard, Suite 201; Anchorage, AK 99503; tel: 907-246-3377 or 907-562-0648.

This King Salmon inn was opened in 1943 and expanded in 1998. King Ko has 14 modern cabins with private baths, some with kitchenettes. The inn is situated next to the airport, near the boundary of Katmai National Park and within walking distance of King Salmon. $$

Kulik Lodge

4550 Aircraft Drive; Anchorage, AK 99502; tel: 800-544-0551 or 907-243-5448.

Set on the crystalline Kulik River in the northern section of Katmai National Park, this lodge specializes in fishing excursions on Kulik and Nonvianuk Lakes and to remote areas within a 100-mile radius. Guest cabins, which sleep two people, have private baths with showers. The spruce lodge has a large stone fireplace, dining area, and an open bar. Round-trip transportation is provided between Anchorage and the lodge, as is a fishing license and fishing gear. Open early June to October. $$$$

Quinnat Landing Hotel

2015 Merrill Field; Anchorage, AK 99501; tel: 800-770-3474 or 907-272-6300.

Overlooking the Naknek River in King Salmon, this year-round hotel is 15 minutes by car from the boundary of Katmai National Park and an hour by boat from the bear-watching section of the park. The hotel has more than 40 modern guest rooms, all with private baths, half with river views. A restaurant and two lounges, one with a fireplace, are on the premises. A variety of guide services, including boat and plane excursions, are available. $$$$

TOURS & OUTFITTERS

Bald Mountain Air Service

P.O. Box 3134; Homer, AK 99603; tel: 800-478-7969.

Brown-bear photo safaris leave daily by floatplane from Homer to Katmai.

Branch River Air

P.O. Box 545; King Salmon, AK 99613; tel: 907-248-3539.

Floatplane service is provided to remote areas of Bristol Bay and the Alaska Peninsula for rafting, photography, bear viewing, and fishing. Lodging and both guided and unguided excursions are available.

Coastal Outfitters

HC 67, Box 1263; Anchor Point, AK 99556; tel: 888-235-8492.

Passengers take floatplanes from Homer to the waters of Katmai for guided or unguided bear viewing, wildlife photography, birding, and kayaking.

Hallo Bay Camp/Kodiak-Katmai Outdoor, Inc.

P.O. Box 8630; Kodiak, AK 99615; tel: 907-486-2628.

This remote camp within Katmai specializes in wildlife viewing and wilderness adventure.

Excursions

Aniakchak National Monument and Preserve

P.O. Box 7; King Salmon, AK 99613; tel: 907-246-3305.

The volcanic Aniakchak Caldera is the primary feature of the park, one of the most remote areas on the Alaska Peninsula. Created by the collapse of the volcano's central section, the six-mile-wide caldera spans 30 square miles. Surprise Lake, heated by hot springs, cascades through a 1,500-foot rift in the wall. Area wildlife include caribou, grizzly bears, and eagles. The park is accessed by charter flights out of King Salmon.

Alagnak Wild River

Katmai National Park and Preserve, P.O. Box 7; King Salmon, Alaska 99613; tel: 907-246-3305 (King Salmon Office) or 907-486-6730 (Coastal Unit Office).

The 67-mile Alagnak River flows west through wilderness from the north of Katmai National Park to Kvichak Bay. The river originates in two lakes: the Kukaklek, which involves dangerous Class III rapids, and the Nonvianuk, which has no serious obstacles. The Alagnak River offers outstanding recreational opportunities, including wildlife photography, primitive camping, and float trips. The river is reached by charter flights from Anchorage or King Salmon.

Becharof Wilderness Area

Alaska Peninsula/Becharof National Wildlife Refuge Complex, P.O. Box 277; King Salmon, AK 99613; tel: 907-246-3339.

Salmon-spawning streams in this 477,000-acre wilderness attract one of the densest brown-bear populations in Alaska. Plenty of moose roam the park, along with about 10,000 caribou. Sea otters, sea lions, harbor seals, and whales congregate along the water's edge, as do nesting eagles, peregrine falcons, and thousands of seabirds. Recreational opportunities include camping, hiking, boating, flightseeing, and wildlife observation. Chartered planes are necessary to reach the park.

Kodiak Island

Paddling into a sheltered cove, a family of four decides to pull their sea kayaks onto a black sand beach to stretch their legs. As they approach the bank, the water erupts with scores, perhaps hundreds, of silvery salmon, churning beneath the surface in a single rippling wave. A hundred yards away, a seal pops its head out of the water and surveys the scene. He seems more curious about the boaters and their kayaks than the abundance of fish. After all, he's already eaten his fill. ◆ This is just one of the countless coves and bays in the **Kodiak** archipelago, situated in the Gulf of Alaska about 200 miles southwest of Anchorage. The main island, Kodiak, the second largest in the United States, is a green jewel in the cold sapphire waters of the northern Pacific. Kodiak and nearly 200 surrounding islands encompass 900 miles of untamed coastline. Kodiak itself is 100 miles long and 60 miles wide, but because of its convoluted shoreline, no place on the island is more than 15 miles from the sea. ◆ Warm ocean currents and continual precipitation

Bears of legendary size and rich coastal waters are just two reasons why Kodiak is known as "Island Terrific in the North Pacific."

sustain a profusion of plant and animal life. Summer wildflowers carpet lush hillsides, aquatic life abounds in coastal waters, and Kodiak bears, the world's largest carnivores, prowl the meadows, rivers, and estuaries. The natural bounty of this "Emerald Isle" no doubt appealed to prehistoric settlers. According to archaeologists, the island was home to some of the oldest villages in Alaska. It also attracted trappers and traders of the Russian-America Company, which established its headquarters here in the late 17th century. From the moment you arrive, it's easy to see why Kodiak

Kodiak "brownies" are bigger than other coastal brown bears because the temperate maritime climate in which they live supports abundant resources such as fish, deer, and berries.

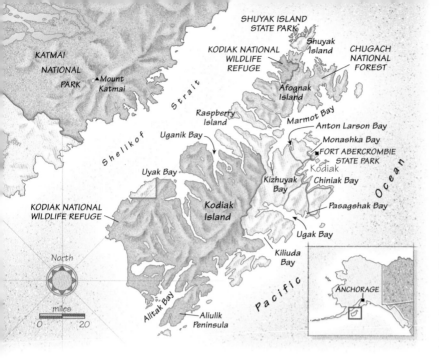

about $100 million. Visitors are encouraged to join a celebration of the sea's bounty at the Kodiak King Crab Festival in spring.

Nearby Wilderness

The island has 83 miles of roads, most of which radiate from the town of Kodiak, a community of about 7,000 people. While many travelers stop here just long enough to catch a boat or plane to more remote areas of the archipelago, there's plenty of wilderness to explore just outside of town.

Trails in **Fort Abercrombie State Park**, just east of town, wind through dense forests, along steep ocean bluffs, and across sandy beaches. Sitka spruce grow only on this northeastern end of the island, their massive, moss-covered trunks rising from a dense undergrowth of feathery ferns. Sitka black-tailed deer are often seen along the trails. Bears, carefully controlled, are less common here than elsewhere on the island.

is one of the largest commercial fishing ports in the United States. Crab boats, shrimp trawlers, and salmon seiners chug in and out of **St. Paul** and **St. Herman Harbors**, where piles of fluorescent buoys, wire crab pots, and enormous nets rarely sit idle. More than 2,500 commercial vessels operate from the island; their annual catch of salmon, halibut, cod, and other fish totals

Another way to discover the beauty of Kodiak without straying too far from town is on horseback. Several ranches offer trail rides or a full resort experience. In a single afternoon, visitors can revel in a meadow painted with fireweed, blue iris, shooting stars, and other late-summer wildflowers, gorge on sweet salmonberries, and gallop along the beaches of **Pasagshak Bay**.

Sea kayaking is another good option for exploring the area, and few modes of travel offer such intimate encounters with aquatic wildlife. Cormorants, black-legged kittiwakes, and glaucous-winged gulls flock to the island's shoreline, and clownlike puffins bob in the water and perch on the cliffs. Marine mammals have little fear of these sleek, silent kayaks, and it's not unusual to have a close encounter with an inquisitive sea lion or to find yourself in the company of humpback whales, orcas, or porpoises.

For a scenic daylong paddle, try **Anton**

Larsen Bay, an 11-mile drive across the island from Kodiak International Airport. The sea is protected and usually calm, and the large island separating the inner and outer bays can be circumnavigated in about three hours. Experienced paddlers can extend the trip into **Kizhuyak** and **Marmot Bays**. Other prime kayaking spots are **Monashka Bay**, just north of town, and, farther afield, **Afognak** and **Raspberry Islands** and **Shuyak Island State Park**. Outfitters in Kodiak offer kayak rentals and guided excursions of varying length. Remember that paddling too far from protected bays and coves can be dangerous. A sudden change in weather can make calm seas treacherous.

Mallards and many other waterfowl (left) winter in the Kodiak National Wildlife Refuge.

A beach-combing bear (opposite, bottom) digs for razor clams in the tidal zone of Kodiak Island.

A weir (below) operated by the Alaska Department of Fish and Game monitors salmon moving into Olga Creek and on to Olga Lakes.

Bears' Refuge

Two-thirds of Kodiak Island is set aside as **Kodiak National Wildlife Refuge**, with access only by charter boat or air taxi. Considering the island's cool, wet weather, the best way to explore the refuge is to base yourself at one of the public-use cabins maintained by the U.S. Fish and Wildlife Service. These simple structures have one or two rooms, kerosene heaters, and bunks; everything else, including food, bedding, kerosene, and a cook stove, is left up to you.

The refuge is home to the majority of the island's 3,000 bears. The Kodiak bear, a subspecies of the brown bear, attains its remarkable size by gorging on summer salmon, berries, and grasses. By the time winter rolls around, a Kodiak bear may

have gained 200 pounds and larded on a six-inch layer of fat. Males can weigh a monumental 1,500 pounds, while females sometimes register a modest 700 pounds.

The dorsal fin (left) of a killer whale can grow as high as 6 feet.

Salmon (below) are the staple fish in Kodiak's commercial fishing industry, which also includes seasonal fishing for crab, halibut, cod, sablefish, and herring.

Kodiak's harbor (right) is home port to dozens of fishing boats.

Pigeon-toed and flat-footed, these overgrown bruins can be seen foraging on beaches, grazing in meadows, or fishing along rivers. This latter activity requires a good deal of skill and often reveals something about the bear's personality. While one bear rushes the river and scoops salmon with noisy abandon, another quietly submerges his head beneath the surface to scope out the goods before sinking his teeth into a tasty morsel.

Needless to say, caution is essential. These are the biggest, strongest bears in the world and can charge at speeds of up to 35 miles per hour. They are extremely protective of cubs and willing to defend favorite fishing holes. Use good bear sense, and always keep your distance.

Other native species include the short-tailed weasel, river otter, brown bat, and red fox, which, in addition to dining on an occasional salmon, feeds mostly on mouselike tundra voles. Birding is quite good, too. More than 200 types of birds inhabit the archipelago, including some 2,000 bald eagles, numerous seabirds, and such forest species as the varied thrush, chestnut-backed chickadee, orange-crowned warbler, and golden-crowned sparrow.

Many of the other animals you may see on Kodiak have been introduced for trapping or sport hunting. Sitka black-tailed deer, brought here in 1924, now number almost 100,000. Mountain goats, occasionally spotted in the high country, were introduced in the 1950s. Roosevelt elk were brought to Afognak and Raspberry Islands in 1929. Other exotic mammals include the muskrat, beaver, red squirrel, arctic ground squirrel, and snowshoe hare.

Kodiak Island embraces the best of many wild habitats in a relatively compact space. From towering rain forests and rolling meadows to glaciated mountains and rich coastal waters, the island's abundance is matched only by the opportunities for discovery.

DETAILS

When to Go

The majority of tourists visit Kodiak from mid-May to late September. Daytime temperatures in summer average about 60°F. Weather is relatively mild by Alaskan standards, but rain and fog are common. Rain- and wind-resistant clothing is a must.

How to Get There

Daily flights are available between Anchorage International and Kodiak Airport. Ferries operated by the Alaska Marine Highway System run between Homer and the island.

Getting Around

There are four roads on Kodiak Island, but the Kodiak National Wildlife Refuge is accessible only by boat, small plane, or on foot. Car rentals are available in Kodiak. Visitors may take their own motor vehicle, bicycle, canoe, or kayak aboard the Alaska Marine Highway System ferry.

Backcountry Travel

A guide to trailheads accessible by road is available at the Convention and Visitors Bureau. The center also offers a kayaking guide to launch points and routes.

INFORMATION

Alaska Division of Parks

Kodiak District Office, 1400 Abercrombie Drive; Kodiak, AK 99615; tel: 907-486-6339.

Alaska Public Lands Information Center

605 West 4th Avenue, Suite 105; Anchorage, AK 99501; tel: 907-271-2737.

Kodiak Island Convention and Visitors Bureau

100 Marine Way; Kodiak, AK 99615; tel: 907-486-6545.

Kodiak National Wildlife Refuge Visitor Center

1390 Buskin River Road; Kodiak, AK 99615; tel: 907-487-2600.

CAMPING

Eight public-use cabins, reserved by lottery, are available in Kodiak National Wildlife Refuge. Cabins may be reached only by floatplane. Contact the visitor center for details. Four additional cabins are available on Shuyak Island. Contact the Alaska Division of Parks, Kodiak District Office, for details and reservations. There are three state campgrounds on Kodiak: Fort Abercrombie State Historic Park, Buskin River State Recreation Site, and Pasagshak River State Recreation Site. Contact the Kodiak District Office for information.

LODGING

PRICE GUIDE – double occupancy

$ = up to $49	$$ = $50–$99
$$$ = $100–$149	$$$$ = $150+

Afognak Wilderness Lodge

P.O. Box 7; Seal Bay, AK 99697; tel: 800-478-6442 or 907-486-6442.

Set on the edge of a saltwater cove in the virgin spruce forest of Afognak Island State Park, this lodge has three large, log cabins, each with two bedrooms, a living room, and bathroom. Included in the package are three daily meals, served in the lodge, and a variety of guide services, including wildlife watching and both fresh- and saltwater fishing. The lodge is about 45 miles north of Kodiak. $$$$

Best Western Kodiak Inn

236 Rezanof Drive West; Kodiak, AK 99615; tel: 888-563-4254 or 907-486-5712.

Perched on Pillar Mountain one

block from downtown Kodiak, the inn has 80 guest rooms and suites, many with views of the harbor and mountains. A restaurant overlooking the ocean specializes in seafood. Also on the premises are an Alaskan-style spa and laundry facilities. $$–$$$

Buskin River Inn

1395 Airport Way; Kodiak, AK 99615; tel: 800-544-2202 or 907-487-2700.

Set on the banks of the scenic Buskin River, one block from the airport and about four miles from downtown Kodiak, this inn has 50 guest rooms, including five suites, all with private baths. The Eagle's Nest Restaurant, which overlooks the river, specializes in seafood and offers an extensive wine list. Free transportation to and from the airport is provided. $$

Shelikof Lodge

211 Thorsheim Avenue; Kodiak, AK 99615; tel: 907-486-4141.

This downtown Kodiak lodge, built in 1965 and recently remodeled, has more than 35 simply appointed rooms with queen-sized or double beds and private baths. A family-style restaurant, lounge, and bar are on the premises. $$

Wintel's Bed-and-Breakfast

1723 Mission, P.O. Box 2812; Kodiak, AK 99615; tel: 907-486-6935.

Built in 1985, this bed-and-breakfast is within walking distance of beaches, hiking trails, and Kodiak's shops and harbor. Four cheery guest rooms have shared baths, country furnishings, handmade quilts, and fine views. A suite has a private bath. Large Alaskan breakfasts are served overlooking the channel. Guests are invited to relax in the Jacuzzi or sauna, or in a den filled with Alaskan art and books. $$

Zachar Bay Lodge

P.O. Box 2609; Kodiak, AK 99615; tel: 907-486-4120.

This converted cannery on Zachar Bay has eight cozy guest rooms, each with two single beds, some with private baths. Fresh fish is served daily. Guide services are available for floatplane, boat, and hiking excursions. $$$$

TOURS & OUTFITTERS

Adventure Charters & Marine Services, Inc.

P.O. Box 1679; Kodiak, AK 99615; tel: 877-872-2527 or 907-486-6400.

Guided fishing and sightseeing adventures are made aboard *The Boat*, which also drops off and picks up campers.

Andrew Airways

P.O. Box 1037; Kodiak, AK 99615; tel: 907-487-2566.

Flightseeing tours of Kodiak Island include wildlife watching from the air.

Kayak Kodiak Adventures

P.O. Box 228; Kodiak, AK 99615; tel: 907-486-2604.

Guides lead eco-sensitive sea-kayaking day tours.

Kodiak Lodge

3204 NE 123rd Street; Seattle, WA 98125; tel: 888-556-3425 or 206-368-8338.

The lodge offers a variety of excursions, including sea kayaking, hiking, photography, bear watching, hunting, fishing, and more.

Kodiak Wilderness Outfitters

431 Main Street, P.O. Box 29; Port Lions, AK 99550; tel: 888-454-2418 or 907-454-2418.

Fishing, kayaking, rafting, and birding trips are available in a variety of packages, some with lodging and meals.

Uyak Air Service

P.O. Box 4188; Kodiak, AK 99615; tel: 800-303-3407.

Around-the-island flights and float trips provide excellent bear-watching opportunities.

Excursions

Alaska Peninsula Refuge

Becharof National Wildlife Refuge Complex, P.O. Box 277; King Salmon, AK 99613; tel: 907-246-4250.

Towering mountains, rolling tundra, rugged coastlines, active volcanoes – this is the wild Alaska Peninsula Refuge. At 8,400 feet, Mount Veniaminof is said to be the largest active volcano on record. Moose, caribou, wolves, brown bears, and wolverines roam the refuge; seals, sea lions, sea otters, and migratory whales inhabit its shores and coastal waters. Flightseeing, wildlife photography, hiking, boating, and camping are popular activities. The refuge is accessed by small aircraft only.

Barren Islands

Alaska Maritime National Wildlife Refuge, 2355 Kachemak Bay Drive, Suite 101; Homer, AK 99603-8021; tel: 907-235-6546.

Thousands of seabirds and sea mammals gather yearly on the Barren Islands to give birth and rear their young. The islands were named in 1778 by Captain James Cook, who thought that they appeared "very naked." In fact, the waters surrounding the islands are rich in marine and plant life, productive feeding grounds for an estimated 500,000 birds of 15 species, and for sea lions, harbor seals, and whales.

Shuyak Island State Park

Kodiak District Office, 1400 Abercrombie Drive; Kodiak, AK 99615; tel: 907-486-6339.

About 54 air miles north of Kodiak is Shuyak Island State Park, with its miles of rugged coastline, beaches, and protected waterways. Veteran kayakers consider the area a true paradise due to an intricate maze of sheltered bays, inlets, and a channel. Abundant wildlife inhabit the island and the surrounding waters. It's not unusual for kayakers to encounter sea otters, seals, or orca whales. The park can be accessed by charter plane from Kodiak or Homer.

Pribilof
Islands

The fur seal approaches with surprising speed, propelled by flippers built primarily for swimming. Awkward but determined, the animal hops and waddles across the boulder beach toward a wooden viewing blind where several people wait with binoculars and cameras. ◆ Stopping just short of the platform, the seal peers at an opening in the blind's plywood wall as the observers contemplate the impressive creature before them. An adult male, it weighs perhaps 300 pounds, though mature bulls can reach twice that weight. Dried and matted from sleeping on the beach, the seal's fur is brownish black. Beneath its outer guard hairs is an underfur with 300,000 or more hairs per square inch, dense enough to be fully waterproof. Wonderfully soft and warm, the underfur is what made the species so popular with traders during the 18th, 19th, and early 20th centuries. ◆ The seal fixes on the blind for several moments. Its face sports big brown eyes, important

Wild and remote, these Bering Sea islands offer close-up views of rare seabirds and northern fur seals.

for an animal that feeds mainly at night; long whiskers; and small, tightly rolled ears designed to keep water out. Finally, it waddles away, stopping once to turn and bark, revealing sharp, predator's teeth. ◆ This male is among the several hundred thousand northern fur seals that inhabit St. Paul Island each summer. About 14 miles long and 8 miles wide, with 45 miles of coastline, **St. Paul** is the largest of the five **Pribilof Islands**, set in the storm-battered **Bering Sea** some 300 miles from Alaska's mainland and nearly 800 miles southwest of Anchorage. ◆ Born from suboceanic volcanoes, the remote Pribilof archipelago is summer home to more than two-thirds of the world's population of northern fur seals. About 80 percent

Northern fur seal rookeries are transformed each spring into a noisy society of bulls, cows, and pups sandwiched among boulders.

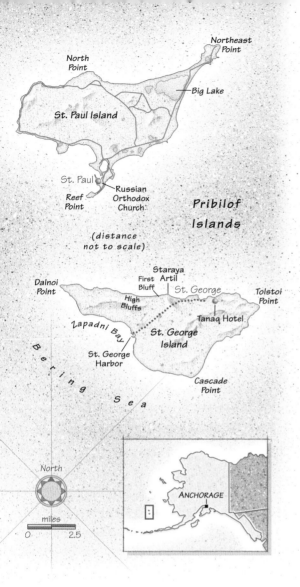

North

miles

0   2.5

ANCHORAGE

by ocean). With a population of nearly 800 people, most of them Native, St. Paul is the world's largest Aleut village. St. George has about 200 year-round residents. The history of both communities is inextricably tied to the northern fur seal.

Seabird Haven

Given their importance to *Callorhinus ursinus*, it's no wonder the Pribilofs are sometimes called the "islands of the seals." But they could just as easily be called the "islands of the birds." The archipelago is widely recognized as a birder's paradise: More than 200 species have been identified here. Some species migrate from as far away as Argentina. Others are year-round residents. Of special note to birders are the rare Asian vagrants, such as the Siberian rubythroat and Eurasian skylark, sometimes blown to the Pribilofs by strong westerly winds. The so-called fallout of Asian species most commonly occurs from mid-May to mid-June, the prime period for birding trips.

Equally impressive, if not more so, is the islands' seabird population. Each summer more than two million seabirds gather at Pribilof nesting grounds. About 90 percent of the Pribilofs' breeders nest on St. George. The precipitous volcanic cliffs here are used by the North Pacific's largest colony of thick-billed murres – an estimated 1.1 million birds – as well as nine-tenths of the world's red-legged kittiwakes, small gulls with black-tipped wings, notched tails, and short red legs. Among those inspired by St. George's thousand-foot-high **Staraya Artil** cliff was renowned ornithologist Roger Tory Peterson, who commented: "Staraya Artil, where the red-legged kittiwakes have their largest colonies, is probably the greatest single bird cliff anywhere in North America."

Other commonly sighted seabird species on St. George and St. Paul include parakeet, least and crested auklets; common murres; red-faced cormorants; northern fulmars; pigeon guillemots; a variety of gulls and terns; and black-legged kittiwakes. Most visitors find the islands' tufted and horned

of the Pribilofs' seals congregate at St. Paul's 14 rookeries and nonbreeding haul-out sites. The remainder gather at **St. George**, the chain's second-largest island, about 45 miles south. Not coincidentally, St. Paul and St. George are also the only islands within the group to be inhabited by humans.

The Pribilofs' two communities – like the islands, they're named St. Paul and St. George – are home to Aleuts, whose ancestors migrated from Asia to Alaska during the Ice Age via the Bering Land Bridge (now covered

puffins to be especially entertaining. With their penguin-like coats, large, brightly colored beaks, Chaplinesque waddle, and rapid wingbeats, they are among Alaska's most distinctive seabirds. To make a good thing even better, some of the top seabird-viewing sites on St. George and St. Paul are within a short walking distance of the hotels.

Though the Pribilofs are best known for their seabird and fur seal spectacles, the islands' coastal and inland areas also are inhabited by a variety of raptors, waterfowl, shorebirds, and passerines, as well as arctic foxes and sea lions. Whales are occasionally spotted off the coast, and a reindeer herd roams St. Paul's tundra. From late June through mid-July, tundra meadows are

Aleut children (left) climb on a reindeer corral at St. George.

Blue foxes (opposite) aren't a separate species; they're a color phase of arctic foxes on the Aleutians and Pribilofs.

St. George (below) is the smaller of the two Pribilof Islands villages; many birds nest in its rocky cliffs.

brightened by millions of wildflowers in all colors of the rainbow.

Since the Pribilofs' Aleut people ended their commercial seal harvest in the mid-1980s, the local economy has been largely dependent on commercial fishing and, to a lesser degree, tourism. Hundreds of people now visit the Pribilofs each summer. Many of them are serious birders; others are photographers, wildflower enthusiasts, or

generalists who come to experience it all.

Generalists seem to find the seals especially fascinating. The island's viewing blinds provide intimate looks at the seals' breeding rituals while minimizing human disturbance of the already stressed animals. After spending the winter at sea, fur seals begin arriving in May. Large male "beach-masters" show up first and quickly establish territories, which they aggressively defend for up to two months while building harems of up to a hundred females. Pregnant females don't arrive until June; they usually give birth to a single pup within 48 hours, then mate again within a week while still nursing their newborn.

Once breeding bulls have established a territory, they usually don't leave their turf for several weeks, even to eat or drink. During this fast, they may lose up to 25 percent of their body weight. Such fasting, combined with an intense competition for females, inevitably makes the bulls irritable, and vicious fights sometimes explode between rivals. The fighting gets worse as the breeding season progresses and peaks in July. The seals' violence helps to explain their choice of boulder beaches as breeding grounds; newborn pups can find hiding spots where they won't be crushed by marauding bulls.

Remarkable for their ferocity, full-blown fights are rare. Mostly the seal bulls nap or watch over their harems, warning off the occasional challenger with a variety of groans, grunts, and growls. Even when things are peaceful, they may huff or chirp or bleat like sheep; at other

As Bering Sea fog rolls in, murres and kittiwakes (left) soar over nesting cliffs at St. George's High Bluffs.

A Russian Orthodox church in the village of St. George (opposite, top) is a visible reminder of the Russian influence on the islands' Aleut culture.

Tourists follow one of the islands' few roads (opposite); the surface is volcanic scoria, a clue to the Pribilofs' fiery origin.

times they whine and pant and occasionally speak in guttural, gargling voices. The talking never seems to end. From dawn to dusk, the beaches ring with seal songs.

Wildlife and Cultural Tours

Most visitors travel to St. Paul Island, where guided tours are run by the local Native corporation in a joint venture with Reeve Aleutian Airways. Tour packages range in length from three to eight days; participants are lodged at St. Paul's single hotel and, accompanied by guides, are escorted to seal and seabird rook-

eries. More rarely, tourists arrange their own Pribilof trips to St. Paul or to St. George, where there's a small hotel but no restaurant. Fortunately, the 10-room **St. George Tanaq Hotel**, a national historic landmark, has a shared kitchen and dining area.

Some ambitious travelers have been known to bring mountain bikes to St. Paul, which, aside from its unpredictable weather, is ideal for biking. The 50 miles of unpaved, volcanic-cinder roads make almost the entire island accessible to bikes, and several of the best wildlife-viewing sites are near the village. When the weather gets nasty, as it often does, bikers or other independent travelers may, for a reasonable cost, join bus tours of the island.

Though wildlife remains the Pribilofs' main attraction, the culture of the islands' Aleut people is now being incorporated in guided tours. At St. Paul, for example, travelers can take a tour of the **Russian Orthodox Church**, learn about Aleut history, and participate in community activities throughout the summer. "For tourists to get the real [Pribilof] experience," one guide says, "they need to understand

our history. Most people don't realize what we've had to do to survive here, how hard it's been." It only seems appropriate that visitors to the Pribilofs also be introduced to the people whose way of life is so intimately linked to "the islands of the seals."

TRAVEL TIPS

DETAILS

When to Go

The best time to visit the islands is from mid-May through August, when migratory birds and marine mammals are most abundant. Rare Asian birds inhabit the islands from mid-May to early June. Seals begin appearing in May; wildflowers attain peak beauty from late June to mid-July. The climate is typically cool, wet, and windy; rain, fog, and drizzle are the norm. Summer temperatures average from 40° to 59°F; winter temperatures, 20° to 35°F.

How to Get There

Most visitors arrive by commercial flight from Anchorage International Airport to St. Paul Airport. The islands may also be reached by boat. Call Reeve Aleutian Airways, 800-544-2248, for information about flights to St. Paul Island; PenAir, 800-448-4226, for information about flights to St. George Island.

Getting Around

Inter-island travel is by boat or by plane. Tour buses are available for nature-related excursions. For information, call the City of St. Paul at 907-546-2331 or the tour operators listed below.

Backcountry Travel ·

Independent exploration is possible but expensive. Island terrain is subdued; rolling grasslands are easily hiked. Supplies may be purchased on St. Paul and St. George Islands but tend to be limited and expensive. It's best to bring necessary supplies.

INFORMATION

City of St. George
P.O. Box 929; St. George Island, AK 99591; tel: 907-859-2263.

City of St. Paul
Pouch 1; St. Paul Island, AK 99660; tel: 907-546-2331.

Tanadgusix Corporation of St. Paul Island
1500 West 33rd Avenue, Suite 220; Anchorage, AK 99503; tel: 907-278-2312.

CAMPING

Camping is not permitted on St. Paul and St. George Islands.

LODGING

PRICE GUIDE – double occupancy	
$ = up to $49	$$ = $50–$99
$$$ = $100–$149	$$$$ = $150+

King Eider Hotel
St. Paul, AK 99660; tel: 907-546-2477.

Built in the 1880s, this landmark was originally a government bunkhouse for non-Native seal harvesters. The hotel, which has sky-blue wood siding, offers 25 simple rooms with shared bath and shower facilities. Within walking distance is the town's lone restaurant, an all-you-can-eat operation. A gift shop and tour desk are available. Open summer only. $$$–$$$$

Lillian Capener's Bed & Breakfast
P.O. Box 105; St. Paul, AK 99660; tel: 907-546-2334.

Homey, English-style bed-and-breakfast accommodations are available year-round at this house, built in 1966. The inn's two guest rooms have double beds and a shared bath. One room is decorated with a bird motif and a lovely wall tapestry; the other has elegant velvet curtains and rose wallpaper. Hearty breakfasts are served; an open kitchen is available for guests who wish to cook their own lunch and dinner. $$

St. George Tanaq Hotel
P.O. Box 939; St. George Island, AK 99591; tel: 907-859-2255.

Also known as the Aikow (or Fox) Inn, this 1935 hotel once housed seal hunters. Today, the establishment offers St. George Island's only commercial lodging. Ten guest rooms share three bathroom and shower facilities. Meals are not served, but guests are welcome to use the large kitchen. The hotel arranges local tours. Open year-round. $$

TOURS & OUTFITTERS

Field Guides, Inc.
9433 Bee Cave Road, Building 1, Suite 150; Austin, TX 78733; tel: 800-728-4953 or 512-263-7295.

Birding tours of the Pribilof Islands include accommodations and transportation. Tours depart in early June, during the exciting courtship season of seabirds.

Gray Lines of Alaska
Anchorage Office, 745 West 4th Avenue, Suite 200; Anchorage, AK 99501; tel: 907-277-5581 or 800-478-6338.

Three-day wildlife-watching excursions depart from Anchorage May to August. Air transportation, sightseeing, and lodging are included in the package.

High Lonesome Ecotours
570 South Little Bear Trail; Sierra Vista, AZ 85635; tel: 800-743-2668.

This week-long birding excursion to the Pribilof Islands includes round-trip transportation from Anchorage, lodging, meals, and guides. Conducted at the end of May, the tour offers opportunities to see smews, common pochards, green sandpipers, Eurasian skylarks, long-toed stints, and many other species.

Nunivak Island Guide Service
P.O. Box 31; Mekoryuk, AK 99630; tel: 888-223-2289 or 907-827-8213.

Wilderness trips with beach-combing and wildlife viewing take place on the Nunivak National Wildlife Range.

PenAir
6100 Boeing Avenue; Anchorage, AK 99502; tel: 800-448-4226 or 907-243-2323.
PenAir offers year-round flights from Anchorage to the Pribilof Islands. Planes depart three days a week.

Reeve Aleutian Airways
4700 West International Airport Road; Anchorage, AK 99502-1091; tel: 800-544-2248.

Three- to eight-day tours of St. Paul Island are designed for wildlife enthusiasts, birders, and photographers from May to September. Lodging is included.

Society Expeditions
2001 Western Avenue; Seattle, WA 98121; tel: 800-548-8669.

Expedition-style cruises head to the Pribilof Islands. Passengers go ashore on remote islands, accompanied by staff scientists.

TDX Corporation of St. Paul Island
1500 West 33rd Street; Anchorage, AK 99503; tel: 907-278-2312.

St. Paul Island tours offer opportunities to view thousands of seals, birds, and wildflowers, as well as visit the historic Russian Orthodox Church and examine the island's geology and Aleut culture.

Excursions

Alaska Maritime National Wildlife Refuge

2355 Kachemak Bay Drive, Suite 101; Homer, AK 99603; tel: 907-235-6546.

This 4.5 million-acre refuge preserves thousands of coastal units – islands, islets, headlands, spires, reefs – from southeastern Alaska to the west coast. The refuge encompasses tundra, rain forests, sea cliffs, and lagoons, and contains the most diverse wildlife of any Alaskan park. Fifty million seabirds nest in the refuge, which includes the Aleutian Islands. Commonly seen marine life includes sea lions, seals, walrus, and sea otters. Permission must be obtained from the refuge for backpacking. Visitors are encouraged to view wildlife from boats.

Izembek National Wildlife Refuge

Box 127; Cold Bay, AK 99571; tel: 907-532-2445.

The Izembek Lagoon and surrounding estuaries and grasslands provide critical habitat for a vast array of migrant waterfowl and shorebirds. Located at the tip of the Alaska Peninsula, this refuge is known for its large brown-bear population. The park also supports caribou, ptarmigan,

and several species of fur-bearing animals. Backcountry travelers interested in observing bears or waterfowl can arrange a flight to Cold Foot or take a ferry operated by the Alaskan Marine Highway System.

Yukon Delta National Wildlife Refuge

P.O. Box 346; Bethel, AK 99559; tel: 907-543-3151.

Backcountry adventure opportunities are excellent in this 19.6-million-acre refuge, located at the deltas of the Yukon and Kuskokwim Rivers in western Alaska. Varied and abundant wildlife live among the park's maze of lakes, ponds, and streams. Swans, geese, ducks, and shorebirds nest in the coastal areas of the refuge, while moose, caribou, brown and black bears, and wolves prowl the upland areas. Prolific herds of musk oxen and reindeer roam the Nunivak Island portion of the reserve. The herds are an important source of food and income for the island's Native residents. Most backcountry travelers arrive by air.

Denali
National Park

CHAPTER 18

Across much of **Denali National Park and Preserve**, the ground looks as if a flash flood had swept over the land, washing away upright trees and leaving only arctic tundra with coarse, indestructible grasses, bog mosses, reindeer lichens, low stubborn alpine willows, and blueberry bushes. As a consequence, the spare terrain freely reveals its essentials: megalithic boulders abandoned by dying glaciers on the sides of hills, clear tarns scattered wherever the ice has surrendered its frost to the sun, and extremely cold rivers wandering over slopes of pulverized rock. Above it all towers 20,320-foot **Mount McKinley**, known to the native Athabascans as Denali, or "The High One." Rising over 18,000 feet from its base near Wonder Lake, it is the tallest peak in North America. Eternally wrapped in snow, Mount McKinley is truly one of the great mountains of the world. ◆ The High One is the centerpiece of the park and, drawing more than 350,000 visitors annually, one of the

Denali offers recreation as rough as you like it, from flightseeing tours of North America's highest peak to going solo in the backcountry.

most popular tourist attractions in Alaska. Established in 1917, largely through the efforts of hunter-conservationist Charles Sheldon, the national park was substantially expanded in 1980. Today the park and preserve is the third largest site in the National Park System. It protects more than six million acres of wilderness, an area larger than Massachusetts. Because of the park's wide-open spaces and tremendous size, there is no better place in the world to view such elusive species as the grizzly bear and the sub-arctic wolf. Other tundra fauna, such as barren-ground caribou, moose, and Dall sheep, also are commonly seen. Most visitors to Denali drive from

Morning mist hovers over a mountain lake as a cow moose approaches, perhaps to feed off the lake bottom.

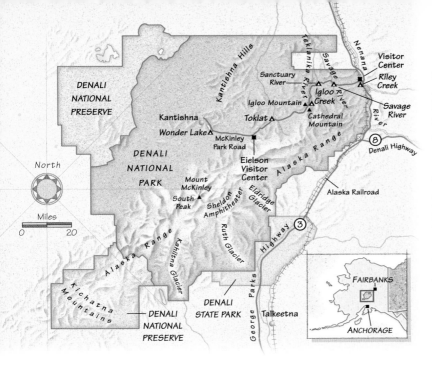

Map labels:
DENALI NATIONAL PRESERVE
Kantishna Hills
Teklanika River
Savage River
Nenana River
Visitor Center
Riley Creek
Sanctuary River
Igloo Mountain
Igloo Creek
Savage River
Kantishna
Toklat
Cathedral Mountain
Wonder Lake
McKinley Park Road
Denali Highway
8
DENALI NATIONAL PARK
Eielson Visitor Center
Alaska Range
Mount McKinley
South Peak
Sheldon Amphitheater
Eldridge Glacier
Alaska Railroad
North
Miles
0   20
Ruth Glacier
Kahiltna Glacier
Highway 3
Alaska Range
Kichatna Mountains
DENALI STATE PARK
George Parks Highway
Talkeetna
DENALI NATIONAL PRESERVE
FAIRBANKS
ANCHORAGE

months in advance. Accommodations also can be found in Healy, about 12 miles north, and in Cantwell, about 30 miles south.

Denali's Seasons

Timing is important in planning a trip to the park, for each month during the busy summer season offers distinct attractions and weather conditions. The Alaska Range tends to be stormy and cold through the middle of May, when winter snows begin to melt on the south-facing slopes and the first grizzlies arrive in the

Fairbanks (120 miles to the north) or Anchorage (240 miles to the south) on the **George Parks Highway**, a two-lane, all-season asphalt road that runs between Anchorage and Fairbanks. In summer, the Alaska Railroad also offers regular passenger service between Anchorage and Fairbanks and makes daily stops at the station near the park entrance. Limited air taxi service is available to small airstrips near the park from Anchorage, Fairbanks, and Talkeetna (north of Anchorage off the George Parks Highway). Motels, hotels, cabins, campgrounds, restaurants, and stores are conveniently situated along the highway near the park entrance. More than 90 percent of all park visitors concentrate their activities in this gateway area and along the road that bisects the northern range of the park. Therefore, reservations for the peak summer season should be made at least six

river bottoms to scavenge wolf kills, dig for plant roots, and consume overwintered blueberries. Caribou and moose are readily seen in the valleys, but Dall sheep remain hidden in the still-snowy highlands. Wolves occasionally appear along the park road and in the river valleys as they begin to hunt for moose and caribou calves. Days are quite long in May, with 16 hours of daylight, and the temperatures gradually warm above freezing by month's end. There are few visitors during May, except for resident Alaskans.

With 24 hours of daylight around the solstice and generally sunny weather, June is an excellent time to visit Denali. June is the height of the grizzly breeding season. It also is the period of maximum bear and wolf predation on moose and caribou calves and Dall sheep lambs, and it's not uncommon for visitors to witness encounters of predator and prey. Bluebells, saxifrage, shooting stars, paintbrush, bistort, and other wildflowers come into bloom, and such migratory tundra birds as the Lapland longspur, long-tailed jaeger, and wandering tattler arrive from their wintering grounds. Mosquitoes become a nuisance in June and continue unabated until the first heavy frosts. July can be rainy. It's also the peak month of tourist visitation, so campsites, bus tickets, and lodging can be difficult to find.

Wild blueberries, cranberries, dewberries, raspberries, and strawberries are abundant in August. Beginning in early September, though, heavy frosts return and the tundra begins to change color. Many people believe Denali is most beautiful at this time of year, when fresh snow falls in the high country, caribou and moose antlers are fully developed, and great numbers of cranes, ducks, and geese pass through during their spectacular fall migrations. Visitors can expect cold and blustery weather off and on from late August (when park visitation drops off dramatically) through early October, when winter returns in full force. The moose and caribou rut, or breeding season, occurs in September, followed by Dall sheep a few weeks later. Most winter visitors schedule their activities, such as dog-sledding and cross-country skiing, for February and March, when the days are longer and the temperatures are somewhat milder – though nights of 30°F or 40°F below zero are still common. Early spring is also the period when wolf and coyote packs breed, and ravens engage in dramatic mating rituals of aerial displays and vocalizations.

Dall sheep (opposite, bottom) live in every Alaskan mountain range except on the Alaska Peninsula.

Caribou (left), in Denali National Park, are especially photogenic.

The Toklat River's East Fork (below) flows through blooming fireweed; the Alaska Range soars in the distance.

aires. The sole exception to this rule is made for campers at the 53-space **Teklanika Campground** on the **Teklanika River** at Mile 29. Teklanika campers are allowed to drive to their campsites, park their vehicles, and then drive back out (no other road driving permitted). A minimum stay of two nights and three days is required at Teklanika.

The 33-site **Savage River Campground** at Mile 12 is in the vehicle-accessible portion of the road. Primitive campsites in **Igloo**

Road to Wonder Lake

The park road runs west from the George Parks Highway into the park for 90 miles. All passenger cars are prohibited beyond Mile 14, and travel for the next 76 miles is restricted to park tour buses and buses operated by park concession-

eastern province of the park, especially if you have good binoculars and are experienced at looking for wildlife. Popular hiking trails in the vicinity of the headquarters include the **Mount Healy Overlook Trail**, which offers a distant view of Mount McKinley; the **Horseshoe Lake Trail**, on which moose are often sighted at dawn and dusk; and the **Savage River** canyon near the ranger station at Mile 14, which can afford views of Dall sheep, caribou, wolves, and grizzlies.

Canyon (Mile 33) and at **Wonder Lake** (Mile 88) are accessible only by bus. More than 100 spaces are available at the **Riley Creek Campground** in the spruce and birch woods near the park entrance.

Visitors who haven't made reservations for a tour bus can explore the first 14 miles of the park road while they're waiting for a ticket. Even during the peak season, it's possible to escape the crowds and have your own private time with the beautiful Alaskan taiga and tundra. All of the "big five" mammals – grizzlies, wolves, Dall sheep, caribou, and moose – can be seen in this

One of the wonders of the National Park System, the park road to Wonder Lake follows an ancient route used first by caribou, then 10,000 to 12,000 years afterward by Athabascan Indians, and more recently by big-game hunters and gold prospectors. In 1923, six years after the park's establishment, Congress appropriated $5,000 for the construction of a gravel automobile road from the interior rail line to the old prospector's camp in the hills beyond Wonder Lake. The primitive road was finally completed in 1938

Peak Experience

Most visitors see Mount McKinley from afar, but a few lucky souls get a close-up view by taking scenic flights around the peak or landing on **Ruth Glacier**. Few sights are more spectacular than the snow-covered slopes of Mount McKinley on a clear day, and, if you visit in May or June, you may see climbing parties as they inch their way toward the summit.

A trip into the great gorge of Ruth Glacier provides a sense of scale and size that you simply can't get from the ground. The mouth of the glacier is about 25 miles northwest of **Talkeetna**, where most flights originate. From there it winds north between sheer rock faces through a narrow canyon called the **Gateway** and then abruptly opens into a 10-mile-wide amphitheater. It is here, within sight of the steep south face of Mount McKinley, that planes land. Some visitors camp on the glacier and are picked up by air taxi the next day. If you visit late or early in the season (between October and April), you may be in for an extra treat – the sight of the northern lights dancing around the High One.

Brown, or grizzly, bears (above) are omnivores and are sometimes seen grazing on summer grasses.

A moose (opposite) wades in Wonder Lake at the end of the park road.

A Cessna 185 (below) soars over the Great Gorge of Ruth Glacier in Denali National Park.

Gray wolves (left), rarely seen from the road, thrive in Denali, where they're protected by Park Service management.

Mount McKinley (bottom), viewed from the north side of the park with Wonder Lake in the foreground, is cloaked in snow year-round.

Three mountaineers (opposite) traverse Ruth Amphitheater on the Southeast Buttress of Mount McKinley.

for hikers and back-country campers: the ascent of **Mount Wright** directly to the north of the cabin and a trek to the headwaters of the

and, to this day, remains gravel and dirt because asphalt or concrete would last only a few seasons in the severe arctic climate.

Hikers are free to leave the buses at any time (except when bears are present or in areas closed for wildlife) to explore the backcountry. There are several excellent sites along the road for landscape photography, wildlife observation, and wilderness hiking. The area around the **Sanctuary River** patrol cabin at Mile 23 offers two superb choices

Sanctuary River to the south. (Those camping in the backcountry are required to obtain and carry a free permit and to attend an orientation at the visitor center.) Ten miles farther, the road enters Igloo Canyon, where many hikers set off to climb **Cathedral Mountain** to the south or **Igloo Mountain** to the north. Both are good locations to observe Dall sheep, which inhabit the high ridges year-round, and grizzly bears, which feed on the plentiful mountain

berries through August and September.

Another favorite destination for hikers is the area around the **Eileson Visitor Center** at Mile 66. Caribou roam this upland region throughout the summer, and grizzlies are often seen. Wonder Lake, near the end of the park road, offers breathtaking views of Mount McKinley when the peak is not obscured by clouds, and some world-class blueberry picking in the fall. For those who enjoy fishing (for trout and grayling), canoes can be rented at Camp Denali just down the road at **Kantishna**, an old mining camp.

Be Prepared

Visitors to Denali should come prepared for some unusual local conditions. A head-net, cotton gloves, trousers, and a long-sleeved shirt are required for protection against the legendary mosquitoes of the Alaskan backcountry. Mosquitoes are generally less numerous in the highlands, where stiff breezes keep them at bay. Hiking on the tundra, which more or less levitates over the permafrost two or three feet below the surface, guarantees unstable and soggy footing. Many hikers choose to wear knee-high rubber boots (inexpensive and available in outdoor stores in Fairbanks and Anchorage) to keep their feet dry. A walking stick also can be helpful. The weather can turn cold and wet at any time of year; hikers should

guard against hypothermia by carrying extra clothing and survival gear.

A fairly dense population of more than 100 grizzly bears inhabits the park's north side, where most visitors spend their time. Black bears are seldom seen on the high-altitude tundra west of the Savage River and east of Wonder Lake, but the species is common in the taiga and forested regions of the park at lower elevations. Standard precautions should be taken with respect to hiking, food preparation, and camping. All backcountry campers are required to attend a bear orientation at the visitor center and to carry special bear-proof food containers.

One thing is certain. A visit to Denali, whether for a couple of busy days or a couple of lingering weeks, will allow you to see the North Country at its finest. For years after, images will come to mind of vast steppes sprawling under clear autumn skies, of a mighty river making its way to a distant sea, of a snowy forest where the only darkness is the eye of a wolf, and of soaring mountain peaks rising majestically on the horizon.

TRAVEL TIPS

DETAILS

When to Go

Denali National Park is open year-round, but the access road is closed in winter. The majority of travelers visit from late May to mid-September. Summer in the park is cool and damp, with temperatures ranging from 40° to 70°F. High winds and storms occur year-round.

How to Get There

Most people arrive via the George Parks Highway. Alaska Direct Bus Lines, 800-770-6652, services the park from Fairbanks and Anchorage. The Alaska Railroad, 800-544-0552, provides daily service to the park in summer.

Getting Around

Travel beyond the first 15 miles of the park road is limited to shuttle buses, tour buses, bicycles, and hiking. Shuttle buses will drop off or pick up anywhere along the route. Shuttle seats may be reserved by calling 800-622-7275 or purchased up to two days in advance at the visitor center. To reserve seats on a tour bus, call 800-276-7234.

Backcountry Travel

A backcountry use permit, required for overnight camping, must be obtained in person at the visitor center in summer and at park headquarters in winter. A quota system is enforced.

INFORMATION

Alaska Public Lands Information Center

250 Cushman Street, Suite 1A; Fairbanks, AK 99701; tel: 907-456-0527.

Denali National Park

P.O. Box 9; Denali Park, AK 99755-0009; tel: 907-683-2294.

Greater Healy/Denali Chamber of Commerce

P.O. Box 437; Healy, AK 99743; tel: 907-683-4636.

CAMPING

The park's seven campgrounds have more than 290 campsites. Three campgrounds (Riley Creek, Savage River, Teklanika) are open to private vehicles. One campground (Morino) is situated near the railroad depot. The remaining campgrounds (Sanctuary River, Igloo Creek, Wonder Lake) must be accessed by shuttle bus. Only Riley Creek is open year-round. To reserve a campsite, call 800-622-7275 or 907-272-7275, or write to Denali Park Resorts VTS, 241 West Ship Creek Avenue; Anchorage, AK 99501.

LODGING

PRICE GUIDE – double occupancy

$ = up to $49 $$ = $50–$99

$$$ = $100–$149 $$$$ = $150+

Camp Denali

P.O. Box 67; Denali National Park, AK 99755; tel: 907-683-2290.

Founded in 1952 by two female bush pilots, the camp is set in the remote Kantishna area at the end of the park road. Seventeen log cabins simply furnished, each with a wood-burning stove and outhouse. A modern bathroom and shower facility is situated nearby. Prices include meals, served in the historic log lodge. The Natural History Resource Center offers exhibits, lectures, and weeklong programs. Amenities include a library, darkroom, canoes, and bicycles. Open early June to early September. $$$$

Denali Backcountry Lodge

P.O. Box 189; Denali National Park, AK 99755; tel: 907-683-1341

(June 1 to September 15) or P.O. Box 810; Girdwood, AK 99587; tel: 907-783-1342 (September 16 to May 31).

Built in 1989, this secluded lodge in the Kantishna area offers 30 comfortable cedar cabins with heat and private baths. Meals are served in a spacious lodge. Extras include free shuttle service, a large resource library, and nature programs. Open June to September. $$$$

Denali Crow's Nest

P.O. Box 70; Denali National Park, AK 99755; tel: 907-683-2723.

Cabins perched on Sugar Loaf Mountain overlook Horseshoe Lake and the Nenana River. The cabins accommodate up to four people in basic comfort and include two double beds and a private bath. Free shuttle service, a restaurant, and tour desk are available. Open late May to early September. $$$–$$$$

Denali Princess Lodge

Mile 238.5, George Parks Highway, P.O. Box 110; Denali National Park, AK 99755; tel: 800-426-0500 or 907-683-2282.

One mile north of the park entrance, this lodge offers 280 rooms with private baths and two double beds, including secluded bungalows with wood stoves and sun porches. Outdoor hot tubs have great views of the Nenana River. A restaurant, exercise room, lounge, and tour desk are available. Open May to September. $$–$$$$

Denali Windsong Lodge

P.O. Box 221011; Anchorage, AK 99522; tel: 800-208-0200 or 907-245-0200.

Built in 1991 and enlarged in 1996, the lodge is set on a bluff overlooking the Nenana River about a mile from the park entrance. Guest rooms have private entrances, two double beds, full baths, log furniture, and mountain views. Shuttle service to the railroad depot and park visitor center is provided. $$–$$$$

Kantishna Roadhouse
P.O. Box 81670; Fairbanks, AK
99708 (off-season) or P.O. Box
130; Denali National Park, AK
99755 (summer); tel: 800-942-
7420 or 907-479-2436.

Set near Wonder Lake at the end
of the park road, the roadhouse
offers 27 cabins with private
baths and three smaller cabins
with shared baths. Prices include
round-trip transportation from
Denali Park Station, three daily
meals, guided hiking, horse-
drawn wagon rides, gold panning,
interpretive programs, and
mountain bikes. A full-service
saloon is on the premises. Open
June to September. $$$$

TOURS & OUTFITTERS

Denali Backcountry Guides
P.O. Box 540; Healy, AK 99743;
tel: 907-683-2419

Day and overnight trips are led
by naturalists and mountaineers.

Denali Raft Adventures
Drawer 190; Denali National
Park, AK 99755; tel: 888-683-
2234 or 907-683-2234.

Two-hour, four-hour, full-day,
and overnight raft trips are
offered on the Nenana River.

Denali Saddle Safaris
P.O. Box 435; Healy, AK 99743;
tel: 907-683-1200.

One-hour to 10-day horseback
tours along the northern edge of
the park are this group's specialty.

**ERA Helicopter Flightseeing
Tours**
6160 Carl Brady Drive;
Anchorage, AK 99502; tel: 800-
843-1947 or 907-266-8351.

"Heli-hiking" tours of Mount
McKinley and the Alaska Range
are available.

Talkeetna Air Taxi
P.O. Box 73; Talkeetna, AK
99676; tel: 800-533-2219 or 907-
733-2218.

This group offers glacier landings,
wildlife tours, and flightseeing
tours of Mount McKinley.

Excursions

Denali State Park
*Alaska State Parks, HC 32, Box 6706;
Wasilla, AK 99654-9719; tel: 907-745-3975.*

This 324,000-acre state park is often
overshadowed by the adjoining national
park, but it offers first-rate paddling and
backpacking opportunities in its own
right. Paddlers on the Chulitna, a mostly
serene river with some stretches of
whitewater, can expect to see bears,
moose, and eagles. The park's Kesugi
Ridge has some of Alaska's best hiking
trails, ranging from 27 to 36 miles long,
one rising to alpine tundra, another with tremendous views
of the Alaska Range. Elsewhere in the park, the view from
Peters Hills is said to have inspired Sydney Laurence's
famous painting of Mount McKinley.

Nowitna National Wildlife Refuge
P.O. Box 287; Galena, AK 99741; tel: 907-656-1231.

The refuge, approximately 45 air miles
from Denali National Park, occupies a
solar basin surrounded by hills capped
with alpine tundra. The main feature of
the refuge is the Nowitna River, which
knifes through a breathtaking 15-mile-
long canyon, whose peaks top 2,100 feet.
Abundant waterfowl – including ducks,
geese, cranes, and swans – are drawn to
the shelter's ponds and waterways. A
mixed habitat of spruce forests, meadows, and wetlands
sustain martens, grizzly bears, black bears, moose, wolves,
and lynx. Fishing for northern pike and sheefish is excellent.

White Mountains National
Recreation Area
*Bureau of Land Management, 1150 University Avenue;
Fairbanks, AK 99709-3844; tel: 907-474-2200.*

About 30 miles north of Fairbanks, this recreation area
encompasses a million acres. Beaver Creek National Wild River
passes through the park below the craggy White Mountains.
Hiking, camping, gold panning, wildlife watching, and float
trips are popular in summer; a network of trails and a number
of public-use cabins
are maintained in
winter, when dog
mushing, cross-country
skiing, snowshoeing,
and snowmobiling
are common activities.

Yukon-Charley Rivers National Preserve

CHAPTER 19

magine a place where there are no roads and time is measured by the melting snow; a place where the sun never sets in summer and winter nights last for 21 hours, flushed now and then with the ghostly green of the northern lights. Imagine a place where each spring the skies are filled with cranes and geese and ducks like a scene from the Book of Genesis, and where every fall the streams are choked with spawning salmon. Imagine standing on the banks of a river as wide as a lake and holding a smooth river stone born in the bowels of the Earth more than 500 million years ago. ◆ Such heart-stilling scenes are common in **Yukon-Charley Rivers National Preserve**, a 2½ million-acre parkland on the U.S.–Canada border. The preserve, established in 1980, encompasses a 128-mile stretch of the **Yukon River** and the entire 106-mile length of one of its main tributaries, the **Charley River**. Because much of the preserve was free of glaciers during the Ice Age, the region is a unique botanical sanctuary in the Far North.

Explore human and geologic history and the wild haunts of moose, bears, and caribou along a remote stretch of the mighty Yukon River.

Remnants of ancient Pleistocene steppe in the Yukon-Charley highlands include the same boreal vegetation once consumed by woolly mammoths and steppe bison. ◆ A century ago, this area was the bustling center of Alaska's world-famous gold rush, and 57 sternwheelers plied the waters of the Yukon carrying prospectors, miners, and hangers-on – the characters who inspired Jack London's best-selling stories. With gold's decline, most of the fortune hunters disappeared, and only a handful of homesteaders remain today. ◆ The preserve lies between the communities of **Eagle** and **Circle**, remote Alaskan bush towns accessible

Backcountry rangers, operating from the village of Eagle, oversee the 2½ million acres of the Yukon-Charley Rivers National Preserve with little manpower.

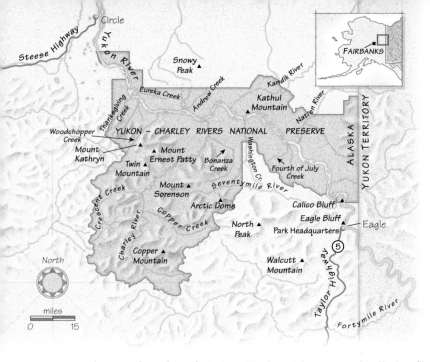

journey of about 160 miles that usually takes five to ten days, depending on how many stops you make along the way. Both towns offer guide services, canoe and raft rentals (with or without motors), and basic food service, lodging, gasoline, groceries, and other supplies. As a safety measure, travelers should always file a float plan at the preserve's field office in Eagle before embarking.

The only practical time to float the Yukon is after breakup in May, when the river is clear of massive and deadly ice floes. Spring here is a spectacle of migratory waterfowl: Sandhill cranes, white-fronted geese, mergansers, buffleheads, green-winged teal, pintails, and widgeons fill the sky by the hundreds. A major flyway passes through the preserve. Sometimes birds stop briefly to feed and rest along the river on their way north to summering grounds in the Yukon Flats or to the Arctic Plain north of the Brooks Range.

Summer is surprisingly mild for such a northern latitude, with average daily highs in the upper 70s. Sudden cloudbursts are not unusual, however, and temperatures can dip below freezing at night. Mosquitoes and other biting insects can be a problem until the first frost in mid-August; a good insect repellent and head-net are essential. Tents should have insect netting and rain flies, and should be able to withstand strong winds. Floaters typically camp on open, sandy beaches, gravel bars, and brushy islands where wind keeps the pests at bay. Five public-use cabins along the river also are available without advance reservation.

The first run of king salmon appears by early July, followed by dog salmon (so called because mushers feed them to their dogs) from

by gravel roads and air taxi. Eagle, with about 200 year-round inhabitants, is south of the preserve at the end of the 160-mile **Taylor Highway**, which begins at **Tetlin Junction** on the **Alaska Highway** west of the Canadian border. The route is passable in summer by cars and trucks but is usually closed by snow from mid-October through April. The highway is one of the more scenic remote roads in Alaska, especially in the alpine heights west of 5,541-foot **Mount Fairplay**, where barren-ground caribou and Dall sheep can be spotted near the road. Drivers of large RVs and those pulling long trailers should exercise caution, as the road is narrow and winding in places with hairpin curves and steep hills.

Circle, northwest of the preserve, can be reached in summer via the **Steese Highway** about 160 miles northeast of Fairbanks.

Starting Out

Most float trips through the preserve run on the Yukon River from Eagle to Circle, a

Male moose (left), or bulls, grow antlers, while cow moose do not; the rack of a mature bull can stretch more than five feet across.

Caribou bulls (opposite, middle) vie for dominance during the spring rut.

Mushrooms (opposite, bottom) grow large under the midnight sun; this one is fives inches in diameter.

The Yukon River (below) continually reinvents its course and is a nightmare for the uninitiated marine pilot.

August through October. September brings the return of the northern lights and, in the valleys, the moose rut. In the highlands, the autumn tundra turns beautiful shades of burgundy and orange, and the caribou begin to run. Winter is a brutal season, with some of the coldest temperatures ever recorded on Earth. An all-time low of −81°F was recorded in January 1989. Streams and rivers ice over, and the Yukon – a vital winter corridor used for millennia by wildlife and humans – runs clear and cold under as much as six feet of ice.

Float through Geologic History

Swift but smooth and free of rapids, the Yukon falls only a little more than 200 feet in the 160 miles between Eagle and Circle. Over this distance, boaters pass through country scoured for a century by gold

Circle City

The first "stampeders" to the Klondike didn't come from Seattle but from Circle City in Alaska. Prior to the 1897–98 Klondike gold rush, it was the largest gold-mining town on the 1,950-mile Yukon River, and at its zenith it was called the "Paris of the North."

Trader Jack McQuesten founded Circle, as it was first known, in the early 1890s to serve gold miners working on upper Birch Creek. Miners misnamed the town, thinking it lay on the Arctic Circle, which is actually 50 miles north. By 1896, Circle had 1,200 residents, a music hall, two theaters, and 28 saloons. Paddle-wheelers churned busily up and down the Yukon to Circle, and wagon roads led off into the wilderness. That summer, George Carmack discovered gold on the Klondike. When the news reached Circle, bartender Henry Ash reportedly told his clientele to help themselves to the inventory – he was off to the Klondike. After the party, the clientele followed.

The exodus nearly killed the little town on the Yukon, which still clings to the edge of the river, at the end of the Steese Highway northeast of Fairbanks. Today, Circle City supports about 100 year-round residents. In summer, it serves as a wilderness launching point for the Yukon-Charley National Preserve to the south and Yukon Flats National Wildlife Preserve to the north. Visitors will find two stores, a gas station, a cafe, a campground, and an airstrip. The only remnant of the gold-rush days is the Pioneer Cemetery, overgrown with trees, a short walk upriver from the town center. – *Sam Bishop*

A legal library (above) once used by U.S. Customs officers at Fort Egbert can still be seen in Eagle.

The U.S. Courthouse (left), built in 1902, now houses the Eagle Museum.

Gold dredges (below) like this abandoned hulk at Coal Creek once served as floating "factories," sifting gold from the soil.

Water-polished boulders (right) have been sorted and rounded by the Yukon River over thousands of years.

seekers. Their crumbling cabins and equipment still lie on the riverbanks or up the tributary valleys to the south.

Emerging from a mixed forest of black and white spruce and deciduous birch, poplar, willow, and alder, black bears and moose regularly visit the riverbanks in the evening hours. Wolves generally remain unseen, but tracks across sandbars attest to their presence. A few grizzly tracks appear as well, while caribou keep to the mountains visible to the south. Once-endangered peregrine falcons nest on ledges overlooking the river and streams, and drift on thermals over the bluffs.

From the start of the trip, floaters encounter cliffs, outcroppings, and other formations that reveal the area's remarkable geologic history. **Eagle Bluff**, consisting of rust-colored greenstone veined with quartz, rises 1,000 feet just downstream from the village of Eagle. **Calico Bluff**, just inside the preserve boundary, is a near-vertical, 800-foot cliff of sandwiched shale and limestone embedded with marine fossils. The layers, deposited some 300 million years ago, have been bent into dramatic bows by deep geologic pressures.

Nation, **Kandik**, and Charley – and hike the surrounding uplands. Or, for an even more remote and challenging wilderness experience, fly to the headwaters of the Charley River and float down to the Yukon and on to Circle. Another option is to float the **Fortymile River** from the bridge on the Taylor Highway to the Yukon River and then paddle west to the boat landing at Eagle. Only highly experienced paddlers should attempt to negotiate the tributaries' rapids and "sweepers," fallen trees that have become lodged across the current. River water is frigid even in summer; capsizing in midchannel can be fatal.

Come Prepared

Self-sufficiency is the guiding principle in the backcountry. Once you leave the settlements, you're completely on your own. There are no roads or trails in the preserve. Grizzly bears, black bears, and moose are common, so be vigilant and take customary precautions. Be prepared to stay beyond your scheduled pickup due to bad weather or equipment failures. It's not unusual for a sudden storm or a fouled fuel line to delay planes for a day or two.

Farther downstream, **Rock of Ages** is the only formation that churns the placid Yukon into anything resembling a rapid. The name is well deserved, for this lump of dolomite dates back some 800 million years, making it the oldest type of rock in the preserve.

Take time along the journey to explore some of the major tributary rivers – the

Another good way to prepare for your trip is to read John Hildebrand's excellent

Reading the River, a chronicle of his epic float down the Yukon from its source in Canada to its outlet in the Bering Sea. Another superb piece of writing is Barry Lopez's essay "Yukon-Charley: The Shape of a Wilderness" in *Crossing Open Ground*, which relates a boating trip he made shortly after the preserve was established. Although the Yukon-Charley is a relatively young unit in the National Park System, it is inspiring its own distinguished literature in the manner – if not the quantity – of such older parks as Yellowstone and Grand Canyon. Contact the preserve for a list of other books on planning a float trip and on the area's geology, flora, fauna, and history.

This is true Alaskan wilderness. If you wish, you can go for weeks or months without seeing a road, a town, even another human being. Life in these ancient mountains and valleys is virtually timeless. Wolf pups are born every spring, moose lock antlers every fall, and the Yukon River continues to flow to the sea.

The Yukon River (above) winds through the spectacular mountain scenery of Yukon-Charley Rivers National Preserve.

Colorful twists and turns (opposite, top) in exposed sedimentary rocks explain why this section along the Yukon River is named Calico Bluff.

Gravel bars along the Charley River (left) make desirable camp-sites, with plenty of flat spots for tents and light breezes to keep insects away.

The Mighty Yukon

For the 36,000 people who live along the Yukon River, spring is a time of both joy and trepidation. As light and warmth slowly return, the river ice cracks and groans and explodes with thunderous force. Great slabs move downriver like islands set adrift. Chunks the size of automobiles pile up against each other and crash against the bank. If an ice jam forms, the river can overflow in a matter of hours. Floods are sudden and devastating.

The Yukon is the longest river in Alaska, flowing about 2,000 miles from its headwaters near Atlin Lake in northern British Columbia to the Bering Sea. Eighteen species of fish are found in the river basin, including northern pike, arctic grayling, and five species of salmon. At the mouth of the Yukon, and for about 100 miles upstream, whitish beluga whales gorge on salmon in the shallows. Farther upriver, boaters encounter moose, wolves, black bears, grizzly bears, and even caribou swimming alongside them. The migratory waterfowl that inhabit the river's basin each summer – especially Yukon Flats National Wildlife Refuge near Fort Yukon – are legendary in number.

For thousands of years the Yukon and its many tributaries were the sole highways available to Native people in Alaska's interior. Russian explorers traveled upstream from the Bering Sea, and Canadian fur traders moved in from the west in the 1830s and '40s. The entire length of the river was floated by Lt. Frederick Schwatka in 1883. He accomplished the feat in the *Resolute*, a log raft, though the last 100 miles were navigated in a sailboat that he purchased from a trader. Later there appeared gold miners, whose strikes led to the formation of boomtowns such as Eagle, Circle, Fort Yukon, Tanana, and Ruby, as well as to heavy steamboat traffic.

Today the Yukon remains as important as it was in earlier times. During the winter months snowmobilers and mushers race up and down its ice, and in the summer hoards of people arrive in canoes, motorboats, barges, sternwheelers, and floatplanes. The Yukon River basin is still a place that wilderness paddlers can explore in profound solitude, the river murmuring some bit of wisdom just beyond human understanding.

TRAVEL TIPS

DETAILS

When to Go

The preserve is open year-round. The Yukon River begins to freeze in October; break-up usually occurs in early May. The area posts some of Alaska's warmest summer weather; average summer temperatures are in the 60s to 70s, with occasional highs in the upper 80s or lower 90s. Thunderstorms are common in summer; nighttime temperatures occasionally dip below freezing, and high winds can produce whitecaps on the river. Severe cold seizes the area from late November to mid-March; temperatures can drop as low as -70°F.

How to Get There

Eagle can be reached by car on the Taylor Highway, open from mid-April to mid-October; Circle is on the Steese Highway, open year-round. Air taxis serve both towns from Fairbanks. Many travelers boat to the preserve on the Yukon River and its tributaries.

Getting Around

Transportation within the park is limited to air taxi, boat, or foot. Several companies are authorized to provide transportation within the preserve. Contact the park for details.

Backcountry Travel

No fee or permit is required for backcountry travel. Old mining and game trails provide some hiking opportunities. Most summer visitors prefer to hike above timberline, where there are superior views, less brush, and fewer insects. Trails are not marked, and hikers should always be aware of private land. There are no services or facilities in the park. All visitors must be self-sufficient and well-versed in wilderness travel. Proper clothing, insect repellent, quality gear, and careful planning are essential.

INFORMATION

Alaska Public Lands Information Center
250 Cushman Street, Suite 1A; Fairbanks, AK 99701; tel: 907-456-0527.

Bureau of Land Management
Arctic District Office, 1150 University Avenue; Fairbanks, AK 99709-3844; tel: 907-474-2300.

Yukon-Charley Rivers National Preserve
P.O. Box 74718; Fairbanks, AK 99707; tel: 907-456-0593 or 907-547-2233 (field office).

CAMPING

The Bureau of Land Management maintains campgrounds along highways leading to the preserve. Small campgrounds are available throughout the Eagle and Circle areas. Four free public-use cabins, located within the preserve, are available on a first-come, first-served basis.

LODGING

PRICE GUIDE – double occupancy	
$ = up to $49	$$ = $50–$99
$$$ = $100–$149	$$$$ = $150+

Arctic Circle Hot Springs Resort
Mile 8, Circle Hot Springs Road, P.O. Box 30069; Central, AK 99730; tel: 907-520-5113.
The resort offers 24 hotel-style rooms and eleven furnished cabins. Many of the rooms in the main building have views of the Yukon Flats. All but one have a shared bath. Hostel-style accommodations are also available. A restaurant, ice cream parlor, and olympic-sized pool (filled with hot spring water) are on the premises, as are a historic cabin and general store. Open year-round. $–$$$

Eagle Trading Company Motel
1 Front Street, P.O. Box 36; Eagle, AK 99738; tel: 907-547-2220.
Set on the banks of the Yukon River in downtown Eagle, this modern motel offers nine basic guest rooms, each with a private bath and shower, two queen-sized beds, and views of the river. The motel is open year-round; a restaurant serves guests from May to October. Also on the premises are a small grocery store and laundry. $$

Falcon Inn
220 Front Street, P.O. Box 136; Eagle, AK 99738; tel: 907-547-2254.
This unique, three-level log cabin at the end of the Taylor Highway has an observation cupola with a wraparound deck. The inn's guest rooms have views of the Yukon River, private baths, single or queen-sized beds, and redwood furnishings. A common area on the second floor has a woodstove and picture window. Open year-round. $$

Riverview Motel
P.O. Box 9; Circle, AK 99733; tel: 907-773-8439.
About 22 miles upstream of Yukon-Charley Rivers National Preserve, this riverfront motel offers three guest rooms and an efficiency apartment. The no-frills guest rooms are simple but cozy; two rooms have a pair of queen-sized beds, one has twin beds; all have private baths. The apartment has a kitchenette, a double bed, and two single beds. Laundry facilities and a canoe drop-off service are also available. $$

TOURS & OUTFITTERS

Adventure Alaska Tours

P.O. Box 64; Hope, AK 99605; tel: 800-365-7057 or 907-782-3730.

Nine-day kayak and canoe excursions of the Yukon River let paddlers visit abandoned gold-rush towns and take advantage of excellent hiking and wildlife watching along the way.

Alaskan Yukon Tours

P.O. Box 221; Fort Yukon, AK 99740; tel: 907-452-7162.

Native guides lead excursions on the Yukon River from Circle City to Fort Yukon.

Circle City Charters

P.O. Box 9; Circle, AK 99733; tel: 907-773-8439.

Hour-long, half- and full-day tours journey into Yukon-Charley Rivers National Preserve on motorboats.

Frontier Excursions

P.O. Box 543; Skagway, AK 99840; tel: 907-983-2512.

Tours, shuttles, and charters venture to historic mining areas along the Yukon River.

Yukon Experience

P.O. Box 72810; Fairbanks, AK 99707; tel: 907-457-4135

Shuttle service and backcountry support assist Yukon River paddlers.

MUSEUMS

Eagle Historical Society and Museum

P.O. Box 23; Eagle, AK 99738; tel: 907-547-2325.

Exhibits focus on life in mining settlements along the Yukon River.

Excursions

Chena River State Recreation Area

Alaska Division of Parks, Northern Area Office, 3700 Airport Way; Fairbanks, AK 99709-4613; tel: 907-451-2695.

The clear water of the Chena traverses a scenic valley in this recreation area, surrounded by alpine ridges and birch-and-alder forest. A 30-minute drive east of Fairbanks, the 250,000-acre park shelters one of the state's most visible moose populations. Other wildlife includes bears, caribou, wolves, wolverines, lynx, and river otters. Hikes of varying length, from one hour to three days, are possible on the park's trails. The river offers one of the finest float trips in the Fairbanks area.

Fortymile River

Bureau of Land Management, Arctic District Office, 1150 University Avenue; Fairbanks, AK 99709-3844; tel: 907-474-2300.

Part of the National Wild and Scenic River System, Fortymile River is noted both for its excellent whitewater and its convenient access along Taylor Highway. The Fortymile, whose numerous branches snake through the Yukon Territory and Alaska's interior, flows into the Yukon River upstream of Eagle. En route, paddlers pass ruins of mining camps. Prospectors once poled boats northward on the Yukon and up the Fortymile. Rain and snowmelt determine the level of difficulty. Frequent portaging may be necessary during periods of high water.

Yukon Flats National Wildlife Refuge

P.O. Box 20, 101 12th Avenue; Fairbanks, AK 99701; tel: 907-456-0440.

About 100 air miles north of Fairbanks, the Yukon River outruns its canyon walls and stretches into a 200-mile-long floodplain with more than 40,000 lakes and ponds. Millions of birds from four continents migrate to the flats each spring. The result is one of the highest densities of nesting birds in North America. A great variety of other animals, including moose, caribou, Dall sheep, wolves, black bears, and grizzly bears, also inhabits the refuge. Paddling is difficult on all but a handful of waterways.

Kobuk and
Noatak Rivers

t's a July evening along the upper Noatak River, just below Nushralatuk Creek. The jagged peaks of the Schwatka Mountains glow as if lighted from within, cast in surreal clarity above the shadowed valley. ◆ On the gravel bar a brace of canoes lies beached; the river, dimpled by rising grayling, is only slightly less transparent than the air. The wind that's blown all afternoon is silent, and mosquitoes whine around four travelers as they sit around a fire of dry willow brush. Earlier they glimpsed a small band of bull caribou crossing the river with their huge racks sheathed in dark summer velvet and, on the hillside a little behind camp, a honey-colored grizzly. ◆ Three days into the trip and with nearly 300 miles still to go, the land's silence has already filled them.

Any word spoken above a murmur seems an intrusion. They sip at their cups of tea, reluctant to turn in though it's long past midnight. The rose-tinted sky shows no sign of darkening, and the stars won't appear again until mid-August. ◆ The **Noatak** and its sister river, the **Kobuk**,

Two alluring waterways, as different and alike as fraternal twins, offer views of distinctive landforms and diverse wildlife.

are among the finest in Alaska. There may be float trips with better fishing, bigger mountains, or more bears to watch. But it's tough to find places that offer all that the Noatak and Kobuk Valleys do on such a grand scale: hundreds of miles of clear streams, unlimited hiking, varied wildlife, good fishing, and spectacular scenery. In these valleys you can see everything from limestone canyons to dense spruce forest, glacial lakes to shifting sand dunes, vast stretches of rolling tundra to granite spires – all this above the Arctic Circle, in a chunk of roadless country twice the size of Indiana.

An outfitter guides a raft down a stretch of whitewater on the Kobuk River. The Kobuk tends to be calmer than the nearby Noatak River.

From their mountain headwaters, the Noatak and Kobuk drain the western **Brooks Range** and flow west to the **Chukchi Sea**. Though they follow roughly parallel courses and are seldom more than 60 miles apart, these rivers offer distinctly different experiences.

The Noatak, the farther north of the two, cuts through a rugged mountain basin virtually unpopulated over most of its 400-mile length. The Inupiat Eskimo community of Noatak, 80 miles from tidewater, is the only settlement. The Kobuk begins equally wild and remote, but within a hundred miles winds out onto a broad, scenic floodplain, meandering past five Eskimo villages before reaching the coast. The Kobuk's personality over most of its 350 miles could best be described as sedate; the Noatak is steeper and wilder, its pace more urgent.

The weather-making shadow of 8,510-foot **Igikpak** – the highest peak in the western Brooks Range – marks the Noatak's source.

The remote and breathtakingly scenic upper 25 miles of the river are seldom floated because of shallow water and a lack of good landing spots. The air services that provide floatplane access from **Bettles**, **Ambler**, and **Kotzebue** normally use one of the lakes between **Angayu** and **Portage Creeks**.

Most folks, eager to get under way, throw in their kayaks or rafts and head downstream, missing some of the best hiking opportunities of the entire trip. Walking in the Brooks Range is never easy, but here it's worth every slogging step. Though acres of cottongrass tussocks, scrub willow, and marshy ground are common obstacles, the ridgelines on the north side offer a view that you'll carry your whole life. The valleys on the south side invite longer backpacking trips into the gorgeous but steep limestone canyons along the Kobuk-Noatak divide, including some places that haven't heard footsteps in years.

Arctic Wildlife

An added bonus is the wildlife – not always abundant, but thick by Arctic standards. Dall sheep dot the slopes on the

Arctic foxes (left) in the white color phase are found almost exclusively along the coast of the Arctic.

The Noatak River (opposite, top) flows through Gates of the Arctic National Park and Noatak National Preserve.

Siberian asters (opposite, bottom) are hardy perennial wildflowers.

north side of the river for a good 50 miles from the put-in. This area of the valley, all within **Gates of the Arctic National Park and Preserve**, is closed to sport hunters and is beyond the range of most area residents who are allowed to hunt for subsistence purposes. The upper valley is narrow and treeless, with the exception of three or four clusters of balsam poplar that seem to have gotten lost above treeline. What all this means is that animals here are relatively concentrated, fairly easy to spot, and often quite unafraid. Fleeting encounters with grizzlies, musk oxen, wolverine, moose, foxes, and wolves are real possibilities. Ground squirrels, ptarmigan, and caribou are, at times, extremely abundant.

Yet to the unseasoned eye, the land may seem empty. Most folks carry binoculars or spotting scopes, but few take the time to use them often enough. The long arctic evenings and early mornings are especially good times to scan for wildlife. Patches of brush and folds in the land provide a surprising amount of cover; wolves and bears appear and disappear like windblown smoke. Keep in mind the old hunting guide's adage: There are always more than you see, and fewer than you think.

The mountains loom close on both sides of the Noatak as far as **Douglas Creek**, which also serves as the eastern boundary of **Noatak National Preserve**. Cutting a braided, rock-strewn channel through the **Schwatkas**, the Noatak breaks out into a sprawling tundra plain framed by the distant shapes of the **Baird Mountains**. Gathering tributaries, including the **Imelyak**, **Cutler**, and **Anisak Rivers**, the Noatak flows 75 miles through cutbanks and bluffs until, quite abruptly, the mountains close in again at the **Grand Canyon of the Noatak**. Less a true canyon than a long, mountain-rimmed constriction, the stretch below

Arctic Etiquette

Though the Arctic is sparsely populated, travelers should always keep in mind that they share the land with others, including Natives engaged in fishing, hunting, trapping, and other subsistence activities.

Be mindful that many inviting camping or fishing spots are privately owned Native allotments or gathering areas that have been used for generations. Camping below the high-water mark and out of sight of others whenever possible minimizes potential conflicts. Seemingly deserted camps or gear almost always belong to someone. Never disturb equipment or interfere with activities such as hunting or seining; Natives rely on them for their livelihood, and, on federal land, subsistence use has priority by law. Other lands may be owned by Native corporations and require permission to enter.

When you encounter local residents, be polite and circumspect. Graciously accept any hospitality they may offer, but if your presence makes people uncomfortable, move on. Natives often feel overwhelmed by outside pressures, especially in heavy-use areas such as the upper Kobuk. And remember, ask permission before you pull out a camera and start snapping pictures.

If you want to be really alone, spend time away from the main river corridors. Careful research and planning and the services of a bush pilot can help you have a remote wilderness experience.

An Inupiat Eskimo woman (left) cleans and cuts fish at her family's seasonal fish camp.

Caribou shed their antlers (below) at different times; bulls lose theirs in early winter, cows lose theirs in spring.

Golden eaglets (opposite, top) will mature into expert predators that feed on small mammals.

The Great Kobuk Sand Dunes (opposite, bottom) are an unexpected natural phenomenon, a desert in the Arctic.

the first stunted black spruce appear. Soon the Noatak enters a true canyon, with rook walls rising from the water's edge and Dall sheep grazing on the slopes above. This is the last good chance for high-country hiking. From here on down, the valley broadens. Spruce forest alternates with tundra for the next 50 miles, and the mountains fade back.

the **Nimiuktuk River** is another good spot to take a break from paddling and explore for a day or two. Fishing for grayling, chum salmon, and Dolly Varden char can be good in July and August. Before you warm up the skillet, remember that the 16-inch grayling you've caught could be 20 years old. More and more, anglers are releasing fish unharmed.

A dozen miles below the **Nakolik River**,

Migrating Caribou Herd

Boat traffic from Noatak village and Kotzebue can be heavy, especially from mid-August to September, when caribou of the immense Western Arctic Herd start moving south. Subsistence hunters sometimes venture as far as the **Nimiuktuk**, hoping to fill their outboard-powered skiffs with meat. You'll find even more activity along the Kobuk. Watching the fall caribou migration means sharing the river with a fair number of both sport and subsistence hunters.

The mouths of two major tributaries, the **Kugururok** and **Kelly Rivers**, are late summer spots for sea-run Dolly Varden, and chum salmon boil in the riffles downstream of Noatak village. Grizzlies prowl side sloughs and channels littered with fish carcasses

and bear tracks. Though most Noatak and Kobuk valley bears work hard to avoid humans (in recent memory, only one death has resulted from bear attacks in this region), a few close brushes happen every year.

Most "floaters," as the Inupiat call them, take out at Noatak village and catch one of several scheduled mail planes to Kotzebue. To keep from missing this settlement of 375, keep track of your progress in the heavily braided section from the Kelly on down. Bear right as you get close. Airport traffic and the town's diesel generators point the way to the cluster of buildings perched on a high bank.

The last 80 miles to Kotzebue are a fine way to cap off a trip, though there's nothing here to match the wild, otherworldly feeling you find upriver. Still, the country is huge and wilder than anywhere in the Lower 48. Here (and on any stretch of either the Kobuk or Noatak), some river runners prefer to rest during the day and travel through the long, cool evenings when headwinds die down, bear and moose rustle in the willows, and the light is haunting.

The Noatak flows on, first through a web of braided channels, then past the brief but impressive **Lower Canyon**. Beyond lies the windswept delta, amid a maze of sandbars and rough water seven miles across **Hotham Inlet** to Kotzebue. You can do this leg by canoe or skiff, but it's best left to strong, experienced paddlers.

Floating the Kobuk

Just to the south is the Kobuk River. Its source, near the **Arrigetch Peaks** in Gates of the Arctic National Park, is fewer than 20 miles from the Noatak's birthplace. Some 40 miles downstream, the Kobuk is joined by the outlet of 14-mile-long **Walker Lake**, more than doubling the flow. With few exceptions, travelers start at the lake after being dropped off by the same air services that specialize in the Noatak.

This is the best area along the Kobuk for

Fly-fishing (left) for Dolly Varden, char, or grayling can be good in late summer; day- or half-day charters by floatplane are available in bigger towns.

Barefoot river crossings (below) save hikers from having to dry out, but arctic streams can be painfully cold.

Moose give birth in spring (right) after an eight-month gestation.

mountain hiking. Conditions around Walker Lake are about as good as they get in the Brooks Range – open spruce-and-birch forest, sharply rising peaks, and rolling sandy country carpeted with gray lichen. Hikes in any direction, from a few minutes to a few days, are bound to be interesting.

A thousand yards down the outlet stream,

the current rushes into a short but major rapid that you'll hear before you see. Don't run this scary series of drops, rocks, and keepers in a raft; use the well-worn portage trail on the left bank. Swamping here could mean losing your gear a long way from help.

The Kobuk swirls green and clear to the **Upper Kobuk Canyon**. This stretch can have strong rapids when the water's high, but you can line the worst spot on the right if you have to. The **Lower Kobuk Canyon**, just under 20 miles downstream, is another place to pay attention. Except at flood levels, the rapids aren't that bad, but rocks in awkward places, a couple of strong drops, and canyon walls can make for some tense moments, especially at the last chute, which is unrunnable. There isn't a portage; skirt to the right and line down the jagged rock ledge.

From here, the Kobuk relaxes, pouring through tall stands of spruce and birch interspersed with tundra. Moose, beaver, and black bear forage along the banks. The southern edge of the Brooks Range rises to the north, tempting but out of reach to all but the most determined hikers.

Lining the Kobuk banks from the **Mauneluk River** on down are Eskimo fish camps made up of white canvas tents and plywood cabins with fish racks out front. The upper Kobuk people, the Kuuvanjmiut, have made their homes here for generations, and most camps are built near ancient gathering sites. Here, as on the Noatak, archaeological sites ranging in age from a

hundred to thousands of years are common. Visitors sometimes find "house pits" – roughly circular or square depressions where sod huts once stood. Alone at dusk in one of these places, you can almost hear the rustling of ghosts.

From mid-July through September, casting big spoons and flies can be excellent for sheefish, an exotic species of whitefish commonly topping 30 pounds. Time of day, persistence, and plain luck all play a part in success. Keep smaller ones for an occasional meal, but gently play and release the big spawning females.

A few bends below the mouth of the **Kogoluktuk River** is the small village of **Kobuk**, which consists of a few houses, a store, and a gravel airstrip. You can make connections from here to Kotzebue or Fairbanks on scheduled mail planes. Eight miles downstream is **Shungnak**, with another airstrip and two stores. Unless you're determined to see the **Kobuk Sand Dunes**, more than 100 miles downstream, this is the place to take out.

Though Shungnak and the next village downstream, **Ambler**, are only 25 miles apart, the Kobuk takes such extravagant loops that the actual river distance is more than double that figure. The current slows to a crawl, and headwinds can become a nuisance. Besides the usual mail planes, Ambler offers its own air service, with connections to Fairbanks as well as floatplane charters.

From Ambler, it's about 40 miles downstream to the Kobuk Sand Dunes, well within the boundaries of **Kobuk Valley National Park.** Formed from windblown glacial debris, the dunes sprawl across 30 square miles. This is a unique biological

Summer on the Kobuk River (opposite, top) can be warm and dry, and the midnight sun makes days long.

Shelf ice (opposite, bottom), or *aufeis*, can be found stacked along riverbanks during spring breakup.

Caribou (below and right) follow migration routes that have been used for thousands of years. The herds travel hundreds of miles between summer and winter feeding grounds.

Moving As One

Alaska's barren ground caribou, numbering about one million animals in 13 different herds, are New World reindeer. Three major herds inhabit arctic Alaska: the Porcupine, Central Arctic, and 400,000-strong Western Arctic. All migrate seasonally to find adequate food. This movement distributes feeding and prevents overgrazing. Mature cows weigh 200 to 300 pounds, adult bulls 350 to 400 pounds. Seven hundred pounds is the record. Both sexes have antlers, which are shed annually. Bull caribou lose their outsized rack in early winter after the October rutting season; cows lose theirs in April and May.

Pregnant cows keep their antlers until calving time in early June. Then, a single 13-pound calf is born; twins are rare. A healthy calf will double its weight in 10 to 15 days. Within an hour newborn calves are able to walk and follow their migrating mothers. Within a few days they can outrun a human, and swim lakes and rivers. Many, however, are lost to drowning and other accidents or to predatory wolves and bears.

The name caribou comes from a Canadian Indian name meaning "the paw-er," a reference to the way they uncover lichens hidden beneath the snow. The caribou's most important adaptation to the northern environment may be its ability to subsist on lichens, which it locates by smell even under two feet of snow. Its scientific name, *Rangifer tarandus*, the wanderer, speaks of far, arctic lands.

In its sleek summer pelage, a caribou dancing over the tundra displays a supple grace and strength refined over the centuries by the harsh environment, long migrations, and its predators. Thick winter coats are shed in spring for thin coats suitable for summer heat. By autumn, the dark summer coat is replaced by a thick brown-and-white one. By early winter the pelage is comprised of a tight layer of long, hollow guard hairs over a coat of fine, curly wool that allows undiminished function even in the most severe wind and cold. – *Tom Walker*

and scenic area, and well worth the hike in. You'll need to pay close attention to a good map, though. Ten miles past the mouth of the **Hunt River**, start looking for **Kavet Creek**, which drains the western edge of the dunes. The creek's mouth is on the south side of the river, a quarter-mile before a prominent bluff on the same side, and roughly across from a forested hill. From the mouth, bushwhack inland and follow the crests of sandy ridges on either side of the stream; the two-mile walk through lichen-carpeted forest is easy after the first few hundred yards. The edge of the dunes is abrupt and impressive. Orient yourself carefully before venturing out. The dunes are deceptively large, and landmarks are few.

The village of **Kiana**, 30 miles downstream of the dunes, is the last commonly used take-out point. Paddling downstream another 20 miles takes you to the community of **Noorvik** on the edge of the Kobuk's huge delta – a swampy maze of channels and sloughs where it's easy to get lost. Wind, currents, and irregular sandbars make a trip down **Hotham Inlet** to Kotzebue difficult to foolhardy.

For many folks, a river trip in the Arctic is a once-in-a-lifetime experience, and, although the journey itself is thrilling, the real reward may come long after you've returned. Time will polish the memory as smooth as a river stone and make your adventure as precious as the wild Arctic itself.

TRAVEL TIPS

DETAILS

When to Go

The Kobuk and Noatak Rivers usually thaw by the end of May and freeze by mid-October. Summer is short, cool, and sunny, with nearly 24 hours of daylight in June. Be prepared for high winds and sudden weather changes. Winter is long and harsh, with long periods of sub-zero temperatures. The region receives only about one hour of daylight by December 1.

How to Get There

Reaching the area is neither easy nor inexpensive. Many visitors take a scheduled flight from Anchorage or Fairbanks to Kotzebue and then arrange a bush plane to drop them off at one of the rivers or nearby villages. Call Ambler Air Service, 907-445-2121, or Bering Air Service, 907-442-3943, for information about charter flights.

Getting Around

There are no roads or rail service. Summer visitors travel through the region by boat or plane or on foot. Snowmobiles are used in winter.

Backcountry Travel

There are no restrictions on backcountry hiking or camping, but travelers should be respectful of Native camps and villages. There are no developed campgrounds or facilities. Supplies at nearby villages are limited and costly. Visitors must be properly equipped, experienced in wilderness travel, and completely self-sufficient.

INFORMATION

Alaska Public Lands Information Center

605 West 4th Avenue, Suite 105; Anchorage, AK 99501; tel: 907-271-2737.

City of Kotzebue

P.O. Box 46; Kotzebue, AK 99752; tel: 907-442-3401.

Gates of the Arctic National Park and Preserve

P.O. Box 74680; Fairbanks, AK 99701; tel: 907-465-0281.

Kobuk Valley National Park and Noatak National Preserve

Northwest Alaska Areas, P.O. Box 1029; Kotzebue, AK 99752; tel: 907-442-8300 or 907-442-3760 (Kotzebue Public Lands Information Center).

CAMPING

No fee or permit is required for primitive camping in the park and preserve, which have no developed campsites.

PRICE GUIDE – double occupancy

$ = up to $49 $$ = $50–$99

$$$ = $100–$149 $$$$ = $150+

Bettles Lodge

P.O. Box 27; Bettles, AK 99726; tel: 800-770-5111 or 907-692-5111.

This year-round, fly-in establishment is a popular jumping-off point for travelers on their way to Kobuk Valley and Gates of the Arctic National Parks. Built in 1948, the lodge is a National Historic Site. It offers a bunkhouse, efficiency apartments, and suites with private baths and Jacuzzis. A restaurant, tavern, and gift shop are on the premises. Hiking, backpacking, fishing, river floats, air charters, and winter adventures are available. $$–$$$

Kiana Lodge

P.O. Box 210269; Anchorage, AK 99521; tel: 907-333-5866.

This newly constructed lodge is operated by Eskimo descendants with almost 40 years of experience as river guides. Situated in the town of Kotzebue, which overlooks the confluence of the Kobuk and Squirrel Rivers, the lodge has six guest rooms, an open kitchen, and a great room with a cathedral ceiling. Meals are included. Boat and raft tours, as well as rentals and drop-off service, are available. Open from June to October. $$$$

Kobuk River Lodge

P.O. Box 30; Ambler, AK 99786; tel: 907-445-2166.

On the banks of the Kobuk River, 14 miles downstream from Kobuk Valley National Park, the lodge has two rooms with a pair of twin beds, one room with a double bed, and two cabins that sleep up to three people each. Guests share bath and shower facilities. Kitchenettes are available in the cabins, which overlook the river. Prices include three meals a day. Extras include a general store, guided or unguided river tours, and backpacking trips. $$$–$$$$

Nullagvik Hotel

P.O. Box 336; Kotzebue, AK 99752; tel: 907-442-3331.

This modern hotel set on Kotzebue Sound has 80 guest rooms, each with a private bath and two twin beds. A restaurant has views of the sound and, in summer, the midnight sun. The hotel's gift shop sells arts and crafts made by Inupiat Eskimos, who live in and around Kotzebue. Open-year round. $$$–$$$$

TOURS & OUTFITTERS

Alaska Discovery

5449 Shaune Drive #4; Juneau, AK 99801; tel: 800-586-1911 or 907-780-6226.

Ten-day raft trips traverse the Noatak River in Gates of the Arctic National Park.

Brooks Range Aviation

General Delivery; Bettles, AK 99726; tel: 800-692-5443.

Floatplane charters are available to the western and central Arctic.

Kobuk River Jets

General Delivery; Kiana, AK 99749; tel: 907-475-2149.

Jet boats transport passengers to the Great Kobuk Sand Dunes on the Kobuk River.

Sunlight North Expeditions

P.O. Box 112983; Anchorage, AK 99511; tel: 907-346-2027.

Arctic treks include completely outfitted 10-day raft trips on the Noatak River.

Wilderness Alaska-Mexico

1231 Sundance Loop; Fairbanks, AK 99709; tel: 907-479-8203.

The service offers guided backpacking, kayaking, and rafting adventures on the Noatak and Kobuk Rivers.

Wild Kobuk River Runners

P.O. Box 110605; Anchorage, AK 99511; tel: 907-345-5956.

River guides lead passengers down the Kobuk and Noatak Rivers. Rafts, canoes, cabins, and tent camps are available.

MUSEUMS

NANA Museum of the Arctic

100 Shore Avenue, P.O. Box 49; Kotzebue, AK 99752; tel: 907-442-3304.

The museum, which features Inupiat storytelling and slide shows, has a wildlife diorama and collections of Inupiat artifacts. The museum hosts Eskimo dancing and blanket tosses in summer.

Excursions

Bering Land Bridge National Preserve

P.O. Box 220; Nome, AK 99762-0220; tel: 907-443-2522.

Situated on the Seward Peninsula, this preserve memorializes the arrival of prehistoric people from Asia, who traversed the land bridge between Siberia and Alaska about 13,000 years ago. Of contemporary interest is the culture of neighboring Eskimos – their villages, reindeer herds, and arts and crafts. The area is home to raptors, waterfowl, and rare Asiatic birds. Visitors can also explore remains of the gold-rush era and visit Serpentine Hot Springs. Float trips and backcountry camping are popular activities at the preserve. Access is by bush plane. Facilities are limited; visitors must be self-sufficient.

Cape Krusenstern National Monument

P.O. Box 1029; Kotzebue, AK 99752; tel: 907-442-3890 or 907-442-3760.

This treeless park is girded by lagoons and limestone hills and marked by long bluffs and ridges formed over thousands of years by the advance and retreat of the sea. About 25 miles north of the Arctic Circle, the area is an important archaeological site, having been inhabited by prehistoric people and Eskimos for more than 8,000 years. Resident wildlife includes caribou, Dall sheep, moose, brown bears, polar bears, arctic foxes, wolves, walrus, and a reintroduced herd of musk-oxen. The park is reached by bush plane or boat from Kotzebue.

Koyukuk National Wildlife Refuge

P.O. Box 287; Galena, AK 99741; tel: 907-656-1231.

This four-million-acre refuge is laced with 14 rivers and hundreds of creeks, ponds, and lakes, providing vital habitat for a great variety of waterfowl. Elsewhere, forests of spruce, birch, and aspen merge with tundra vegetation. The refuge also encompasses the 10,000-acre Nogahabara Dunes in the western section of the preserve. Koyukuk offers prime habitat for large populations of moose, caribou, and small, fur-bearing animals. Black bears range the forest; grizzly bears roam the open tundra. Canoeing and kayaking are good on the Koyukuk River.

Brooks Range

Shadows creep across the thin forests, streams, and ponds of the **Yukon Flats** just north of the **Arctic Circle**. From a small plane flying at an altitude of 4,000 feet, the muskeg seems to stretch on forever with no hint of human habitation. To the north, growing closer, a jumble of peaks rises on the horizon. ◆ Leaving the flats behind and passing over the foothills of the **Brooks Range**, the plane's four passengers excitedly point and call out to one another. "That peak looks like the Matterhorn," says one. "Those look like the Tetons." ◆ "Sheep! Those white spots are Dall sheep." ◆ As planned, the pilot deviates from his usual route and turns west, then north up a river valley choked with willow and surrounded by tundra rising to bare, austere peaks sugared with fresh snow. For the passengers, this is a once-in-a-lifetime trip, and they've paid extra for flight-seeing on the way to their drop-off point.

Beyond the boreal mountains lies a vast, Arctic wilderness described by some writers as the "Serengeti of the North."

The pilot grows animated, too, peering left and right at the summits and tundra below. ◆ "That peak, the one like the Matterhorn," he says, "is **Mount Doonerak**, a Native name for a supernatural being." A minute or two later, as the valley narrows and the mountains lean in, he points to his left and says, "Those are **Frigid Crags** and that one, to the east, is **Boreal Mountain**. These are the **Gates of the Arctic**." ◆ In 20 minutes, after crossing eastward over the trans-Alaska pipeline and **Dalton Highway**, the pilot begins a gradual descent and circles a small airstrip hewn from the gravel of a north-flowing river. The approach and landing on the short strip is flawless. No time is spent on small talk. It's growing late, and

Snowy owlets leave the nest after a few weeks but are still fed by their parents. Adult snowy owls feed on lemmings and other small creatures.

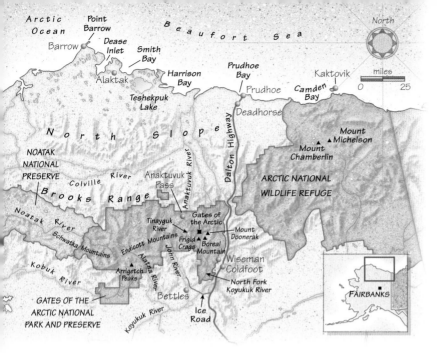

the measure of the river, the tundra, the shadowy mountains. All are experienced backcountry hikers, but here is *wilderness* beyond their previous understanding of the word. They will see no other people or structures of any kind. There will be no way out until they reach their destination, the Eskimo village of **Kaktovik** on **Barter Island**, more than 80 roadless miles away. This is no place for novices or the unprepared. No one speaks, but they're all thinking the same thing: "Did we make the right decision in not hiring a guide? Do we have what it takes? Can we really do this?"

A Cold Desert

The 600-mile-long Brooks Range runs east to west across the Arctic from the Canadian border nearly to the **Chukchi Sea**. Many times older than the Rocky Mountains, this vast mountain range, one of the northernmost in the world, encompasses what one writer called "the last great wilderness in North America." Only one road bisects it, and the remainder is almost completely protected by two national parks, a national preserve, and an immense wildlife refuge. Here the Continental Divide

Winter campers (left) see the sun's midday arrival.

A golden eaglet (opposite, top) waits for an adult to return, perhaps with the remains of a ground squirrel.

Gates of the Arctic National Park (right) straddles the Arctic Divide. The landscape is treeless north of the divide and lightly forested to the south.

before heading back to Fairbanks the pilot must pick up a party of hikers on the south side of the range. Hurriedly he unloads the plane – raft, paddles, backpacks, and other gear. After a quick goodbye, he starts the engine and, with an ear-splitting roar, hurtles into the air.

The drone of the engine fades quickly, and all that's left is the murmuring river and the distant cawing of a raven. The four friends shake out cramps from the long flight, laugh and joke, and pull on coats against the chill. They look around and take

separates the watersheds that flow north into the **Arctic Ocean** from those that flow south and west into the **Bering Sea**.

Beyond the mountains stretches more than 80,000 square miles of tundra laced with meandering rivers and countless ponds. Beneath a cover of thin tundra plants lies permanently frozen ground, called permafrost, which extends to depths of 2,000 feet. For only a few days each summer the top few inches thaw, allowing a spare growth of small willows, wildflowers, grasses, and sedges.

With annual precipitation of less than 10 inches, the **North Slope** of the Brooks Range is a cold desert. Rain and snowmelt, trapped by the ice below, turn the surface into a bog and a prime breeding ground for mosquitoes and other voracious pests. With the exception of **Teshpuk Lake**, the third-largest in Alaska, most of the ponds are small. Because most freeze solid in winter, few have fish. The North Slope is characterized in summer by cool, dry, often foggy weather, and in winter by severe cold and harsh winds. South of the divide, summers are warm, calm, and relatively dry, but snow is possible in any season.

The entire region lies north of the Arctic Circle and is therefore subject to extremities of light and dark. At **Barrow**, the northernmost point in Alaska, the sun doesn't rise for 67 days in winter and doesn't set for

84 days in late spring and summer. Visitors soon learn that continuous daylight can be as unsettling as constant darkness.

Pristine Wilderness

The 8,472,000-acre **Gates of the Arctic National Park and Preserve** lies at the heart of the Brooks Range. Here 8,510-foot **Mount Igikpak** and the black granite **Arrigetch Peaks** have been carved into dramatic spires by long-vanished glaciers. Six national wild and scenic rivers – **Noatak**, **Alatna**, **John**, **Kobuk**, **Tinayguk**, and **North Fork Koyukuk** – flow from the mountains into lowland forest. The only human settlement is a Native village, **Anaktuvuk Pass**, the home of the Nunamiut Eskimos, which sits astride an ancient caribou migration route.

The park has no tourist facilities, roads, or marked trails. You're free to go wherever you wish, although most people combine float trips and hiking along one of the major rivers. First-time visitors, even those experienced in the outdoors, are well advised to enlist the aid of a guide or outfitter, and all must be fit and properly equipped.

The **Alatna River** is a good choice for less experienced paddlers. It flows gently for about 75 miles from the **Endicott Mountains** in the southwest corner of the park to the little village of **Allakaket** at its confluence with the **Koyukuk River**. The journey takes about a week; most paddlers put in at **Takahula** or **Circle Lakes**.

Both the John River and North Fork Koyukuk offer a more exhilarating ride. The John runs for about 100 miles from **Hunt Fork Lake** to the Koyukuk River just south of **Bettles**. The North Fork Koyukuk passes between Boreal Mountain and Frigid Crags in the eastern flank of the park and flows on to the Koyukuk River at Bettles.

Extreme weather, rugged terrain, and difficult river crossings present the greatest challenges.

Adventure Road North

The 414-mile, gravel Dalton Highway is the longest road in Alaska. The pipeline Haul Road was built in 1974 by an army of workers in just 154 days, but its entire length wasn't opened to the public until December 1994.

From its junction with the **Elliott Highway** north of Fairbanks, the 28-foot-wide road parallels and sometimes crosses the pipeline. The route traverses forests, rolling hills, and muskeg south of the Brooks Range and treeless tundra to the north. The high point of the road is 4,800-foot **Atigun Pass**. The Bureau of Land Management oversees 2.7 million acres of public land along the route and maintains a pull-out and campsite at the **Arctic Circle**, a popular stopping place. The historic mining village of **Wiseman** can be accessed from Mile 188.6. There's a general store, food service, camping, bed-and-breakfast inn, and the **Wiseman Mining Museum**. Farther on the road passes within several miles of Gates of the Arctic National Park.

Food, fuel, repairs, and lodging are available at only three sites along the route: the **Yukon River Bridge**, Mile 56; **Coldfoot**, Mile 175; and **Deadhorse**, near the end of the road. Delays are common due to dust, truck traffic, road construction, mud, and snow. Minor damage to headlights and windshields from flying rocks is common, and flats are to be expected. Travelers should carry extra fuel, spare parts, and at least two full-sized, mounted spare tires.

Breaking down on the Dalton is a nightmarish experience and can be very expensive. Towing by private wrecker can cost $5 per mile both ways. Auto rental agencies prohibit the use of most vehicles on the road, but every year foolhardy souls end up in a financial morass by violating the restriction.

Wiseman Trading Post (above, left) is a meeting spot for a village that's still home to gold miners.

A Dalton Highway mile marker (left) is a raven's perch in a treeless region.

Remote lodges in the Brooks Range (opposite, top) are accessible mainly by floatplane.

Musk oxen (right) seem to be throwbacks to the Ice Age; their underwool, or *qiviut*, is highly valued.

Temperatures in the mountains can dip below freezing in summer, and even a light wind can make a relatively mild day feel chilly and bring on the risk of hypothermia.

Insects, too, can be more than a little annoying. Mosquitoes and gnats are at their worst from June to early August and can make life miserable for humans and wildlife alike. Sometimes drawing a breath without inhaling a bug or two is nearly impossible. Repellents, head-nets, gloves, and a good waterproof tent with sewn-in netting are absolutely essential, although a stiff wind is probably your best protection. Sweaty hikers struggling over boggy tundra or up steep hillsides are prime targets for the swarming pests. Tundra hikers rarely cover more than five miles a day, and prolonged exposure to biting insects is typical.

Bountiful Wildlife

To the east, the Brooks Range is protected by the 19,285,923-acre **Arctic National Wildlife Refuge**. Created in 1960 and doubled in size in 1980, this immense parcel of real estate encompasses three national wild and scenic rivers and two of the chain's tallest peaks – 9,020-foot **Mount Chamberlin** and 8,855-foot **Mount Michelson**. It is best known, however, for wildlife. Snowy owls, peregrine falcons, gyrfalcons, and golden eagles are commonly sighted, and the region is a vital stopover for such migratory species as Canada geese, northern pintails, and tundra swans.

Mammals include polar bears, arctic foxes, and musk oxen, which were successfully reintroduced here in 1969 after nearly being eliminated in the region in the late 19th century. The refuge also protects the calving grounds of the Porcupine caribou herd, which numbers more than 125,000 animals. Their annual migration is one of the most spectacular events in the natural world. The herd begins to congregate in May on the north side of the Brooks Range on the coast of the **Beaufort Sea**, and it peaks in size in late June or early July. On hot, breezeless days, it's not uncommon to find caribou wading into the frigid sea seeking relief from the relentless mosquitoes. By early July the cows have given birth and the herd begins its long journey to wintering grounds on the south and east sides of the mountain range. Tens of thousands of caribou pour over the tundra under the light of the midnight sun. It's an extraordinary event but highly unpredictable. Being at the right place at the right time is a tricky business. Your best bet may be to hire an outfitter who can guide you on a river or hiking trip across the migration route.

Whether you see the migration or not, the mountains and tundra are at their most beautiful in July. Dwarf willows and shrubby plants have leafed out, and a succession of wildflowers – avens, lousewort, campion, buttercup, saxifrage – carpets the tundra. Delicate, decades-old lichens experience their only growth of the year. Fledgling birds beg for food, and wolf pups romp around their dens. It's an exuberant outpouring of life but all too short. Fall arrives in August, and serious cold and darkness clamp down soon after.

Winter is a harsh reality in this remote wilderness. Summer is little more than wishful thinking.

Trans-Alaska Pipeline

Alaska was changed forever when the largest oil field in North America was discovered in 1968 at Prudhoe Bay. Before even a single drop of oil was pumped, the state raked in $900 million from its sale of oil leases.

Oilmen initially believed that a pipeline could be built here as anywhere else. Permafrost and government regulation taught them otherwise. Suits filed by environmentalists and Alaska Natives delayed actual line construction until 1974. Later, the oil experts admitted that they didn't know how to build the line safely when first proposed.

Eight oil companies pooled their resources and formed the Alyeska Pipeline Service Company. A pipeline 800 miles long, 48 inches in diameter, was needed to move the oil south to the marine terminal at Valdez. The route led across three mountain ranges, tundra that was underlain in places with 2,000 feet of permafrost, and 600 streams and rivers, as well as several seismically active zones. Thirty construction camps, five to eight pumping stations, and a haul road that stretched more than 400 miles had to be established for the work to proceed.

In mid-December 1973, an ice bridge was built across the Yukon River, and in just over 80 days, 33,700 tons of equipment and supplies were delivered to points north. The haul road was declared complete on November 15, 1974. The Yukon River bridge was built in 1975 as a major link in the supply route, and on March 27, 1975, the first pipe was laid below the Tonsina River near Valdez. The pipeline took three full years to complete with a work force that numbered 28,000 at its highest point.

The economic and social impact on Alaska was overwhelming. Work proceeded despite 90°F summer heat and swarming mosquitoes, and winter temperatures that fell to −80°F and induced a lot of frostbite. Four hundred and twenty miles of pipe were suspended above frozen ground; only 380 miles were buried. Oil, flowing over Atigun Pass at 7.35 miles per hour, entered the pipeline on June 19, 1977. A few glitches along the way slowed its passage, but eventually oil reached Valdez. At peak capacity the pipeline carried two million barrels a day. Total cost: $8 billion.

Arctic fox pups (top) born in spring are hunting on their own by fall.

The trans-Alaska pipeline (left) parallels the Dalton Highway, also known as the Haul Road, which was used to build the pipeline.

Polar bears weigh as much as 1,000 pounds and are second in size only to brown bears. They inhabit the Beaufort Sea coast and prey primarily on seals.

TRAVEL TIPS

DETAILS

When to Go

The region receives almost round-the-clock sunlight in June and July. Summer weather is generally cool and breezy, but temperatures sometimes soar into the upper 80s or fall below freezing. Thunderstorms are common in summer, especially in August; snowfall is possible in any season. Winter is long and severe.

How to Get There

Most visitors take a scheduled flight from Fairbanks to Bettles, then charter a bush plane to Brooks Range destinations. Scheduled flights from Fairbanks to Anaktuvuk Pass are available.

Getting Around

There are no roads in the Arctic National Wildlife Refuge or Gates of the Arctic National Park. Dalton Highway, which runs north from Fairbanks to Prudhoe Bay, is the only maintained road in the Brooks Range. Transportation in the region is limited to plane, boat, and foot. Air-taxi service is expensive and unavailable for much of the year. Advanced planning is essential.

Backcountry Travel

Strong wilderness skills and complete self-sufficiency are necessary for travel in the Brooks Range, which has few developed trails. Rain gear, insect repellent, a head net, and quality clothes and equipment are essential. The use of guides and outfitters is highly recommended. The national park requires a backcountry orientation program, offered in Bettles, Coldfoot, and Anaktuvuk Pass.

No fee or permit is required for backcountry travel.

INFORMATION

Alaska Public Lands Information Center

250 Cushman Street, Suite 1A; Fairbanks, AK 99701; tel: 907-456-0527.

Arctic National Wildlife Refuge

P.O. Box 20; Fairbanks, AK 99701; tel: 907-465-0250.

Bureau of Land Management

1150 University Avenue; Fairbanks, AK 99709; tel: 907-474-2300.

Gates of the Arctic National Park and Preserve

P.O. Box 74680; Fairbanks, AK 99701; tel: 907-465-0281.

CAMPING

Public campgrounds are available from June to September in Wiseman and Coldfoot, located near the park's southeast border. Camping on public lands is permitted throughout the Brooks Range; no fee or permit is required. Campers should take care to avoid private land.

LODGING

PRICE GUIDE – double occupancy

$ = up to $49 $$ = $50–$99

$$$ = $100–$149 $$$$ = $150+

Arctic Getaway Bed-and-Breakfast

Mile 189, Dalton Highway; Wiseman, AK 99790 tel: 907-678-4456.

The lone stopping place in Wiseman is housed in a log cabin behind historic Pioneer Hall. Built in 1995, the cabin is cozily appointed with four beds, a kitchen, and a private bath. The town borders the southeast corner of the national park. Open year-round. $$

Iniakuk Lake Wilderness Lodge

P.O. Box 80424; Fairbanks, AK 99708; tel: 907-479-6354.

The lodge, 60 miles north of the Arctic Circle, has sheltered travelers since 1974. It offers many extras seldom found in wilderness retreats: gourmet meals, professional massage, and morning cafe latte (delivered via canoe). Five guest rooms, housed in two buildings, have shared baths and fabulous views, some of Iniakuk Lake. Also included in the package are guided adventures, natural-history presentations, use of canoes, and round-trip air service from Bettles. $$$$

Peace of Selby Wilderness

90 Polar Road, P.O. Box 86; Manley Hot Springs, AK 99756; tel: 907-672-3206.

Situated in the wilderness surrounding Selby and Narvak Lakes in Gates of the Arctic National Park and Preserve, this lodge is reached by floatplane only. Basic accommodations are offered in the main building and in outlying cabins near the Kobuk River and Minakokosa and Nutuvukti Lakes. Guests bathe in a wood-fired hot tub on the lakeshore. The rustic lodge, decorated with Native arts and crafts, has an open lounge and common room. Meals are served home-style. Included in the cost are the use of canoes, camping equipment, and cooking facilities. Hiking, floating, and dog-mushing expeditions are available. $$$$

Slate Creek Inn

Mile 175, Dalton Highway, P.O. Box 9041; Coldfoot, AK 99701; tel: 907-678-5201 or 907-678-5224 (May to September).

Located in the hamlet of Coldfoot, this Brooks Range inn offers 50 rooms, each with twin beds and a private bath. The Bureau of Land Management Visitor Center, within walking distance of the inn, conducts evening programs in summer. A bar and a 24-hour cafe are on the premises. Open year-round. $$$

TOURS & OUTFITTERS

Arctic Tours/ Sourdough Outfitters

P.O. Box 90; Bettles, AK 99726; tel: 907-692-5252.

Guided and unguided wilderness trips explore the Brooks Range by canoe, raft, kayak, and on foot. Also offered are dog-mushing, cross-country skiing, and snowmobiling trips. Raft and canoe rentals are available.

Arctic Treks

P.O. Box 73452; Fairbanks, AK 99707; tel: 907-455-6502.

Backpacking and rafting trips in the Brooks Range last from seven to 14 days. Hikers stay in national park or refuge base camps.

Bettles Air Service

P.O. Box 27; Bettles, AK 99726; tel: 800-770-5111 or 907-692-5111.

Bush planes transport passengers and equipment into the Brooks Range.

Ouzel Expeditions

P.O. Box 935; Girdwood, AK 99587; tel: 800-825-8196 or 907-783-2216.

Guided float trips are offered throughout the Brooks Range.

MUSEUMS

Wiseman Museum

Mile 188, Dalton Highway; Wiseman, AK 99790.

Housed in the historic Carl Frank cabin, the museum displays old miners' journals, hotel registers, and photos.

Excursions

Kanuti National Wildlife Refuge

101 12th Avenue, P.O. Box 11; Fairbanks, AK 99701; tel: 907-465-0329.

This refuge sprawls to either side of the Arctic Circle. Though less visited than many of the state's refuges, the Kanuti provides vital waterfowl habitat when prairies in Canada and the Lower 48 states experience dry periods. The refuge offers excellent opportunities for raft trips on remote rivers surrounded by unspoiled wetlands. Wolves, grizzly bears, black bears, moose, caribou, and wolverines range throughout the region. Fishing for northern pike and grayling is very good.

Selawik National Wildlife Refuge

P.O. Box 270; Kotzebue, AK 99752; tel: 907-484-2123.

The delta of the Selawik and Kobuk Rivers, popular among rafters and kayakers, provides prime feeding and nesting habitat for migratory birds from five continents. About 360 miles northwest of Fairbanks, the two million-acre refuge also shelters caribou, moose, grizzly bears, foxes, wolves, and river otters. Inupiak Eskimo and Athabascan Indians use the region for subsistence hunting, fishing, and gathering.

Wind River

Arctic National Wildlife Refuge, 101 12th Avenue; Fairbanks, AK 99701; tel: 907-456-0250.

One of three designated Wild Rivers in the Arctic National Wildlife Refuge, Wind River flows through the park from open tundra in the north to boreal forest in the south. The northern stretch of the river offers good whitewater for experienced rafters and kayakers, while the southern stretch flows more gently. Wildlife watching is excellent along the entire route. Sightings of Dall sheep, caribou, moose, brown bears, and a variety of arctic and migratory birds are common. Be sure to leave time for angling and hiking. The river is accessible by bush plane from Fort Yukon and Bettles.

Resource Directory

FURTHER READING

History & Culture

Alaska: A Bicentennial History, William R. Hunt (W. W. Norton, 1976).

Alaska: A History of the 49th State. 2nd ed., Clause M. Naske and Herman E. Slotnick (University of Oklahoma Press, 1987).

Alaska Aviation History, Robert W. Stevens (Polynyas Press, 1990).

Alaskan Eskimos, Wendell H. Oswalt (Chandler and Sharp, 1967).

Alaskans: Life on the Last Frontier, Ron Strickland (Stackpole Books, 1992).

Alaska: Reflections on Land and Spirit, Gary Holthaus (University of Arizona Press, 1989).

Alaska's History: The People, Land, and Events of the North Country, Harry Ritter (Alaska Northwest Books, 1993).

Art and Eskimo Power: The Life and Times of Alaskan Howard Rock, Lael Morgan (Epicenter Press, 1988).

Beyond the Wall, Essays from the Outside, Edward Abbey (Holt, Rinehart and Winston, 1984).

Big Game in Alaska: A History of Wildlife and People, Morgan B. Sherwood (Yale University Press, 1981).

Bush Pilots of Alaska, Kim Heacox (Graphic Arts Center Publishing Company, 1989).

Captain James Cook, Alan Villiers (Charles Scribner's Sons, 1967).

Children of the Midnight Sun: Young Native Voices of Alaska, Tricia Brown (Alaska Northwest Books, 1998).

Coming into the Country, John McPhee (Farrar, Straus, & Giroux, 1976).

Earth and the Great Weather: The Brooks Range, Kenneth Brower (Friends of the Earth, 1973).

The Eskimos of Bering Strait, 1650-1898, Dorothy Jean Ray (University of Washington Press, 1975).

The Forgotten War: Pictorial History of World War II in Alaska, Stan Cohen (Pictorial Histories Publishing Co., 1981).

Iditarod Silver: 25 Years of the Last Great Race, Lew Freedman (Epicenter Press, 1997).

The Klondike Fever: The Life and Death of the Last Great Gold Rush, Pierre Berton (Alfred A. Knopf, 1958).

The Last Light Breaking: Living Among Alaska's Inupiat Eskimos, Nick Jans (Alaska Northwest Books, 1994).

The Life of Captain James Cook, John Cawte Beaglehole (Stanford University Press, 1974).

Make Prayers to the Raven: A Koyukon View of the Northern Forest, Richard Nelson (University of Chicago Press, 1983).

North of 53°: The Wild Days of the Alaska-Yukon Mining Frontier, 1870-1914, William R. Hunt (Macmillan, 1974).

People of the Noatak, Clair Fejes (Alfred Knopf, 1966).

A Place Beyond: Finding Home in Arctic Alaska, Nick Jans (Alaska Northwest Books, 1996).

Russian Alaska, Hector Chevigny (Viking, 1965).

Sadie Brower Neakok: An Inupiaq Woman, Margaret B. Blackman (University of Washington Press, 1989).

The Thousand-Mile War: World War II in Alaska and the Aleutians, Brian Garfield (Doubleday and Co., 1969).

Thomas Merton in Alaska: The Alaska Conferences, Journals, and Letters, Thomas Merton (New Directions, 1989).

Travels in Alaska, John Muir (Houghton Mifflin, 1979).

Voyages on the Yukon and Its Tributaries, Hudson Stuck (New York: Charles Scribner's Sons, 1975).

Wager With the Wind: The Don Sheldon Story, James Greiner (Rand McNally and Co., 1974).

The Wake of the Unseen Object: Among the Native Cultures of Bush Alaska, Tom Kizzia (Henry Holt, 1991).

Natural History

Alaska, Fred Hirschmann and Suzan Nightingale (Graphic Arts Center Publishing, 1994).

Alaska's Bears, Alaska Geographic (Alaska Geographic Society, 1993).

Alaska's Bears: Grizzlies, Black Bears, and Polar Bears, Bill Sherwonit (Alaska Northwest Books, 1998).

Alaska's Mammals, Dave Smith (Alaska Northwest Books, 1995).

Alaska's Saltwater Fishes and Other Sea Life, Doyne W. Kessler (Alaska Northwest Books, 1985).

Alaska from the Air, Fred Hirschmann (Graphic Arts Center Publishing, 1999).

Alaska Trees and Shrubs, Leslie A. Viereck and Elbert L. Little, Jr. (University of Alaska Press, 1986).

An Alaskan Reader, 1867-1967, Ernest Gruening, ed. (Meredith Press, 1966).

Arctic Dreams: Imagination and Desire in a Northern Landscape, Barry Lopez (Charles Scribner's Sons, 1986).

Bears: Monarchs of the Northern Wilderness, Wayne Lynch (The Mountaineers, 1993).

A Beast the Color of Winter: The Mountain Goat Observed, Douglas Chadwick (Sierra Club Books, 1983).

Checklist of Alaska Birds, D.D. Gibson (University of Alaska Museum, 1993).

Degrees of Disaster: Prince William Sound: How Nature Reels and Rebounds, Jeff Wheelwright (Simon and Schuster, 1994).

The Freshwater Fishes of Alaska, J.E. Morrow (Alaska Northwest Books, 1980).

The Great Alaska Nature Factbook, Susan Ewing (Alaska Northwest Books, 1996).

The Great Bear: Contemporary Writings on the Grizzly, John A. Murray, ed. (Northwest Books, 1992).

Hunters of the Northern Forest, Richard Nelson (University of Chicago Press, 1980).

In the Wake of the Exxon Valdez: The Devastating Impact of the Alaska Oil Spill, Art Davidson (Sierra Club Books, 1990).

Monarch of Deadman Bay: The Life and Death of a Kodiak Bear, Roger Caras (Little, Brown, 1969).

Moose Country: Saga of the Woodland Moose, Michael W. P. Runtz (NorthWord Press, 1991).

Mount McKinley: The Pioneer Climbs, Terris Moore (The Mountaineers, 1981).

A Naturalist in Alaska, Adolph Murie (Devin-Adair Co., 1961).

Oomingmak: The Expedition to the Musk-Ox Island in the Bering Sea, Peter Matthiessen (Hastings House, 1967).

The Pinnipeds: Seals, Sea Lions, and Walruses, Marianne Riedman (University of California Press, 1990).

A Republic of Rivers: Three Centuries of Nature Writing from Alaska and the Yukon, John Murray, ed. (Oxford University Press, 1990).

Shadows on the Koyukuk, Sidney Huntington and Jim Rearden (Alaska Northwest Books, 1998).

Sierra Club Handbook of Whales and Dolphins, Stephen Leatherwood and Randall R. Reeves (Sierra Club Books, 1983).

The Stars, the Snow, the Fire, John Haines (Greywolf Press, 1989).

Stalking the Ice Dragon: An Alaskan Journey, Susan Zwinger (University of Arizona Press, 1991).

Wildlife Notebook Series, Cheryl Hall, et al. (Alaska Department of Fish and Game, 1994).

Of Wolves and Men, Barry Holstun Lopez (Charles Scribner's Sons, 1978).

The World of the Sea Otter, Stefani Paine (Sierra Club Books, 1993).

Wild, Edible, and Poisonous Plants of Alaska, Christine Heller (Cooperative Extension Service, University of Alaska, 1989).

Yukon Summer, Eugene Cantin (Chronicle Books, 1973).

Field Guides

Alaska National Wildlife Refuge, Alaska Geographic (Alaska Geographic Society, 1993).

Alaska Paddling Guide, 3rd ed., Jack Mosby and David Dapkus (J&R Enterprises, 1986).

Alaska Region, National Audubon Society Field Notes, T. G. Tobish, Jr. (National Audubon Society, 1994).

The Alaska River Guide: Canoeing, Kayaking, and Rafting in the Last Frontier, 2nd ed., Karen Jettmar (Alaska Northwest Books, 1998).

Alaska's Accessible Wilderness: A Traveler's Guide to Alaska's State Parks, Bill Sherwonit (Alaska Northwest Books, 1996).

The Alaska Wilderness Guide, 7th ed., Kris Valencia, ed. (Vernon Publications, 1993).

The Alaska-Yukon Wildflowers Guide (Alaska Northwest Books, 1990).

The Audubon Society Master Guide to Birding, J. Farrand, Jr., ed. (Alfred A. Knopf, 1983).

Backcountry Bear Basics: The Definitive Guide to Avoiding Unpleasant Encounters, Dave Smith (The Mountaineers, 1997).

Basic River Canoeing, Robert E. McNair (American Canoeing Association, 1987).

The Complete Tracker: Tracks, Signs, and Habits of North American Wildlife, Len McDougall (The Lyons Press, 1997).

The Cordes/LaFontaine Pocket Guide to Outdoor Photography, Mary Mather (Graycliff Publishing, 1994).

Discovering Wild Plants: Alaska, Western Canada, the Northwest, Janice J. Schofield (Alaska Northwest Books, 1989).

Easy Access to National Parks: The Sierra Club Guide for People with Disabilities, Wendy Roth (Sierra Arts Foundation, 1992).

Fast and Cold: A Guide to Alaska Whitewater, Andrew Embick (Alpine Books, 1994).

A Field Guide to the Ecology of Western Forests, John C. Kricher (Houghton Mifflin Company, 1993).

Field Guide to the Gray Whale, Oceanic Society Staff (Sasquatch Books, 1989).

A Field Guide to the Mammals: North America North of Mexico, William H. Burt and Richard P. Grossenheider (Chapters Pub Ltd, 1998).

Grizzly Bears: An Illustrated Field Guide, John A. Murray (Roberts Rinehart Press, 1995).

A Guide to Alaskan Seabirds, N. E. Stomsem (Alaska Natural History Association/U.S. Fish and Wildlife Service, 1982).

Guide to the Birds of Alaska, 4th ed., Robert Armstrong (Alaska Northwest Books, 1995).

Hiking Alaska, Dean Littlepage (Falcon Publishing Co., 1997).

Making Camp: A Complete Guide for Hikers, Mountain Bikers, Paddlers & Skiers, Steve Howe, Alan Kesselheim, Dennis Coello, and John Harlin (The Mountaineers, 1997).

Marine Mammals of Alaska, Kate Wynne (Alaska Sea Grant College Program, 1992).

Marine Mammals of Eastern North Pacific and Arctic Waters, 2nd ed., Delphine Haley (Pacific Search Press, 1986).

National Audubon Society Field Guide to North American Birds: Western Region, Miklos D. F. Udvardy and John Farrand, Jr. (Knopf, 1994).

The Sierra Club Family Outdoors Guide, Marilyn Doan (Sierra Club Books, 1995).

The Sierra Club Handbook of Whales and Dolphins, Stephen Leatherwood and Randall R. Reeves (Sierra Club Books, 1993).

Snow Sense: A Guide to Evaluating Snow Avalanche Hazard, 4th ed., Jill Fredston and Doug Fesler (Alaska Mountain Safety Center, 1994).

U.S. National Parks West, John Gattuso, ed. (Apa Publications, 1995).

A Walker's Companion, David Rains Wallace, ed. (Time-Life Books, 1995).

Walking Softly in the Wilderness: The Sierra Club Guide to Backpacking, John Hart (Sierra Club Books, 1994).

Watching Nature: A Beginner's Field Guide, Monica Russo (Sterling Publications, 1998).

The Whale Watcher's Guide, Patricia Corrigan (Northword Press, 1994).

Wilderness Basics: The Complete Handbook for Hikers and Backpackers,

Jerry Schad (The Mountaineers, 1993).

Regional Guides

Admiralty Island: Fortress of the Bears (Alaska Geographic Society, 1991).

Alaska Peninsula (Alaska Geographic Society, 1994).

Alaska's Glacier Bay, Karen Jettmar (Alaska Northwest Books, 1997).

Alaska's Ocean Highways: A Travel Adventure Aboard Northern Ferries, Sherry Simpson (Epicenter Press, 1995).

Alaska Wilderness: Exploring the Central Brooks Range, Robert Marshall (University of California Press, 1956).

The Aleutian Islands, Penny Rennick, ed. (Alaska Geographic Guides, 1995).

Along the Alaska Highway, Gloria Maschmeyer (Alaska Northwest Books, 1992).

The Brooks Range (Alaska Geographic Society, 1997).

Denali (Alaska Geographic Society, 1995).

55 Ways to the Wilderness of Southcentral Alaska, 4th ed., Helen Nienhueser and Johnson Wolfe (The Mountaineers Books, 1994).

Guide to the Killer Whales of Prince William Sound, Craig O. Matkin (Prince William Sound Books, 1994).

In Denali, Kim Heacox (Companion Press, 1992).

Katmai Country (Alaska Geographic Society, 1989).

The Kenai Canoe Trails, Daniel L. Quick (Northlite Publishing Co., 1995).

Kenai Pathways: A Guide to the Outstanding Wildland Trails of Alaska's Kenai Peninsula (Alaska Natural History Association, 1995).

Kenai Peninsula (Alaska Geographic Society, 1997).

Kuskowkim (Alaska Geographic Society, 1990).

Midnight Wilderness: Journeys in Alaska's Arctic National Wildlife Reufge, Debbie S. Miller (Sierra Club Books, 1990).

Minus 148°: The Winter Ascent of Mount McKinley, Art Davidson (W. W. Norton and Co., 1969).

The Nature of Southeast Alaska: A Guide to Plants, Animals, and Habitats, Rita M. O'Clair, Robert H. Armstrong, and Richard Carstensen (Alaska Northwest Books, 1992).

Rivers of the Yukon: A Paddling Guide, Ken Madsen and Graham Wilson (Primrose Publishing, 1990).

Southcentral Alaska: Including Anchorage, Kenai Peninsula, Susitna Valley and Prince William Sound, Scott McMurren (Epicenter Press, 1995).

To the Top of Denali: Climbing Adventures on North America's Highest Peak, Bill Sherwonit (Alaska Northwest Books, 1990).

Magazines

Alaska Magazine
619 East Ship Creek Avenue,
Suite 239; Anchorage, AK 99501.

Alaska's Mountain Magazine
1200 R Street, Unit B; Anchorage, AK 99501.

Alaska People Magazine
P.O. Box 190648; Anchorage, AK 99519.

Audubon
National Audubon Society, 950 Third Avenue; New York, NY 10022.

Backpacker
Rodale Press, 33 East Minor Street; Emmaus, PA 18098.

Explore
301 14th Street NW, Suite 420; Calgary, Alberta, T2N 2A1.

National Parks
National Parks and Conservation Association, 1701 18th Street NW; Washington, DC 20009.

National Wildlife
National Wildlife Federation, 1400 16th Street NW; Washington, DC 20036.

Natural History
American Museum of Natural History, Central Park West at 79th Street; New York, NY 10024.

Nature Conservancy
The Nature Conservancy, 1815 North Lynn Street; Arlington, VA 22209.

Outdoor Photographer
12121 Wiltshire Boulevard, Suite 1220; Los Angeles, CA 90025-1175.

Outdoor Traveler
WMS Publications, One Morton Drive, Suite 102; Charlottesville, VA 22903.

Outside
Outside Plaza; 400 Market Street; Santa Fe, NM 87501.

Sierra
The Sierra Club, 730 Polk Street; San Francisco, CA 94109.

Wilderness
The Wilderness Society, 900 17th Street NW; Washington, DC 20006-2300.

GOVERNMENT AGENCIES

Alaska Department of Fish and Game
Juneau Headquarters, P.O. Box 25526; Juneau, AK 99802-5526; tel: 907-465-4112.

Anchorage Office
333 Raspberry Road; Anchorage, AK 99518-1599; tel: 907-344-0541.

Fairbanks Office
1300 College Road; Fairbanks, AK 99701-1599; tel: 907-459-7200.

Alaska Department of Natural Resources
Anchorage Office, P.O. Box 107005; Anchorage, AK 99510-7005; tel: 907-269-8400.

Fairbanks Division of Forestry
3700 Airport Way, Fairbanks, AK 99709; tel: 907-451-2700.

Juneau Division of Forestry
400 Willoughby Avenue, Juneau, AK 99801; tel: 907-465-3379.

Alaska Division of State Parks
Southeast Area Office, 400 Willoughby Avenue, Fourth Floor; Juneau, AK 99801; tel: 907-465-4563.

Chugach State Park Office
Potter Section House, HC 52, Box 8999; Indian, AK 99540; tel: 907-345-5014.

Kenai/Prince William Sound Area Office
P.O. Box 1247; Soldotna, AK 99669; tel: 907-262-5581.

Kodiak District Office
1400 Abercrombie Drive; Kodiak, AK 99615; tel: 907-486-6339 or 907-486-6550.

Mat-Su/Valdez-Copper River Area Office
HC 32 Box 6706; Wasilla, AK 99687-9719; tel: 907-745-3975.

Northern Area Office
3700 Airport Way; Fairbanks, AK 99709-4613; tel: 907-452-2695.

Alaska Public Lands Information Center
605 West 4th Avenue, Suite 105; Anchorage, AK 99501; tel: 907-271-2737.

Bureau of Land Management
Alaska State Office, P.O. Box 13; Anchorage, AK 99513; tel: 907-271-5960.

Anchorage Office
6881 Abbott Loop Road; Anchorage, AK 99507; tel: 907-267-1246.

Fairbanks Office
1150 University Avenue; Fairbanks, AK 99709-3844; tel: 907-474-2302.

Glennallen Office
P.O. Box 147; Glennallen, AK 99588; tel: 907-822-3217.

Juneau Mineral Information Center
100 Savikko Road; Douglas, AK 99824; tel: 907-364-1553.

Kotzebue Office
P.O. Box 1049; Kotzebue, AK 99752; tel: 907-442-3430.

Nome Office
P.O. Box 925; Nome, AK 99762; tel: 907-443-2177.

Tok Office
P.O. Box 309; Tok, AK 99780; tel: 907-883-5121.

U.S. Forest Service
U.S. Department of Agriculture, Forest Service Information Center, 101 Egan Drive; Juneau, AK 99801; tel: 907-586-8751.

Southeast Alaska Visitor Center, Tongass National Forest
50 Main Street; Ketchikan, AK 99901; tel: 907-228-6214.

Chugach National Forest
3301 C Street, Suite 300; Anchorage, AK 99503; tel: 907-271-2500 or 800-280-2267 (cabin reservations).

Craig Ranger District
P.O. Box 500; Craig, AK 99921; tel: 907-826-3271.

Cordova Ranger District
612 Second Street; Cordova, AK 99574; tel: 907-424-7661.

Girdwood Ranger Station
Alyeska Highway and Monarch Mine Road; Girdwood, AK 99587; tel: 907-783-3242.

Hoonah Ranger District
P.O. Box 135; Hoonah, AK 99829; tel: 907-945-3634.

Juneau Ranger District
8465 Old Dairy Road; Juneau, AK 99801; tel: 907-586-8800 or 907-586-8790 (Admiralty Island National Monument).

Ketchikan and Misty Fiords National Monument Ranger District
3031 Tongass Avenue; Ketchikan, AK 99901; tel: 907-225-2148.

Petersburg Ranger District
P.O. Box 1328; Petersburg, AK 99833; tel: 907-772-3871.

Seward Ranger District
334 Fourth Avenue; Seward, AK 99664; tel: 907-224-3374.

Sitka Ranger District
201 Katlian Street, Suite 109; Sitka, AK 99835; tel: 907-474-4220.

Thorne Bay Ranger District
P.O. Box I; Thorne Bay, AK 99919; tel: 907-828-3304.

Wrangell Ranger District
P.O. Box 51; Wrangell, AK 99929; tel: 907-874-2323.

Yakutat District
P.O. Box 327; Yakutat, AK 99826; tel: 907-784-3359.

National Park Service
Alaska Regional Office, 2525 Gambell Street; Anchorage, AK 99503; tel: 907-256-2696.

Aniakchak National Monument and Preserve
P.O. Box 7; King Salmon, AK 99613; tel: 907-246-3305.

Bering Land Bridge National Preserve
P.O. Box 220; Nome, AK 99762; tel: 907-443-2522.

Cape Krusenstern National Monument
P.O. Box 1029; Kotzebue, AK 99752; tel: 907-442-3890.

Denali National Park
P.O. Box 9; Denali National Park, AK 99755; tel: 907-683-2294.

Gates of the Arctic and Yukon-Charley Rivers
P.O. Box 74680; Fairbanks, AK 99707; tel: 907-456-0281.

Glacier Bay National Park and Preserve
P.O. Box 140; Gustavus, AK 99826; tel: 907-697-2232.

Kenai Fjords National Park
P.O. Box 1727; Seward, AK 99664; tel: 907-224-3175.

Klondike Gold Rush National Historic Park
P.O. Box 517; Skagway, AK 99840; tel: 907-983-2921.

Kobuk Valley National Park
P.O. Box 1029; Kotzebue, AK 99752; tel: 907-442-3890.

Lake Clark National Park
Alaska Pacific University, Grace Hall, Suite 311, 4230 University Drive; Anchorage, AK 99508; tel: 907-271-3751.

Noatak National Preserve
P.O. Box 1029; Kotzebue, AK 99752; tel: 907-442-3890.

Sitka National Historical Park
P.O. Box 738; Sitka, AK 99835; tel: 907-747-6281.

Wrangell-St. Elias National Park and Preserve
P.O. Box 29; Glennallen, AK 99588; tel: 907-822-5234.

U.S. Fish and Wildlife Service
Alaska Regional Office, 1011 East Tudor Road; Anchorage, AK 99503; tel: 907-786-3353.

Alaska Maritime National Wildlife Refuge
2355 Kachemak Drive, Suite 101; Homer, AK 99603-8021; tel: 907-235-6546.

Alaska Peninsula National Wildlife Refuge/Becharof

National Wildlife Refuge,
P.O. Box 277; King Salmon, AK 99613; tel: 907-246-3339.

Aleutian Islands Unit/Alaska Maritime National Wildlife Refuge
P.O. Box 5251; Adak, AK 99546-5251; tel: 907-592-2406.

Arctic National Wildlife Refuge, Federal Building
101 12th Avenue, P.O. Box 20; Fairbanks, AK 99701; tel: 907-465-0253.

Innoko National Wildlife Refuge
P.O. Box 69; McGrath, AK 99627; tel: 907-524-3251.

Izembek National Wildlife Refuge
P.O. Box 127; Cold Bay, AK 99571-0127; tel: 907-532-2445.

Kanuti National Wildlife Refuge
Federal Building, 101 12th Avenue, P.O. Box 20; Fairbanks, AK 99701; tel: 907-456-0329.

Kenai National Wildlife Refuge
P.O. Box 2139; Soldotna, AK 99669-2139; tel: 907-262-7021.

Koyukuk National Wildlife Refuge/Nowitna National Wildlife Refuge
P.O. Box 287; Galena, AK 99741; tel: 907-656-1231.

Selawik National Wildlife Refuge
P.O. Box 270; Kotzebue, AK 99752; tel: 907-442-3799.

Tetlin National Wildlife Refuge
P.O. Box 779; Tok, AK 99780; tel: 907-883-5312.

Togiak National Wildlife Refuge
P.O. Box 2770; Dillingham, AK 99576; tel: 907-842-1063.

Yukon Delta National Wildlife Refuge/Nunivak National Wildlife Refuge and Wilderness/ Andreafsky National Wilderness and Wild River
P.O. Box 346; Bethel, AK 99559; tel: 907-543-3151.

Yukon Flats National Wildlife Refuge, Federal Building
101 12th Avenue, P.O. Box 20; Fairbanks, AK 99701; tel: 907-456-0440.

TOURISM INFORMATION

Alaska Tourism
P.O. Box 110801; Juneau, AK 99811; tel: 907-465-2010.

Alaska Native Tourism Council
1577 C Street #304; Anchorage, Alaska 99501, tel: 907-274-5400.

Anchorage Convention and Visitors Bureau
524 4th Avenue; Anchorage, AK 99501; tel: 907-276-4118.

Cordova Visitors Center
P.O. Box 391; Cordova, AK 99587; tel: 907-424-7443.

Fairbanks Convention and Visitors Bureau
550 First Avenue; Fairbanks, AK 99701; tel: 800-327-5774 or 907-451-1724.

Greater Copper Valley Visitor Information Center
P.O. Box 469; Glennallen, AK 99588; tel: 907-822-5555.

Haines Visitor Information Center
P.O. Box 518; Haines, AK 99827; tel: 907-766-2234.

Juneau Convention and Visitors Bureau
76 Egan Drive, Suite 300; Juneau, AK 99801; tel: 907-586-1737.

Kachemak Bay Convention and Visitors Association
Box 1001; Homer, AK 99603; tel: 907-235-8897.

Kenai Visitor Information Center
P.O. Box 1991; Kenai, AK 99611; tel: 800-535-3624 or 907-283-1991.

Ketchikan Convention and Visitors Bureau
131 Front Street; Ketchikan, AK 99901; tel: 907-225-6166.

Kodiak Island Convention and Visitors Bureau
100 Marine Way; Kodiak, AK 99615; tel: 907-486-6545.

Seward Visitor Information Cache
P.O. Box 749; Seward, AK 99664; tel: 907-224-8051.

Sitka Convention and Visitors Bureau
P.O. Box 1226; Sitka, AK 99835; tel: 907-747-5940.

Skagway Convention and Visitors Bureau
P.O. Box 415; Skagway, AK 99840; tel: 907-983-2854.

Tok Visitor Center
P.O. Box 389; Tok, AK 99780; tel: 907-883-5775.

Valdez Convention and Visitors Bureau
P.O. Box 1603; Valdez, AK 99686; tel: 800-770-5954 or 907-835-4636.

TRANSPORTATION

By Air
The secret to conquering Alaska's vastness is air travel. Commuter airlines and charter aircraft are everywhere. Virtually every community found on the map is served by an air carrier. Per capita, six times as many Alaskans have a pilot's license as do residents of the rest of the country.

By Sea
Many visitors arrive in Alaska on cruise ships, which sail through the spectacular Inside Passage arriving at Skagway, Ketchikan, Sitka, Juneau, Seward, and Anchorage. About a dozen cruise lines serve Alaska, with several small vessels offering excursions. Cruises normally start from Vancouver, Seattle, or San Francisco. Cruise lines normally operate between May and September. For further information about cruise options and to make reservations, contact a travel agent. The Alaska Marine Highway operates passenger ferries between many coastal towns.

By Rail
There is no rail service directly to Alaska from the Lower 48. However, the Alaska Railroad provides passenger service within the state, connecting Anchorage with Fairbanks to the north and Whittier and Seward to the south.

By Road
Traveling the Alaska Highway is a great adventure, but it should be considered only by visitors with plenty of time. For more information about driving in Alaska, refer to The Milepost (All-the-North Guide), published by Alaska Northwest Publishing. A free state-

published brochure on the Alaska highways may be obtained from the Alaska Division of Tourism, P.O. Box 110801; Juneau, Alaska 99811, tel: 907-465-2010.

Alaska Airlines
19300 Pacific Highway South; Seattle, WA 98188; tel: 800-426-0333.

Alaska Direct Bus Lines
P.O. Box 501; Anchorage, AK 99510; tel: 800-770-6652 or 907-277-6652.

Alaska Marine Highway
P.O. Box 25535; Juneau, AK 99802; tel: 800-642-0066 or 907-465-3941.

Alaskan Express (inter-city bus transportation)
745 West 4th Avenue; Anchorage, AK 99501; tel: 800-544-2206 or 907-277-5581.

Alaska Railroad
411 West 1st Avenue, P.O. Box 107500; Anchorage, AK 99510; tel: 800-544-0552 or 907-265-2494.

ERA Aviation
6160 Carl Brady Drive; Anchorage, AK 99502; tel: 800-866-8394 or 907-248-4422.

L.A.B. Flying Service
P.O. Box 272; Haines, AK 99827; tel: 800-426-0543 or 907-766-2222.

Parks Highway Express
P.O. Box 82884; Fairbanks, AK 99708; tel: 888-600-6001 or 907-479-3065.

Seward Bus Lines
3339A Fairbanks Street; Anchorage, AK 99503; tel: 907-278-0800.

White Pass & Yukon Route Railroad
P.O. Box 435; Skagway, AK

99840; tel: 800-343-7373 or 907-983-2217.

ORGANIZATIONS

Alaska Natural History Association
P.O. Box 230; Denali National Park, AK 99755; tel: 907-683-1258.

American Birding Association
P.O. Box 6599; Colorado Springs, CO 80255; tel: 800-835-2473.

American Cetacean Society
P.O. Box 1391; San Pedro, CA 90731; tel: 310-548-6279.

American Hiking Society
P.O. Box 20160; Washington, DC 20041-2160; tel: 703-319-0084.

National Audubon Society
950 Third Avenue; New York, NY 10022; tel: 212-832-3200.

National Campers and Hikers Association
4804 Transit Road, Building 2; Depew, NY 14043; tel: 716-668-6242.

National Parks and Conservation Association
1776 Massachusetts Avenue NW, Suite 200; Washington, DC 20036; tel: 202-797-6800.

National Recreation and Park Association
2775 South Quincy Street, Suite 300; Arlington, VA 22206-2204; tel: 703-671-6772.

National Wildlife Federation
1400 16th Street NW; Washington, DC 20036; tel: 202-223-6722.

The Nature Conservancy
1815 North Lynn Street;

Arlington, VA 22209; tel: 703-841-5300.

Sierra Club
730 Polk Street; San Francisco, CA 94109; tel: 415-923-5630.

Wilderness Society
900 17th Street NW; Washington, DC 20006; tel: 202-833-2300.

CALENDAR OF EVENTS

January

Anchorage Folk Festival
Anchorage; tel: 907-566-2334.

Copper Basin 300 Sled Dog Race
Glennallen; tel: 907-822-3663.

Great Alaska Beer Festival
Anchorage; tel: 907-562-9911.

Willow Winter Carnival
Willow; tel: 907-495-6633.

February

Peninsula Winter Games
Kenai/Soldotna; tel: 907-262-9322.

Iditasport Races
Big Lake; tel: 907-345-4505.

Sled Dog Races
Anchorage; tel: 907-562-2235.

Homer Winter Carnival
Homer; tel: 907-235-7740.

Yukon Quest International Sled Dog Race
Fairbanks; tel: 907-452-7954.

Iditarod Days Festival
Wasilla; tel: 907-376-1299.

March

Festival of Native Arts
Fairbanks; tel: 907-474-7181.

North Pole Winter Carnival
North Pole; tel: 907-488-2242.

Iditarod Trail Sled Dog Race
Anchorage; tel: 907-376-5155.

Fairbanks Winter Carnival
Fairbanks; tel: 907-452-1105.

Windfest
Skagway; tel: 907-983-1898.

April

Annual Spring Carnival
Girdwood; tel: 907-754-2259.

Jazz Week
Anchorage; tel: 907-786-1684.

Whale Fest
Kodiak; tel: 907-487-5961.

Alaska Folk Festival
Juneau; tel: 907-364-2658.

Alaska State Community Theatre Festival
Haines; tel: 907-766-2708.

May

Copper River Delta Shorebird Festival
Cordova; tel: 907-424-7260.

Celebration of the Sea
Ketchikan; tel: 907-225-6177.

Kachemak Bay Shorebird Festival
Homer; tel; 907-235-7740.

Juneau Jazz and Classics
Juneau; tel: 907-463-3378.

Kodiak King Crab Festival
Kodiak; tel: 907-486-5557.

June

Kenai River Festival
Kenai; tel: 907-262-9225.

Sitka Summer Music Festival
Sitka; tel: 907-747-6774.

Alaska Mardi Gras
Haines; tel: 907-766-2234.

Midnight Sun Festival
Nome; tel: 907-443-5535.

Summer Solstice Festival
Fairbanks; tel: 907-452-8671.

Gold Rush Days at Gold Rush Fields
Juneau; tel: 907-586-2497.

July

July 4th Celebration
Wrangell; tel: 907-367-9745.

Wasilla Water Festival
Wasilla; tel: 907-376-1299.

Bear Paw Festival
Eagle River; tel: 907-694-4702.

Moose Dropping Festival
Talkeenta; tel: 907-733-2487.

World Eskimo-Indian Olympics
Fairbanks; tel: 907-452-6646.

Kodiak Bear Country Music Festival
Kodiak; tel: 907-486-4829.

Fairbanks Summer Arts Festival
Fairbanks; tel: 907-474-8869.

August

Funny River Festival
Soldotna; tel: 907-260-4660.

Gold Rush Days
Valdez; tel: 907-835-4232.

Tanana Valley State Fair
Fairbanks; tel: 907-452-3750.

Southeast Alaska State Fair
Haines; tel: 907-766-2476.

Kenai Peninsula State Fair
Ninilchick; tel: 907-567-3670.

Alaska State Fair
Palmer; tel: 907-745-4827.

September

Kodiak State Fair and Rodeo
Kodiak; tel: 907-486-4959.

Discovery Days Celebration
Valdez; tel: 907-835-2764.

Make It Alaskan Festival
Anchorage; tel: 907-279-0618.

October

Oktoberfest
Homer; tel: 907-235-7721.

Oktoberfest
Kodiak; tel: 907-486-5557.

Alaska Days Festival
Sitka; tel: 907-747-5940.

November

Annual Sitka Whalefest
Sitka; tel: 907-747-5940.

Athabascan Fiddling Festival
Fairbanks; tel: 907-452-1825.

Alaska Bald Eagle Festival
Haines; tel: 907-766-2202.

Juneau Public Market
Juneau; tel: 907-586-1166.

December

Colony Christmas
Palmer; tel: 907-745-2880.

Talkeetna Winter Fest
Talkeetna; tel: 907-733-2330.

Winter Solstice Celebration
Fairbanks; tel: 907-452-8671.

PHOTO AND ILLUSTRATION CREDITS

AlaskaStock Images 8R, 24T, 134B, 190T

Anchorage Museum/Alaska-Stock Images 83T, 84T

Chris Arend/AlaskaStock Images 112M

Arend-Pinkerton/AlaskaStock Images 201T

John Baston 41 (2nd from bottom)

Randy Brandon/AlaskaStock Images 31T, 102T, 122

Craig Brandt 1, 41 (2nd from top), 147B, 205B

Robin Brandt 41T, 163M, 183T, 191

Matt Breiter/Ken Graham Agency 41 (3rd from bottom)

John Burcham/Ken Graham Agency 20-21, 48T

Luigi Ciuffetelli 37T

Michael DeYoung/AlaskaStock Images 9B, 38T, 48B, 127M, 127B, 135B, 187T, 188B

Patrick J. Endres/AlaskaStock Images 30

Patrick J. Endres/Wide Angle Productions 8L, 14-15, 40T, 98, 100, 101B, 102B, 104, 115T, 119T, 125B, 138, 141T, 148, 166, 169, 177T, 200T, 202B

Tom Evans/AlaskaStock Images 12-13, 46, 49B

Kevin Fleming Photography 42

Jeff Foott Productions 56B, 67B

John K.B. Ford/Ursus Photography 152T

Francois Gohier 107B

Ken Graham/Ken Graham Agency 5B, 119B

Al Grillio/AlaskaStock Images 102M

Calvin W. Hall/AlaskaStock Images 33B

Bob Hallinen/AlaskaStock Images 92T

Kim Heacox Photography/Ken Graham Agency 6-7, 39, 52-53, 54, 59T, 69B, 70, 83B, 173B, 205T

Fred Hirschmann Wilderness Photography 2-3, 16, 25T, 40 (2nd from bottom), 44, 45B, 56T, 58T, 61T, 61M, 61B, 69M, 72, 73B, 74, 75T, 75B, 79T, 79M, 79B, 80, 85B, 87B, 90, 91B, 93B, 94, 97T, 97B, 103T, 105B, 107T, 107M, 108, 114T, 117, 120, 123B, 124B, 128, 130, 131T, 131B, 132, 133T, 134T, 135T, 137T, 137M, 140, 144T, 153, 155M, 155B, 156, 158, 159B, 160, 161T, 163T, 168B, 173T, 177B, 178T, 178M, 179, 180T, 181, 183M, 183B, 187B, 189B, 195T, 195M, backcover (bottom)

Randi Hirschmann 95B, 167B, 200B

John Hyde/AlaskaStock Images 36T, 62

Nick Jans 193B, 195B, 198, 199B

David J. Job/Ken Graham Agency 40 (3rd from top), 88, 97M

Johnny Johnson/AlaskaStock Images 19

R.E. Johnson/AlaskaStock Images 51T

Mike Jones/Ken Graham Agency 10-11

Mark Kelley/AlaskaStock Images 5T, 28, 66

Ken Graham Agency 69T, 127T

Thomas Kitchin/Tom Stack & Associates 25B, 65T, 167T

Grant Klotz/AlaskaStock Images 87T

Bob Krist 159T, 161B

Lon E. Lauber/AlaskaStock Images 113

Tom & Pat Leeson 22, 36B, 84M, 103B, 116B, 119M, 142T, 142B, 144B, 145B, 150, 170T, 186, back cover (top)

Chlaus Lotscher/AlaskaStock Images 40 (3rd from bottom)

Clark James Mishler/Alaska-Stock Images 34

Mark Newman/Tom Stack & Associates front cover, 26, 112B

Jim Nilsen/Tom Stack & Associates 152B

Glenn Oliver/Ken Graham Agency 137B

Jo Overholt/AlaskaStock Images 173M

Terry Parker/Ursus Photography 123T, 193T

Margo Pinkerton/AlaskaStock Images 190T

Don Pitcher 64, 65B, 101T, 111B, 112T, 151B

Allen Prier/AlaskaStock Images 58-59, 124T, 170-171

Joel W. Rogers 18, 29B, 33T, 37B, 38B, 40 (2nd from top), 50B, 51B, 116T, 171T, 174, 176B, 178B, 184, 188T, 192T

Carl R. Sams II 151T

Jeff Schultz/AlaskaStock Images 4, 40B, 45T, 50T, 93T, 110

Bill Sherwonit 41 (3rd from top), 125T, 133B, 147T, 206-207

Bill Silliker, Jr. 73T

Kevin G. Smith/AlaskaStock Images 41B

Tom Soucek 32, 87M, 95T, 105T, 115B, 147M

Tom Soucek/AlaskaStock Images 143

Ursus Photography 111T, 201B

Harry M. Walker/AlaskaStock Images 85T

Tom Walker 49T, 84B, 115M, 141B, 164, 176T, 202T, 203

Steve Warble 82

John Warden/AlaskaStock Images 24B

Art Wolfe 9T, 57, 76T, 76B, 77, 91T, 114T, 155T, 163B, 168T, 189T, 192B, 196, 199T

George Wuerthner 29T, 31B, 67T, 92B, 145T, 180B, 190B, 205M

Maps by Karen Minot
Design by Mary Kay Garttmeier
Layout by Ingrid Hansen-Lynch

T = top, B = bottom, M = middle,
R = right, L = left

INDEX

Note: page numbers in italics refer to illustrations